Technical Analysis

FOR

DUMMIES®

2ND EDITION

Technical Analysis

FOR

DUMMIES®

2ND EDITION

by Barbara Rockefeller

WILEY

Wiley Publishing, Inc.

Technical Analysis For Dummies®, 2nd Edition

Published by
Wiley Publishing, Inc.
111 River St.
Hoboken, NJ 07030-5774
www.wiley.com

WILEY

About the Author

Barbara Rockefeller is a writer specializing in international economics and finance, with a focus on foreign exchange. She also trades in the foreign exchange market. She is the publisher of a daily newsletter on the foreign exchange market, "The Strategic Currency Briefing." Her newsletter combines technical and fundamental observations. Additionally, she publishes separate daily "Trader's Advice" reports for spot and futures foreign exchange traders. Newsletter subscribers include central banks, investment banks, hedge funds, multinational corporations, investment managers and individuals. Miss Rockefeller also prepares custom charts on a consulting basis for individuals and institutions.

Before starting the newsletter business, Barbara was in the credit, foreign exchange, and risk-management departments at several U.S. banks, including Citibank and Brown Brothers Harriman. Conventional economic theory failed to generate valid currency forecasts at Brown Brothers, which led her to spearhead a technical analysis system at Citibank. This decision was in 1980, long before technical analysis went mainstream and at a time when it was considered at least a little crackpot.

Barbara has a B.A. in Economics from Reed College in Portland, Oregon, and a M.A. in International Affairs from Columbia University. While at Citibank, she traveled the world, training staff and clients on the fundamentals of foreign exchange, international economics, and risk management. Favorite country? Turkey. Smartest traders? Hong Kong.

Barbara is the author of *How to Invest Internationally*, published in Japanese in 1999 (Franklin Covey), *CNBC 24/7, Trading Around the Clock, Around the World*, published in 2000 (John Wiley & Sons), and *The Global Trader*, published in 2001 (John Wiley & Sons). She also writes a monthly column for *Currency Trader Magazine*.

Dedication

This book is dedicated to Robert James Deadman, founder of Technical Systems Analysis Group, who taught as much of "the scientific way of thinking" as it's possible to cram into a "social science" mind, and with endless patience.

I also dedicate the book to Alfred A. "Chip" Olbrycht, who forces me to question the easy way and to look at everything a second time, and a third time, too.

Author's Acknowledgments

For Dummies editors Mike Baker and Alissa Schwipps, who caused much suffering. I'm wrung-out, but you, dear reader, have a better book.

And the usual suspects: Jim Sullivan, head of the Fairfield County Technical Traders' Club, contributed numerous gentle nudges on perspective as well as how traders really use indicators and think about trading risk. Ed Dobson, founder of Traders Press, and Perry Kaufman, author of Trading Systems and Methods, always generous. Most generous of all over the years is Desmond MacRae, whose ideas I gladly and routinely steal.

Publisher's Acknowledgments

We're proud of this book; please send us your comments at http://dummies.custhelp.com. For other comments, please contact our Customer Care Department within the U.S. at 877-762-2974, outside the U.S. at 317-572-3993, or fax 317-572-4002.

Some of the people who helped bring this book to market include the following:

Acquisitions, Editorial, and Media Development

Senior Project Editor: Alissa Schwipps

   (Previous Edition: Mike Baker)

Acquisitions Editor: Michael Lewis

Copy Editor: Sarah Westfall

Assistant Editor: David Lutton

Technical Editor: Charles LeBeau

Senior Editorial Manager: Jennifer Ehrlich

Editorial Assistants: Rachelle Amick, Jennette ElNaggar

Cover Photo: © iStockphoto.com/Nikada

Cartoons: Rich Tennant
   (www.the5thwave.com)

Composition Services

Project Coordinator: Sheree Montgomery

Layout and Graphics: Vida Noffsinger, Lavonne Roberts

Proofreaders: John Greenough, Lindsay Littrell, Bonnie Mikkelson

Indexer: Estalita Slivoskey

Publishing and Editorial for Consumer Dummies

   Diane Graves Steele, Vice President and Publisher, Consumer Dummies

   Kristin Ferguson-Wagstaffe, Product Development Director, Consumer Dummies

   Ensley Eikenburg, Associate Publisher, Travel

   Kelly Regan, Editorial Director, Travel

Publishing for Technology Dummies

   Andy Cummings, Vice President and Publisher, Dummies Technology/General User

Composition Services

   Debbie Stailey, Director of Composition Services

Contents at a Glance

Table of Contents

Introduction

● ●

*T*iming is everything.

Timing is critical in cooking, romance, music, politics, farming, and a hundred other aspects of life on this planet. Putting money into a securities market is no different — you need good timing to get the best results.

Technical traders all over the world, amateur and professional alike, earn a living by using technical analysis to time their trades in many different markets. They not only earn a living, but are also still standing after a market crash. In this book, I try to explain how they do that, and how you can do it, too.

About This Book

The technical analysis industry is positively blooming. Go to an Internet search engine and type in **technical analysis,** and you get over 45 million responses. The phrase **support and resistance** results in over 10 million hits. Okay, everyone knows the limitations of Web searches, but even after weeding out the mismatches, that's still a huge amount of material. Don't be intimidated. In this book, I include core concepts, some of which you can apply *today* with no further research.

I want you to grasp the mindset of the technical trader or investor: To think independently, to take responsibility for actions, and most of all, to act on observation rather than conventional wisdom. Try to leave your preconceptions about trading and investing behind. For example, a core technical concept is that the technical trader cuts losses and lets the winning trades run. Chances are you think that, after taking a loss, you should continue to hold the security, because if it's a true value investment, it'll come back.

But try to think like a 10-year-old as you read this book. In fact, go find a 10-year-old, if you have one handy, and ask him, "Which is better to hang on to: a thing that has already let you down (losses) or a different thing that's delivering exactly what you wanted (profits)?" See? Technical analysis is subversive that way.

Beating the system is fun and rewarding. The market doesn't know you, your age, gender, ethnicity, good looks or lack of them, singing talent, or anything else about you except whether you're a successful trader. The market is blind. In fact, the market is indifferent. It's the one place you can go to be judged solely on your merits. Use this book to help you find your way.

The good news is that *For Dummies* books are designed so that you can jump in anywhere and get the information you need. Don't feel that you have to read every chapter — or even the entire chapter. Take advantage of the table of contents and index to find what you're looking for, and check it out.

Conventions Used in This Book

To help you navigate this book, I use the following conventions:

- ✔ *Italic* is used for emphasis and to highlight new words or terms that are defined.
- ✔ **Boldfaced** text is used to indicate keywords in bulleted lists or the action part of numbered steps.
- ✔ Monofont is used for Web addresses.

What You're Not to Read

I intend for this book to be a pleasant and practical read so that you can quickly find and absorb the information you want. However, I sometimes couldn't help going a little bit deeper or relaying information that expands on the basics. You might find this information interesting, but you don't need it to understand what you came to that section to find.

When you see a sidebar (a gray-shaded box of text) or text flagged with the Technical Stuff icon, know that the information is optional. You can lead a full and happy life without giving it a glance. (But aren't you curious? A little?)

Foolish Assumptions

Every author must make assumptions about her audience, and I've made a few assumptions that may apply to you:

- ✔ You've never put a dime into a security but you plan to; and when you do, you intend not to lose it.
- ✔ You're reasonably well versed in the trading game, but you're looking for new tools to become a more effective trader and improve your profits.
- ✔ You're tired of the buy-and-hold approach in which your returns seem unrelated to the supposed quality of the security you bought.
- ✔ You want to find out how to sell. You know how to buy, but timing your sales ties you up in knots.

> ✔ You've experienced some setbacks in the market, and you need an approach to make that money back.
>
> ✔ You want to know whether technical analysis has any basis in reason and logic — or whether all technical analysts are crackpots.

If any of these descriptions fits the bill, then you've picked up the right book.

How This Book Is Organized

I've arranged *Technical Analysis For Dummies* into six parts. Parts I and II introduce you to the field of technical analysis, and Parts III through V introduce you to nuts and bolts — the indicators. What's that leave? The famous *For Dummies* Part of Tens — Part VI.

Part 1: Defining Technical Analysis

The point of technical analysis is to help you observe prices in a new way and to make trading decisions based on reasonable expectations about where "the market" is going to take the price. This part shows you how to view security prices as the outcome of crowd psychology.

Part 11: Preparing Your Mind for Technical Analysis

Before you plunge into risking hard-earned cash on securities trading, you have to realize that it's not the security that counts; it's the trade. Each trade has two parts — the price analysis and *you*. Price analysis tools are called *indicators,* and you have to select the indicators that match your personality and preference for risk. But most people don't know their risk preference when they start out in securities trading (which changes over time, anyway), so you have a chicken-and-egg situation. By studying the kinds of profit and loss outcomes that each type of indicator delivers, you can figure out your risk preferences.

Part 111: Observing Market Behavior

The price bar and its placement on the chart deliver a ton of information about market sentiment. It doesn't take much practice to start reading the mind of the market by looking at bars and small patterns. The payoff is cold, hard cash, but you have to be patient, imaginative, and thoughtful.

Part IV: Finding Patterns

If all you can see on a security's price chart at first are meaningless squiggles, this section shows you core tools for organizing your vision. With a little practice, you can quickly start throwing around technical jargon like *support and resistance* with the best of them. Better yet, this part provides the concepts you need to start making informed decisions.

Part V: Flying with Dynamic Analysis

This part deals (mostly) with math-based indicators. Relax — it's only arithmetic. Math indicators are the workhorses of technical analysis. They help you identify whether your price is trending, the strength of the trend, and when the trend is at a reversal point. Applying these indicators carefully and consistently is the key to trading success. If you're mathematically competent, you can take a giant leap into system building, and remove most of the day-to-day judgmental decision making that trading involves.

Part VI: The Part of Tens

As I say in Part I, there's the trade, and then there's you. You can be merely competent at using indicators and still achieve excellence as a trader. I show you how in this part, by sharing ten rules that every top trader follows, ten technical things you can do that will help you make money trading, and ten ways in which the market has changed. Finally, I include a brief listing of the top resources to follow up on.

Icons Used in This Book

Icons are small pictures in the margins of this book that flag certain material for you. The following icons highlight information you want to pay special attention to.

When you see this icon, you don't want to forget the accompanying info — pretty subtle, huh?

This icon clues you in on hands-on time- and hassle-saving advice that you can put into practice. In many cases, this icon tells you directly how to conduct a trade on a technical principle, usually an indicator crossing something, breaking something, or dancing a jig.

Ignore this information at your own financial peril. I use this icon to warn you about mistakes, missteps, and traps that can sink even the best trading professional.

This icon flags places where I get really technical about technical analysis. Although it's great info, you can skip it and not miss out on the subject at hand.

Where to Go from Here

If you're new to technical analysis, take a close look at Parts I and II for the scoop on the field. If you are already a good chart reader, what you probably need is help on managing the trade (Chapter 5). Applying indicators is better than willy-nilly trading decisions, but to get The Traders' Edge, you also need the discipline of a winner. How do you become a winner? The same way you get to Carnegie Hall — practice, practice, practice, and hanging out with other winners. Figuring out how to trade technically is a journey of self-discovery, corny as that sounds. Luckily, it's a journey with a lot of fellow travelers to keep you company. I hope you enjoy the road.

Part I
Defining Technical Analysis

"The one thing I've learned about technical analysis is, timing is every... SMOOF!"

In this part . . .

Get ready to set aside everything you think you know about trading and investing. In technical analysis, you look only at what prices are doing, not at fundamentals or what some theory says they "should" do. In this part, I explain how the price behavior of securities is the outcome of crowd psychology. Technical analysis is all about observing how prices actually move and trying to use past regularities in price movements to predict future regularities.

Chapter 1

Opening the Technical Analysis Toolbox

*W*elcome to technical analysis, which may be a new way of looking at stocks and other securities for you. Simply put, technical analysis is a set of forecasting methods that can help you make better trading decisions.

In this chapter, I take you on a quick tour of key technical concepts and review why technical analysis works (and why sometimes it doesn't). You may think that technical analysis is all about reading charts full of squiggles and lines, and although I give you plenty of material about squiggles and lines in this book, technical analysis is also about managing market risk.

Does that sound a bit too grand? Well, building a house isn't chiefly about hammers and nails, although you need them. Squiggles and lines are just tools. Think of tackling technical analysis as a project to build better trading practices. Yes, you need the squiggles and lines, but your goal is to use those tools to make money.

Introducing Technical Analysis

Technical analysis is the study of how securities prices behave and how to exploit that information to make money while avoiding losses. The technical style of trading is opportunistic. Your immediate goal is to forecast the price of the security over some future time horizon in order to buy and sell the security to make a cash profit. The emphasis in technical analysis is to make profits from trading, not to consider owning a security as some kind of savings vehicle. Therefore, technical analysis dictates a more active trading style than you may be used to.

Trading or investing: The many faces of technical analysis

Both traders and investors use technical analysis. So what's the difference between a trader and an investor? Most people consider that a trader is someone who holds securities for only a short period of time, anywhere from a minute to a year. An investor is someone who holds securities anywhere from many months to forever, depending on whom you ask. Holding period is not the only factor, though. You may think of an investor as someone who also seeks income from dividends or bond coupon payments, and the timing of those payments influences the investor's holding period, too.

Actually, the dividing line between trader and investor isn't fixed (except for purposes of taxation). Be careful not to fall into the semantic trap of thinking that a trader is a wild-eyed speculator while an investor is a respectable guy in a pinstriped suit. I use the word *trader* in this book, but don't let it distract you. People who consider themselves *investors* use technical methods, too.

You can use technical methods over any investment horizon, including the long term. If you're an expert in Blue Widget stock, for example, you can add to your holdings when the price is relatively low, take some partial profit when the price is relatively high, and dump it all if the stock crashes. Technical analysis has tools for identifying each of these situations. You can also use technical tools to rotate your capital among several securities, allocating more capital to the ones delivering the highest gains. At the other end of the investment horizon spectrum, you can use technical analysis to spot a high-probability trade and execute the purchase and sale in one hour.

Setting new rules

You may have the preconceived notion that because technical analysis entails an active trading style, you're about to embark on a wild and risk-laden adventure — like the one-hour trade, for example. Nothing is further from the truth. Executing the one-hour trade has less inherent risk of loss than buying and holding a security indefinitely without an exit plan. The existence of an exit plan is what defines and limits the risk.

The one-hour trade entails risk management, whereas holding a security without an end in mind on some concept of hypothetical "value" is to take 100 percent risk. That supposedly "valuable" security can quickly tank and go to zero. Think of Enron, WorldCom, Lehman Brothers, or Bear Stearns — all failed companies whose stock price went to zero, even though "experts" said that these names were buying opportunities right up to the last minute.

Preventing and controlling losses is more important than outright profit seeking to practically every technical trader you meet. The technical analysis approach is demonstrably more risk averse than the value-investing approach.

To embrace technical analysis is to embrace a way of thinking that's always sensitive to risk. *Technical trading* means to trade with a plan that identifies the potential gain and the potential loss of every trade ahead of time. The technical trader devises rules for dealing with price developments as they occur in order to realize the plan. In fact, you select your technical tools (from the many available) specifically to match your trading style with your sensitivity to risk. I talk about this in Chapter 4.

Using rules is the key feature of lasting success in trading. Anybody can get lucky — once. To make profits consistently requires that you not only identify the trading opportunity, but also manage the risk of the trade. Most of the "trading rules" that you hear about, such as "Cut your losses and let your winners run," arise from the experience of technical traders. (I come back the subject of managing the trade in Chapter 5.)

Making the case for managing the trade

To buy and hold securities for a very long period of time is a well-documented path to accumulating capital, but only if your timing is good and you got in at the best time. Consider the following:

- ✔ If you had bought U.S. stocks at the price peak just ahead of the 1929 Crash, it would've taken you over 20 years to recover your initial capital.

- ✔ Since the end of World War II, the Dow Jones Industrial Average has fallen by more than 20 percent (a *bear market* — see the "Keeping your bulls and bears straight: A word about words" sidebar in this chapter) on 12 occasions.

- ✔ From January 2000 to October 2002, the S&P 500 fell by 50 percent. If you owned all the stocks in the S&P 500 and held them throughout the entire period, you lost 50 percent of your stake, which means you now need to make a gain equivalent to 100 percent of your remaining capital to get your money back, as Table 1-1 shows. Ask yourself how often anyone makes a 100 percent return on investment.

- ✔ Oil rose from $18.03 a barrel in November 2001 to $147.27 a barrel in July 2008, a gain of 720 percent. But if you bought at the high and expected the gravy train to keep flowing, you faced a humungous loss as oil fell to $33.87 by December 2008 — unless you exited.

Table 1-1	Recovering a Loss
Loss	*Gain Needed to Recover Loss*
10%	11.1%
20%	25.0%
30%	42.9%
40%	66.7%
50%	100.0%
60%	150.0%
75%	300.0%

Timing your entry and exit from the market is critical to making money and controlling losses. The central part of the book, Chapters 6 through 17, covers technical methods that aim to improve the timing of your entries and exits.

Making the Trend Your Friend

You can look at most charts and see that in some time frame, securities prices tend to move in trends, and trends often persist for long periods of time. A *trend* is a discernible directional bias in the price — upwards, downwards, or sideways. If you can't see a trend, widen the time frame from a few days to many months or narrow the time frame from a few days to an hourly basis.

The trend is your friend. If you identify trends and trade with them, you can make more money trading securities than if you ignore trendedness. Trend identification gives you an advantage and helps you perform two functions near and dear to the heart:

✓ **Create capital:** As a general rule, you want to buy securities only when their prices are rising, called an *uptrend*. Buying into an uptrend usually improves the probability of making money, providing you can figure out at what price point to sell.

✓ **Preserve capital:** You tend to make fewer mistakes and preserve capital by not buying a security when the price is falling (a *downtrend*) — no matter how charming the salesman or fascinating the story. In addition, you preserve capital by selling your security when it starts downtrending. You don't know where or when a downtrend might end.

Focusing on the price is right (and respectable)

Securities prices are the product of the collective decision making of buyers and sellers. Prices incorporate (or *discount*) all known information, including assumptions, about the security, and prices change as new information becomes available. *All known information* consists of hundreds of factors ranging from accurate facts to opinions, guesses, and emotions — and previous prices. They all go into the supply and demand for a security and result in its price. I talk about supply and demand in Chapter 2 and environmental factors that affect the price in Chapter 3 as well as in Chapter 10.

Charles Dow, one of the founders of *The Wall Street Journal,* observed around the turn of the 20th century that no matter what the true facts are about a security and what people are saying about it, the price neatly cuts through all the clutter of words and is the one piece of hard information you can trust. Nowadays traders have to qualify that statement with the caveat "unless the computers made an error."

Note, however, that prices on a chart don't tell you anything about the underlying value of the security. Where the price "should" be is a totally different subject, named *fundamental analysis.* Most technical traders use both forms of analysis, because technical analysis isn't antithetical to fundamental analysis, as some critics think. The two can be used together. You can choose to trade only the highest-quality securities on a fundamental basis, but time your purchases and sales according to technical criteria.

 Technical analysis and fundamental analysis are compatible. The core ideas of technical analysis aren't some new and crackpot flash in the pan, but rather, they came into being over 100 years ago. Technical ideas have a respectable origin and have been embraced and explored by some very brainy and successful figures in American finance.

Check out the following basic observations underlying technical analysis that are attributed to Dow himself:

- ✔ Securities prices move in trends much of the time.

- ✔ Trends can be identified with patterns that you see repeatedly (which I cover in Chapter 9) and with support and resistance trendlines (see Chapter 10).

- ✔ Primary trends (lasting months or years) are punctuated by secondary movements (lasting weeks or months) in the opposite direction of the primary trend. Secondary trends, today called *retracements,* are the very devil to deal with as a trader. (See Chapter 2 for more on retracements.)

- ✔ Trends remain in place until some major event comes along to stop them.

These ideas and many more attributed to Dow (sometimes wrongly) are called *Dow Theory*, although he never called it that as far as anyone knows. An Internet search of the phrase *Dow theory* yields over a quarter of a million hits. A key point to take away from knowing about Dow is that traders were using technical ideas long before the advent of electronic communication and software programs — technical analysis is hardly a new-fangled fad that will have a short shelf life. It has already survived over 100 years.

Charting your path

Prices and trends rule, so you have to be able to track and identify them. And to identify prices and trends, you have to see them. After you become proficient, you can order your software to "see" trends, but if you are a beginner, you need to become familiar with the price chart (see Figure 1-1). This chart shows a classic uptrend following a downtrend.

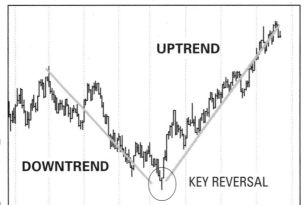

Figure 1-1:
Uptrend and downtrend.

UPTREND

DOWNTREND

KEY REVERSAL

At the most basic level, your goal as a technical trader is to shun the security shown on the chart while it's downtrending and to identify the *reversal point* — the best place to buy (shown in the circle) — as early as possible. Figure 1-1 is a good example of the kind of chart with which you spend most of your time. A chart is the workspace of technical analysis. Technical analysts have developed numerous indicators based on price and volume that can be expressed as statistics, tables of numbers, and other formats, but the core method remains a graphic display of prices in a chart.

Taking a Closer Look at the Many Faces of Trendedness

Trend means different things to different people. Trend is such a wide and flexible concept that a large variety of definitions is possible. In fact, to be pragmatic, you can say that a trend is a price move that your indicator identifies. In other words, you can define trend according to technical measures that appeal to your sense of logic and what works for you. In this book, definitions of trendedness are spread out under various technique headings so that you can choose which definition of trendedness suits your personality and trading style.

Quantifying trendedness

Creating a chart like the one in Figure 1-1 is easy. To illustrate classic trend behavior, I could've taken any security out of thousands in my database and found some period of time over which the security's price looked like this chart. However, I could have also found many time periods when this same security was not trending. In fact, some securities are frequently in a trending mode, others seldom trend, or their trends are short lived. To complicate matters, some securities exhibit a "habit" of tidy trending while others trend in a sloppy way (with high variability around the average).

Charles Dow may have started the ball rolling in technical analysis over 100 years ago, but in the grand scheme of things, we're still in frontier days. Ask a group of technical traders, "What percentage of time are securities trending and what percentage of the time are they nontrending?" and you will get a different answer from each person. Each technical analyst has a different idea about the percentage of time securities are trending based on his own personal definition of trendedness and the time frame he looks at.

Choosing a definition

No single definition of trendedness is the universal gold standard on which everyone agrees, so it's hardly surprising that no one can say, "Securities are trended *x* percent of the time." Just about any generalization about trendedness can be demonstrated — or rebutted.

For example, I trade foreign exchange, and in my experience, the pound, the euro, and the yen are trended about 60 percent of the time. I say that because 60 percent of the time, I can identify a directional bias by using *my* tools on *my* time frames. However, someone else may say currencies are trended only

40 percent of the time — using a different, equally valid statistical method to define *trendedness*. In fact, some analysts say foreign exchange prices are mean reverting 60 percent of the time (see Chapter 2 for the mean-reversion concept) but I say "So what?" Mean reversion can coexist with trendedness and doesn't affect my trading.

Only one thing is certain: No security trends all the time. Even the best-behaved security spends some time going sideways (nontrending), which can be considered a trend in its own right.

I give you the key definitions of trendedness in Parts III through V. Chapter 6 describes it as a series of higher highs together with a series of higher lows (for an uptrend). In Chapter 12, trendedness is defined as the price rising above a moving average or a short-term moving average rising above a long-term moving average (also an uptrend). The rest of the chapters contain other definitions, like the linear regression slope I mention at the beginning of this section.

Picking a time frame

If you're looking at ten years of daily prices, you get a different view of trendedness than when you're looking at only two years of data. In other words, you need to consider the time period of the data you analyze. A security may display a trend on data captured every hour but appear to be nontrending when you look at daily data. Some securities may trend in the morning and not in the afternoon. To go to the other extreme, you may not be able to detect a trend on daily data but a weekly or monthly chart shows a trend. You cannot say anything reasonable and useful about trends without specifying the time frame.

Further, a security that trended in one period may not be trending in another. Markets are dynamic. They change (then they change back). Accept it.

Embrace the spirit of empirical investigation embodied in technical research. When you're drawing charts, experiment with different time frames.

Discovering Why Technical Analysis Does and Doesn't (Always) Work

Technical analysis works because people consistently repeat behaviors under similar circumstances. For example, I say in Chapter 10 that support and resistance lines are a simple and effective method to identify the limits of a trend, and when a price breaks a support or resistance line, it's called a *breakout*.

Breakout is a powerful concept and used in other indicators, too. Why does a breakout attract so much attention? Because over decades of analysts following prices, a breakout reliably signaled the end of a trend many, many times.

While "breakout" is powerful, it isn't always correct. You will run into situations where a breakout is not respected and the price resumes the direction it was headed in the first place. In short, some breakouts are "false" — they lead you astray.

The biggest mistake that beginning technical traders make is attributing too much reliability and accuracy to technical methods. (Check out Chapter 3 for more technical analysis forecasting method constraints.) Experienced technical traders know that no technique works all the time. In fact, many techniques work only when the majority of market participants believe that they will work, forming a self-fulfilling prophecy. As long as you can identify what technical theory has a grip on the market's imagination at any one time, you don't need to care whether the theory is scientifically verifiable. Your goal is to make money, not to be scientifically pure.

Understanding that no technique works all the time helps you overcome doubts raised by critics who say that the whole field of technical analysis is not worthwhile because techniques are not 100 percent reliable. Because a method doesn't work all the time isn't the right criterion for evaluating it. Just because the meteorologist is wrong 50 percent of the time doesn't mean you should take off in your Cessna when he's forecasting a violent thunderstorm in the next hour.

In financial markets, the value of an analytical method is determined by whether it helps you to consistently make more money than you lose. Notice that this statement has two components: The method and you. The "you" variable is why two traders — whether newcomers or grizzled old hands — can use the same method but achieve very different results. (I discuss this puzzle in Chapter 17.)

Beating the Market

Every day, hundreds of thousands of traders all over the world beat the market. To *beat the market* means to earn a return higher than the benchmark in that market, such as making more from trading a single stock included in the Dow Industrial Average than the Dow Industrial Average index returned in the same period. Beating the market can also mean to earn a return greater than the return on the return on a risk-free investment, usually defined as the three-month U.S. Treasury bill.

Technical analysis is about making extraordinary gains — beating the market — and if you think that isn't possible, you haven't looked hard enough. Many people try to beat the market and fail. Almost everyone knows the story of the hapless day traders of the 1990s who deluded themselves into thinking that they possessed trading secrets when all they had was a roaring bull market. A few survived — because they adapted their trading techniques to the changing market. To trade well is a skill that takes training, practice, and benefiting from mistakes, just like any other business. You wouldn't open a restaurant without knowing how to cook, but somehow people think they can trade securities without understanding how and why prices move.

Whether you just want to get out ahead of another crash, sharpen your trading skills, or aspire to become a self-supporting trader, use your noggin: This business is going to take some sweat — and some hard choices. You may be disappointed to discover that technical analysis doesn't offer a single, coherent path to market wisdom. You'd think that after 100 years of development, traders would have a rule book with a single set of steps to take and processes to go through. But they don't.

Why not? For the same reason that you can find ten equally good ways to cook an omelet. Each cook selects a different pan, whisking and stirring techniques, amount of salt, amount of heat, and so on. Likewise in trading, each trader sees a different amount of risk on any particular chart, chooses one set of indicators over another, and has a taste for taking a certain amount of profit (or loss) for the capital at stake. Just as no one can dictate a single right way to cook an omelet, no one can name the single best way to trade a particular price situation. Theoretically, you could say that the best way is the way that makes the most money, but that fails to account for the trader — his personality, goals, and experience — and how much money he has to risk.

To blend technical methods with your own personal risk profile isn't the work of one day. It's a lengthy and difficult process that requires some soul-searching. To keep the process manageable, confine your conclusions to what you can observe and verify — the empirical approach. Be careful to avoid the error of composition, like reading that one set of technical traders believes in magic numbers and concluding that all of technical analysis involves magic numbers. (It doesn't.) It's astonishing how many otherwise smart people misjudge technical analysis in exactly this manner, and in widely reviewed books, based on an incomplete understanding of the field. Many critics take one technical idea, fail to integrate it with their personal risk profile, and then blame all of technical analysis for their losses.

Another error to avoid is the overly scientific approach. Like the expert who proved that the Bernoulli principle is mathematically wrong and therefore airplanes can't fly, probability experts say they can prove prices are random. Random numbers do throw up patterns, the argument goes, so technical analysts are deluding themselves that apparent orderliness can be exploited for profit over any length of time. And yet you do see orderliness, and you can exploit it, at least enough of the time to beat the market. Traders have been profiting from technical methods for over a hundred years — longer, if you count 17th-century candlestick charting (for more on this method, see Chapter 8).

Finding Order

Much of the time you can see order in the way securities prices evolve, even though they develop in an infinite variety of configurations and each chart is literally unique. Technical traders attribute that orderliness to the swings of market sentiment. Prices form patterns because the traders in the market behave in regular and repetitive ways. You can identify, measure, and project prices because you can identify, measure, and project human behavior. Most people can do it only imperfectly, but you and I can both do it.

Probably the most intriguing thing about technical analysis is that ideas and insights about price behavior from 1900 are as fresh and valuable today as they were then. Technical analysis never throws anything out — it just finds more-efficient ways to capture price moves. Since the personal computer came along, technical analysis has become more math oriented, but the essence of technical analysis is still to grasp the underlying human behavior that makes prices move.

In the grand scheme of things, technical analysis is a fairly new field of endeavor, and still changing. Traders like you and me have a lot to master. The few things technical traders do know for certain include the following:

- No technique works all the time.
- No technique works on every security.
- Something mysterious is going on that traders don't yet understand. A famous trader named Bernard Baruch said

    Have you ever seen, in some wood, on a sunny quiet day, a cloud of flying midges — thousands of them — hovering, apparently motionless, in a sunbeam? . . . Yes? . . . Well, did you ever see the whole flight — each mite apparently preserving its distance from all others — suddenly move, say three feet, to one side or the other? Well, what made them do that? A breeze? I said a quiet day. But try to recall — did you ever see them move directly back again in the same unison? Well, what made them do that? Great human mass movements are slower in inception but much more effective.

This phenomenon is what technical analysis seeks to explain.

Viewing the Scope of Technical Analysis

Technical analysis focuses on prices. Analyzing prices can take many different forms — from drawing lines on a chart by hand to using high-powered computer software to calculate the most likely path of a price out of all possible paths. Technical analysis is sometimes called by other names, such as *charting, market timing,* and *trend-following.* The press, the public, and even technical-analysis authors all use these terms interchangeably.

When you see these terms in this book and elsewhere, don't fret over a strict interpretation — and don't accept or reject a technical idea because it has a particular label. You can put ten technical traders in a room and get ten definitions of each term. The following sections are my interpretation of these terms and their nuances.

Charting

Charting is probably the oldest generic term used for technical analysis. I cover "charting" techniques in Parts III and IV. Charting refers to reading supply and demand into bars and patterns. Some technical analysts reject the term *charting* because it harkens back to the days of colored pencils and rulers. They see charting as subjective, while statistics-based indicators (which I cover in Part V) are "objective." But many traders use charting conventions developed over decades, and they *work.* I think charting gets you closer to the supply-demand dynamics (the "mind of the market") than math-based indicators that quantify market sentiment in a more abstract way.

Market timing

Market timing is another term used in place of *technical analysis.* All technical trading involves timing, but to my way of thinking, the term *market timing* refers to statistical analysis that goes beyond a single chart. It encompasses many techniques, such as sentiment indicators and calendar effects, that many self-described chartists say aren't charting and at least some technical analysts say aren't technical analysis. I cover these and other tools in Chapter 3.

Trend-following (there's that word again)

The very first thing you look for in a chart is whether the price is trending. Because so much emphasis is put on the presence or absence of a trend, technical analysis is sometimes named *trend-following.* Parts IV and V contain techniques that are trend-following. Some analysts object to the term because you aren't always following, but often anticipating, a trend such as when you use momentum indicators (see Chapter 13).

Keeping your bulls and bears straight: A word about words

A *bullish market* is one that is rising, and a *bearish market* is one that is falling. A *bull* is an optimist who thinks prices will rise; a *bear* is a pessimist who thinks prices will fall. Bull and bear are oversimplifications. But those words are commonly used in discussing securities markets. Accept them. The word *bull* applies to the long-term holder as well as the in-and-out quick-trade artist. The point is that bull and bear, or bullish and bearish, are useful shorthand words that summarize market players and market sentiment as either positive and optimistic (prices will rise) or negative and pessimistic (prices will fall).

A lot of people don't like those words, finding them to be coarse, undignified, and often inaccurate. When you buy a security for an expected long-term holding period, you feel positive about the security, but the word *bullish* sounds emotional and doesn't describe the deeply intellectual process you went through in selecting that particular security. When you sell a security, you may not appreciate being named a bear. You may not have had a negative attitude toward that security — you just wanted the money from the sale for some other purpose.

Some critics complain that technical analysis uses far too much jargon that is not intuitively obvious, and sometimes just plain ridiculous (although bull and bear are not confined to technical analysis). The only answer is that every field has its lingo, and I introduce it as gently as possible. When you take a course in cooking, you have to understand the meaning of *sauté, blanch,* and *braise.* The lingo of technical analysis is no more difficult or silly than the lingo of fine cooking.

But it does have some additional problems. Not everybody agrees on word usage. A *bearish market* is one in which prices are falling. It rises to the status of *bear market* (no *-ish*) when it has fallen by 20 percent or more from a peak for a sustained period. A *bull market* is one that has risen at least 20 percent for a sustained period from a major low. Some writers, even experts, call *any* big move a bull or bear market when they should use a more-careful phrase, such as "the market has a bullish tone." In short, market commentators are prone to exaggeration and sloppy use of language. Be aware of this shortcoming. Check the facts before you go bulling or bearing your way through the market.

Technical analysis

Technical analysis is the broadest of the terms. It covers hand-drawn lines as well as grand theories of price cycles. In short, technical analysis is a term encompassing all the tricks and techniques.

Technical analysis is not confined to just math-based techniques, as some folks may think. Using math is a breakthrough and a curse. Math may outperform human judgment and the human eye, as many an optical illusion has proved, but it's not true that numbers never lie. Numbers lie all the time in price analysis! You can have a textbook-perfect trend with ten confirming indicators, and it can still run into a brick wall — really bad news that trashes the price of the security. Math can never overcome the inconvenient fact that fresh news, which no one can predict, may overwhelm any price trend.

In your quest to define trendedness and formulate trading rules to maximize profits and reduce risk, don't run the risk of turning into an obsessed, nerdy number cruncher. Don't forget that behind the numbers are other human beings who often behave in irrational ways. Technical analysis (so far) remains an art, not a science, even when it uses scientific methods.

What You Need to Get Started

If you don't already know trading basics, you need to get a few things under your belt to get the most out of this book — things like what a securities exchange is, exchange hours, what trades in after hours, what brokers do (and don't do), trading conventions like "bid and offer" and order types, how to read a brokerage statement, and oh yes, what securities you plan to trade.

After that, all you really need is a newspaper that publishes securities prices, a sheet of graph paper, and a pencil. Fortunes have been made with nothing more than that. But these days, a computer, an Internet connection, and at least one piece of software that allows you to collect data and draw charts are also standard issue. You can also do charting directly on technical analysis Web sites without buying software.

Don't skimp on tools to put in your technical analysis tool belt. Buy the data, books, magazines, and software you need. Pay for lessons. Get a trading coach. You wouldn't try to make a cordon bleu dinner on a camp stove with three eggs and a basil leaf, so don't try to make money in the market by using inadequate tools. Your first task when you're ready to take your technical knowledge out for a trial run is to earn back the seed capital you put into the business, the business of technical trading.

Chapter 2

Uncovering the Essence of Market Movement

*T*echnical analysis focuses on the price of a security rather than its fundamentals. The collective behavior of buyers and sellers, also known as "the crowd" or "the market," sets the prices. The market may be rational or irrational, but the market is always "right" in the sense that it sets the price of a security. You and I, as minor members of the market, don't get to set the price, no matter how intelligent our analyses and piercing our judgments.

In this chapter, I suggest one way of looking at the supply-and-demand dynamics of crowd behavior that's consistent with the technical approach — the auction model of supply and demand. Next, an outcome of crowd behavior is the tendency of prices to cluster around the average, even when the average is trending. It's useful to identify clustering, in part to know when to heed the prices that stray from the cluster. Also, a large group of technical traders think that crowd behavior fits a particular model based on a sequence of numbers called the Fibonacci sequence. At the end of the chapter, I address whether this is a useful way to work with technical concepts.

The eBay Model of Supply and Demand

Securities are not regular goods, and to apply orthodox supply-and-demand economics to securities trading can result in some silly conclusions. In the biggest macroeconomic perspective, securities are indeed subject to the standard laws of supply and demand, but as a practical matter for your day-to-day trading, the auction model is more useful.

Securities aren't socks: The demand effect

Securities are different from cars, bread, and socks. You don't buy a security for the joy of owning it and using it. You can't drive it, eat it, or wear it. Aside from getting a dividend or coupon payment, the only reason to buy a security is to sell it again, preferably for more than you paid for it. Unless you're a merchant, you hardly ever buy anything with the idea of selling it again — except securities.

In standard economic thinking, the law of supply and demand states that demand for an item depends on its price, which is a function of scarcity. If something is rare, it's expensive. At higher and higher prices, demand falls off. At some point, the high price induces suppliers to produce more of the thing, whereupon the price falls. *Equilibrium* consists of demanders and suppliers finding the mix of quantity and price that both parties find acceptable. This process is called *price discovery,* and it can take time.

In contrast, in securities trading, the pricing process is like the pricing process in an auction. For one thing, prices move a lot faster. Plus, in an auction (such as the online auctioneer eBay), demand for the item often rises as the price rises. If you ever participated in an auction, you probably paid more for something than you should have. But you just couldn't let the other guy win, right? Every time someone else outbids you, you want the item more than ever and become determined to be the winner. The intrinsic value of the item doesn't matter. Sound familiar? You may even have an object or two in the hall closet you're ashamed of having bought at an auction. I certainly do.

In an auction (whether live or online), what gets your blood running is that someone else also wants to buy the item in question. Visible demand begets more demand. Auction economics are contrary to what traditional economics teaches — that demand will *decrease* as the price rises. In the auction situation, demand *increases* as the price rises. The item may or may not be actually scarce in the real world. It doesn't matter.

The immediacy of the auction is what skews prices, sometimes to absurd levels. Later, when suppliers see the high prices, they may indeed be able to find or produce more of the item — but by then, the specific demand dynamic of that one auction is gone.

Creating demand from scratch

When you are wearing your investor hat, you may buy stocks and bonds chiefly to get the dividend or the interest rate coupon, with capital gain on the price a secondary consideration. When you are wearing your trader hat, you buy a security because you think the price will rise. You decide to sell because you have a profit that meets your needs or because you have taken an intolerable loss. You seldom think about the true supply of the security.

While, technically, the supply of any security is limited by the number of shares outstanding and the like, supply may be considered infinite for all practical purposes. If you really have to have 100 shares of Blue Widget stock, some price you can offer will get you those shares. Turn it around, and you can easily see why. A price exists at which you can be induced to sell the stock for which you paid $10. It might be $20, or $200, or $10,000 — but rest assured, some price will force you to part with it, and *right now*.

In technical trading, think of demand for a security as rising on rising prices, not falling ones. Similarly, the supply of a security dries up on rising prices, at least in the short run. (Later, when the long-term security holder sees how high the price has gone while he wasn't looking, he may say "Holy Toledo!" and call his broker to sell, making more supply available.)

Identifying Crowd Behavior

Technical analysis is the art of identifying crowd behavior in order to join the crowd and take advantage of its momentum. This phenomenon is called the *bandwagon effect*. (A subset of the bandwagon effect is named *momentum investing,* which I talk about in Chapter 13.) Here's how a bandwagon works: A fresh piece of news comes out. Many traders (or a few with deep pockets) interpret the news as favorable to the security, and buying overwhelms selling so that the price rises. You profit by going with the flow. Then when everyone is jumping off the bandwagon, you should jump, too.

Traders are people, and people often behave in predictable ways. When it comes to emotions like fear and greed, people today are not so different from people 100 years ago or maybe even 1,000 years ago. People become reckless and irrational in a mania. They become overly cautious after a bubble bursts. A *mania* is a situation in which traders buy an object or security without regard for its intrinsic value or even whether they'll be able to sell it again later at a higher price. They fear being left out of an opportunity. They're caught up in the moment and temporarily irrational. A *panic* is the opposite — people can't sell the thing fast enough and will accept ever-lower prices just to get any money back at all.

In economic history, a mania or a panic comes along only a few times in a century. However, in the technical world, mania and panic happen every day, in miniature. Emotional extremes lead to price extremes in the context of the hour, day, or week — minimanias and minipanics occur all the time. Those words aren't used in technical trading lingo, but the emotion and the price effects are the same as in big-picture manias and panics. (I lead you through a technical terminology minefield in the "Identifying and Responding to Crowd Extremes" section in this chapter.)

The individual versus the crowd

People behave differently as individuals from the way they act when they're part of a crowd. Crowd behavior encompasses fraternities, sports teams, political parties, gangs, religious sects, mobs, people attending an auction — the list goes on. A crowd is more than the sum of its parts. Otherwise sensible individuals can behave in the most extraordinary ways when they become part of a crowd. One famous case is how people in 17th-century Holland saw tulipmania, the trading of tulip bulbs for sums like $250,000, deflate overnight when someone mistakenly ate one, revealing how ridiculously far prices had diverged from any reasonable concept of value.

You know that if someone shouts, "Fire!" in a crowded theater, people will trample each other to get to the exits. In markets, you see the same thing in the price of a security when bad news about it is released. Also, if someone shouts, "Free ice cream!" people will throw elbows at anyone just to be first in line. The same thing happens to securities prices as they reach new highs, especially if an authority figure pronounces the security a gem and a bargain.

Don't be surprised when traders invent rumors to try to create a stampede — in either direction. As a technical trader, you want to be sensitive to what the crowd is doing without succumbing to the ruling passions of the crowd itself. Technical traders work hard at not listening to chatter about securities, even from experts. You may get information overload — and you may get *disinformation* (deliberately misleading information). All the information you need to make a trading decision is embedded in the price. The price incorporates the crowd reaction to information, and it's more practical to look at prices than to guess what the crowd might be thinking. When you check the news for the cause of a price action, do it with a healthy dose of skepticism.

Playing games with traders' heads

The market is self-regarding — it watches itself. One behavior begets another in a dynamic way. For example, many advisors recommend a rule that if a price falls by x percent from a peak, it's prudent to exit the trade. William O'Neil of *Investor's Business Daily* made the 8 percent rule popular. Famous investor Gerald Loeb and others used the 10 percent rule. Other advisors recommend a 25 percent rule. Because these rules are so well known, many traders use then and cause the rule to be self-fulfilling. Traders know that others will exit at a level of (say) 8 to 10 percent or 25 percent under the peak, and will sell the security specifically to get everyone else to exit, whereupon they're able to buy the security at a cheaper price. Activities like this reveal the game-playing aspect of trading.

Game playing can become incredibly complex, replete with bluffing, cheating, feints, and double crossing. Note that many top traders are also top competitors in fencing, chess, backgammon, bridge, and poker. Each security or class of securities has a different degree of crowd complexity. The crowd that trades the S&P e-mini futures contract is different from the crowd that trades the soybeans futures contract, and in turn, that crowd is different from the one that trades the Swiss franc and the one that trades IBM stock.

Each security has its own crowd, and you will get a payoff if you can figure out what pushes the buttons of the crowd that trades your security. One crowd may always respect a support line, for example, while others enjoy breaking the support line by just a little to induce selling so they can buy at a cheaper price. (For more on support lines, see Chapter 10.) In foreign exchange (FX), the Elliott Wave theory has a grip on many traders' imaginations. You may think the theory is ridiculous, but you still want to know the wave count and the retracement levels in order to know that the FX crowd is thinking. See "The Elliott Wave principle" sidebar in this chapter.

Figuring Out What's Normal: Considering the Normal Distribution

Each crowd, whether a fraternity or a gang, develops criteria for normal behavior, such as wearing certain colors or having a secret vocabulary. In trading, the crowd that trades a specific security has a firm grip on the normal daily high-low trading range and can easily and quickly spot any big price move beyond that normal range. (I cover the high and the low in Chapter 6 and the average range in Chapter 7.)

This section describes how to identify what is "normal" and outlines a trading technique that some traders use. I think it's equally useful to identify what is normal in order to be able to spot what is "abnormal" — in other words, what constitutes an extreme. Alas, I have to throw in a few math terms, but fear not. You can easily wrestle the concepts to the ground.

Reverting to the mean

The phrase *reversion to the mean* refers to a statistical concept that accepts as its core assumption that high and low prices are temporary and a price will tend to go back to its average over time. The first step is to identify the normal trading range of the security, say $5 per day. (For more on the trading range, see Chapter 7.) You can observe that the price varies by about $5 every day around an average price of (let's say) $20 over the past week. Therefore, if the current price is $17.50, that's half of the normal trading range below the average price and a buying opportunity. If the price is $22.50, that's half of the average trading range above the average and a selling opportunity. If prices are normally distributed, you can buy at $17.50 and sell at $22.50 for a $5 profit. In other words, deviations from the average price are expected to revert to the average.

Okay, here it comes — I just introduced a fancy word, *deviation*. The concept of deviation (and its cousin, standard deviation) is not as hard as it sounds. When discussing the idea of normal distribution and deviation from normal distribution, textbooks use the height of a group of people in a room. The average height is (say) 5 feet 8 inches, with some short people distributed out on the left-hand side at 4 feet 10 inches and some tall people out on the right-hand side at 6 feet 4 inches. The height measurement of the majority of people, about 67 percent, falls near the center, while the very short and very tall cases are out near the edges, called the *tails*. In this example, the "normal" height is 5 feet 8 inches — it's the average, and the normal range is 4 feet 10 inches to 6 feet 4 inches. In this crowd, you would instantly spot someone who was 3 feet 2 inches or someone who was 7 feet 10 inches.

Prices clustered around the average are normal and represent the market consensus of the rough equilibrium price for that day. The prices farther away from the normal price tend to deviate by only one unit from the average in each direction: higher or lower. This unit is named a *standard deviation*. Frankly, that's all you need to know about the standard deviation — it's a unit of measurement that describes how far away from an average higher or lower prices are likely to fall, based on the past distribution of highs and lows against a past average.

The one standard deviation region is symmetrical. When you use the normal distribution concept, you assume that an equal number of prices will fall on each side of the average. This assumption isn't always true, of course. Prices are trended at least some of the time, and so if the price is on a generally rising trend, expect to see the distribution curve skewed to one side, toward the higher prices. You'll also see days in which the prices form a double hump or are just flat across the daily range.

Trading mean reversion

To trade the concept of mean reversion means that you find an average price over some past period, figure out the high-low range, and simply buy when the price has deviated to the low side of the range and sell when it gets to the high side.

Does this sound too good to be true? Well, it is. Mean-reversion trading ideas have the appearance of applying basic statistical concepts to securities prices to derive trading rules, but mean-reversion trading faces severe obstacles, such as:

✔ What is the ideal lookback period to determine the average? Say, for example, that Blue Widget stock over the past two years averaged $20 — but that $20 average incorporates a few abnormal prices like $1 and $40. An average can disguise multiple deviations that have already occurred.

✔ Is it true that securities prices are normally distributed? Statisticians say that securities prices are not actually normally distributed — they just look that way sometimes. In technical analysis, your primary goal is to determine whether your security exhibits a price trend. You also want to know how strong the trend is and whether it might be ending soon. To accept the assumption that the distribution of prices will be normal is the same thing as saying that you know in advance where the price trend will end — at or near the price represented by the average plus one standard deviation. If the price goes higher than the price that one standard deviation dictates, the trading rule embedded in the mean-reversion trading technique would have you sell.

You consider the security "overpriced" on a statistical basis. And yet you can't be sure that the other traders in the market performed exactly the same analysis as you did. Even if they are using the mean-reversion concept, maybe they used a different lookback period to calculate the average. Because the other traders in this security don't see the security as overpriced, they may keep buying, and buying, and buying — pushing the price to the equivalent of the guy in the room standing 7 feet 10 inches. The opposite is true, too. The mean-reversion process would not identify the situation where the price keeps going to zero.

Identifying and Responding to Crowd Extremes

Statistical analysis cannot capture the nuances of crowd behavior. One way to get a handle on crowd behavior is to master the key terms referring to crowd behavior. These terms range from general trading-lore descriptions to words that are specific to technical analysis. Notice that most of the lingo applies to crowd extremes. These words and phrases, whether old news or brand-new to you, are important as you navigate the technical trading waters.

Ready to dive right in? Here's what you need to know:

- ✔ **Accumulation:** As market participants get excited about a security, they become increasingly bullish and either buy for the first time or add to positions, a phase named *accumulation*.

- ✔ **Distribution:** When traders become disillusioned about the prospect of their security price rising, they sell, a stage called *distribution*.

- ✔ **Changing your position:** To buy 100 shares of a stock is to *enter a position*. To buy another 100 shares for a total of 200 is to *add to your position*. If you have 500 shares and sell half, you would be *reducing your position*. To sell all the shares you own is to *square your position*. When you're *square* (also called *flat*), you have no position in the security. All your money is in cash. You're neutral. (I talk more about changing your position in Chapter 5.)

- ✔ **Too far:** After traders have been accumulating the security on rising prices, eventually the price goes too far. *Too far* is a relative term and can be defined in any number of equally valid ways. In the mean-reversion case in the "Reverting to the mean" section in this chapter, too far would be a price of $32.50 when the normal distribution would cap the highest price at $22.50.

  If you like to draw support and resistance lines (for more info, see Chapter 10), *too far* is a level beyond the lines, a *breakout*. If you're of a statistical bent, you will determine that *too far* lies just outside a band constructed from the average true range, two standard deviations away from a moving average (called a *Bollinger Band*), or some other nonjudgmental measure. See Chapter 14 for a description of those techniques.

Breaching the limits: Overbought and oversold

When a price has reached or surpassed a normal limit defined by an indicator, that price is at an extreme. In an up move, everyone who wanted to buy has already bought. In this case, you can say that the market is *overbought,* a term specific to securities trading. In a down move, when everyone who wanted to sell has already sold, the security is called *oversold.*

Technical traders apply the concepts of overbought and oversold to market indices as well as individual securities. Overbought and oversold are usually measured by the momentum indicators, which I cover in Chapter 13.

Notice that the terms *overbought* and *oversold* are applied to the security, but what the terms secretly refer to is how much money the traders in that security have available at the moment. By the time most of the market participants have jumped on the bandwagon, the wagon has become so heavy it can't move forward. Traders are tapped out. All their money is in a position. Traders have to get out of their positions just to put cash back into their pockets so they can conduct additional trades.

Position squaring is the closing of positions after a big price move. Position squaring doesn't necessarily imply that market participants think a move is over. They may plan to reenter the security in the same direction later on.

Position squaring occurs for many reasons, including the following:

- ✔ Traders think that the move is exhausted for the moment.

- ✔ Traders have met a price objective — whether profit or loss.

- ✔ Traders have met a time limit, such as the end of the day, week, month, or tax period.

- ✔ Traders want to withdraw money from the security to trade a different security, or for a non-trading purpose.

Position squaring occurs when a large number of traders have big losses, too. Say, for example, a high percentage of traders believe in a particular price-move scenario that then fails to develop in the expected way. Eventually, a few traders throw in the towel. The resulting change in prices causes bigger losses for the remaining traders, and they, in turn, give up. You get a succession of stop-loss orders being hit that turns into a down-market rout, or even a panic. A *stop-loss order* is an order you give to your broker to sell your position if it goes against you too far and reaches the maximum loss you're prepared to accept. (I talk about stop-loss orders in Chapter 5.)

Going against the grain: Retracements

When a price has gone too far and traders deem the security overbought or oversold, the price stops rising or falling. It doesn't just stop, though, and hover at a particular level. As nature abhors a vacuum, traders abhor an unmoving price. Instead, the price moves in the opposite direction for a while, as traders take profits or cut losses, as the case may be. As I mention in Chapter 1, a move in the opposite direction of the main trend is named a *retracement.* A retracement is also called a *correction,* which explicitly recognizes that the security had gone too far and is now correcting course, like a ship. A retracement may also be termed a *pullback* or *throwback.*

Prices seldom move in one direction for long. Even a major trend exhibits retracements. When the market runs out of cash, traders have to close positions to get their cash back so they can put on new trades. If they've been buyers, they need to sell. If they've been sellers (shorting the security), they need to buy. Therefore, at the extreme outside limit of a price move, you should expect a temporary, minor reversal of the previous price move. In an uptrend, a retracement is always a drop in price. In a downtrend, a retracement is always a rise in price. Position squaring generally causes a price move in the opposite direction of the trend.

Retracements can get out of hand and transform themselves into trend reversals, too. At the time a retracement starts, you don't know for sure that it is a retracement. For all you know, it could be a full reversal, with the price switching directions. In this situation, you do well to check the fundamentals — the news and events pertaining to the security. An ordinary retracement caused by normal position squaring can suddenly turn into a full-fledged rout in the opposite direction if fresh news comes out that seems to support a reversal. But also remember that sometimes big traders try to trick you into thinking they have interpreted fresh news in a particular way, when all they're trying to do is push a retracement farther so that they can stampede you into a trading action that is to their benefit.

In Figure 2-1, the chart shows a primary trend with several retracements, each outlined by an ellipse. In this instance, the retracements last only a day or two, but retracements can last a lot longer, even several weeks on a daily chart, for example.

The press often asserts that every retracement is a profit-taking correction. This assumption isn't accurate. If traders took profit on every correction, they'd all be rich. Remember, somebody bought at the high. If the correction goes too far against him, he must get out of the position at a loss. From this observation you should deduce that to stick to a position when it is correcting against you requires the courage of your convictions — and capital. (I talk more about managing money during retracements in Chapter 5.)

Catch a falling knife: Estimating where and when a retracement will stop

To try to estimate where a retracement will stop is called "to catch a falling knife." In other words, no reliable rules exist to tell you *where* a trend correction will end or *when* the primary trend will resume. One of the chief uses of indicators and combined indicators, described in Chapter 16, is to get guidance on where and when a retracement will stop.

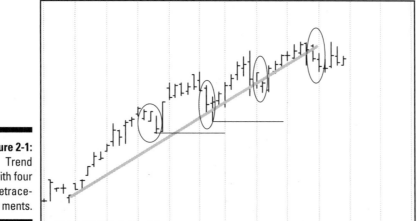

Figure 2-1:
Trend
with four
retrace-
ments.

Your tolerance for retracements is the key to deciding in what time frame you want to trade. If the security you want to trade regularly retraces 50 percent and the prospect of losing 51 percent turns you into a nervous wreck, you need to trade it in a different time frame — or find another security.

Acknowledging that no one can forecast a retracement hasn't stopped technical traders from trying to establish forecast rules. The following rules are generally helpful, but no one can offer reliable statistics to back them up, so take them with a grain of salt.

- **A retracement won't exceed a significant prior high or low.** In Figure 2-1, for example, the second retracement doesn't challenge the lowest low of the first dip, and the third retracement doesn't challenge the second. This is cold comfort, because knowing where it *won't* go doesn't help you figure out where it *will* go.

- **Look for round numbers.** Research shows that support and resistance levels (see Chapter 10) actually do occur more often at round numbers than chance would allow.

- **The 30 percent rule.** Measure the percentage change and assume that a majority of traders will place stops to avoid losing more than x percent, such as 30 percent. The problem with this idea, and it's a chilling one, is that you're measuring from a peak and you don't know the price level where the majority of traders entered. Logically, you should assume that they're protecting 70 percent of their personal cash gain from their entry, not from the peak. To measure from the peak would be to say that traders make decisions based on opportunity loss rather than cash loss, and while this contains a germ of truth, it's not a reliable assumption about crowd behavior. (The germ of truth lies in people feeling worse if they expected to get $10 and got only $1, compared to how they feel if they expected to get $5 and got only $1, as shown by behavioral economics — see the sidebar "Empiricists, 1: Academics, 0.")

Empiricists, 1: Academics, 0

Finance academics assert that the price of a security depends on forecasts of the security's underlying value in the future, such as a company's future earnings. The price today already contains market expectations about the price tomorrow. This idea is called *rational expectations.*

Rational expectations sound okay until you lift up your head and look around. You find many more price changes than you can find information about future earnings! In the 1990s, some dotcom stock prices represented 1,000 times future earnings — for companies that had no earnings. Finance academics said people knew the earnings expectations were absurd fictions, but they didn't care because they expected to unload the stock at a higher price to a greater fool.

Finance academics stopped at the greater-fool theory. If you buy a security whose price is wildly divergent from some estimate of "value," you're the fool. This is profoundly disappointing, because nobody has a certain way to attribute intrinsic value to any security. So how do you know when you're the last fool, the one who will get stuck with the security at its highest price? Even historical comparisons are iffy. To use the price-earnings ratio over the past 50 years, for example, is to assume that those traders knew the right way to merge price and value, so following this logic, you can't find any fools in 1950 or 1960. And which earnings are you talking about, anyway? *Earnings* has more than one definition.

Finance academics treat manias and panics as though they're inconvenient and rare exceptions to the rational expectations rule. In 2000–2003, most technical analysts escaped the appalling losses that accompanied the pricking of the dotcom bubble because to them, manias and panics are normal and familiar market behavior — writ large.

Behavioral economics is just starting to define in exactly what ways people fail to be rational. One key is that most people have a lousy understanding of probability. The gambler's fallacy is the most famous example — in a coin toss, after heads comes up 50 times in a row, just about everybody will bet on tails, ignoring that the coin doesn't remember which way it fell last time and the probability of heads is still 50 percent. In fact, the probability of heads may be higher than 50 percent, because the coin may not be a fair one.

But it's more complicated than misunderstanding probability. For example, people will give up a small certain gain for the chance to deprive their opponent of a larger gain. People go out of their way to avoid small risks but then take wild gambles on the word of a stranger. Most people feel twice as much pain at a loss than they feel pleasure at a gain. Behavioral economists, now winning a few Nobel Prizes, are starting to grasp and quantify these "irrational" behaviors. Eventually this work will lead to a coherent theory of crowd behavior.

Big-Picture Crowd Theories

Some important ideas about the extent of retracements come from theories about the cyclical nature of history. This section deals with these ideas as a stand-alone section because they're pervasive — and controversial.

When you start gathering technical analysis material, you inevitably run into big-picture crowd theories, a school of thought that is very popular today.

Some people swear that the ideas are obvious. But just as beauty is in the eye of the beholder, theories about the ebb and flow of history are just that — theories. No big-picture theory has been proved by statistical measures. To be fair, no theory has been disproved, either.

Technical analysis is a sufficiently crowded field already and offers a bewildering variety of tools and techniques. Why make things more complicated than they have to be? If you use the empirical evidence in front of you — clean and easy techniques like drawing support and resistance lines, for example — you can use technical analysis to make profits and avoid losses. Do you really need to know the secrets of the universe, too? My heartfelt advice to the beginner is, "Don't go there."

But you need to know that these ideas are scattered throughout the field of technical analysis and some smart and successful people in the field believe them. Those who don't are mostly too polite to ridicule the ideas. You'll also run into critics who mistakenly think that all technical analysis involves big-picture crowd ideas. So buckle your seat belt.

Some analysts subscribe to the idea that in the ebb and flow of human affairs, they can perceive cycles, including market cycles. Some of these ideas contain mystical overtones and unproven claims about how the world works, such as "the trading crowd is only the instrument of bigger forces at work."

Because these ideas can never be verified, some critics unfairly color the whole field of technical analysis with the charge of supernatural voodoo. Empiricists and skeptics cast doubt on these theories because they're not proven and by their nature, can't be proven. In particular, economics offers no theoretical basis for cycles that are fixed in size or duration. Economists do observe business cycles — several of them — but they overlap and don't appear regularly. It is undeniable, however, that retracements do occur sometimes near the levels forecasted by market cycle theorists such as J.M. Hurst, who has a large following. As a result, technical traders are reluctant to level the charge of crackpot against cycle theories.

The Gann 50 percent retracement

In the early 1900s, a trader named W.D. Gann discovered that retracements in the securities he was trading at the time tended to occur at one-half of the original move from the low to the high. To illustrate, say the price moved from $10 to $30. At $30, the crowd decided that the security was overbought and started to sell. The ensuing price decline, the retracement, stops near 50 percent of the original $10 to $30 move, namely $20. See Figure 2-2. This chart shows the 50 percent retracement case.

In fact, Gann said that the most profitable retracement is a 50 percent retracement. The area around 50 percent is a danger zone, because the price can keep going and become a full-fledged reversal around there (in which case you lose all the gains). But it's the best place to reenter an existing trend (with an exit planned just below using a stop-loss order in case it doesn't work). If the trend resumes, Gann wrote that it will then exceed the previous high, which gives you an automatic minimum profit target. This observation may be the origin of the phrase, "Buy on the dip."

Gann also saw retracements occurring at the halfway point of a move, such as 25 percent (half of 50 percent), 12.5 percent (half of 25 percent), and so on. Statisticians can't offer proof that retracements occur at 12.5 percent, 25 percent, or 50 percent with more frequency than chance would allow. The absence of statistical proof in a field populated by mathematical sophisticates is puzzling at first.

But when you ask a statistician why he doesn't just run the numbers and test the hypothesis, he points out that defining the low-to-high original move and then defining the stopping point of a retracement is a computational nightmare. No matter what definitions he gives his software, another analyst is sure to want to refine them in some other way. You'll see studies, for example, showing that the actual percentage change of many retracements isn't precisely 50 percent, but rather in a range of 45 to 55 percent. Should you accept a minor retracement of 45 percent but not a major one that correctly predicts a trend resumption at 44 percent?

A critical point about the 50 percent retracement rule is that you may think you want to exit to protect your profit at the 50 percent level. If you bought the security at $10 and it rose to $30, but has now fallen to $20, shown in Figure 2-3, you want to sell at $20 to hang on to the gain you have left. But if the 50 percent retracement rule works this time, you would be getting out exactly when you should by buying *more* (adding to your position), because a resumption of the trend at the $20 level almost certainly means that the price will now go higher than the highest high so far, $30.

A 100 percent retracement, a price that goes from $10 to $30 and back to $10, will often form a *double bottom,* a bullish formation. When the price peaks twice at the same level, you have a *double top,* a bearish formation. (See Chapter 9 for more details on these formations.)

Figure 2-2:
Gann 50
percent
retracement
rule.

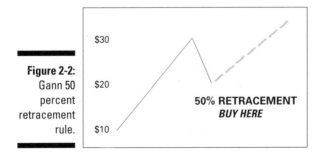

Magic numbers: "The secret of the universe"

Another theory about how retracements should form is based on the Fibonacci sequence of numbers. This theory says that a retracement is most likely to stop at one of a series of numbers, with an emphasis on 38 percent or 62 percent of the original move. Where does this come from?

A 13th-century Italian mathematician named Fibonacci discovered a self-replicating sequence of numbers with curious properties. It starts with 1, 1, 2, 3, 5, 8, 13, 21, 34, 55, 89, 144, and so on to infinity. The sum of two adjacent numbers in the sequence forms the next higher number in the sequence. Most important, the ratio of any two consecutive numbers approximates 1.618 or its inverse, 0.618 (after the first few numbers).

Nature offers many examples of these ratios: daisy petals, ferns, sunflowers, seashells, hurricanes, whirlpools, and atomic particles in a bubble chamber. And many of man's works purportedly embody the Fibonacci ratios as well: the pyramids in Egypt, the Parthenon in Greece, and Cézanne's choice of canvas shape, although some mathematicians dispute some or all of these.

Of course, critics point out that many other events in nature, architecture, and human behavior follow a sequence of 2, 4, 6, 8, and so on. The number 11 can be considered magic, not to mention *pi* (3.14159), used to calculate the circumference of a circle. Prime numbers, which are numbers divisible only by themselves and one (3, 5, 7, 11, 17, and so on), are important numbers. In fact, many other self-replicating number sequences exist. In short, scientists say that to attribute human behavior to any single number sequence is ludicrous, or at least not plausible.

A trader named Ralph Nelson Elliott believed that man's behavior, including his behavior when trading in the stock market, revealed similar characteristics as the Fibonacci sequence and could therefore be charted to predict future behavior. Elliott observed that securities prices appear in a wave-like form on charts, hence the name of his forecasting method, *Elliott Wave*. Elliott wrote that the Fibonacci sequence provides the mathematical underpinnings of the wave principle. Elliott Wave adherents expanded Elliott's use of the Fibonacci sequence and often use Fibonacci levels, with special attention to 38 percent and 62 percent (but also including 23.6 percent, 50 percent, and 100 percent of the high-low span), to predict the extent of retracements. Note that technically, 50 percent isn't a Fibonacci number. It's customary to include it, though, possibly because of Gann's influence.

To make life difficult, some traders who like the Fibonacci sequence aren't strict adherents of the Elliot Wave principle and some Elliot Wave traders don't necessarily believe that price moves will stick to Fibonacci numbers. See the sidebar "The Elliot Wave principle" in this chapter for more about the Elliott Wave, which goes far beyond the subject of retracements.

The Elliott Wave principle

The wave idea became popular in part because one of its proponents, Robert Prechter, called for a massive bull market in 1982 that did materialize — and then he called the top, just ahead of the 1987 Crash. That certainly got the market's attention! And prices do seem to move in waves on many charts.

The basic idea is that all price movements have two segments: impulse waves and corrective waves. The *impulse wave* is the way the crowd wants to take the price in a trend. Considering that the right way to look at price developments is through the lens of crowd psychology, impulse is an excellent choice of words. Each impulse wave has five parts: three waves that go in the trend direction, alternating with two that go in the opposite direction.

In a correction, each *corrective wave* has three parts: two that go against the main trend and one that goes with it. If a bull market reaches a new high in five waves instead of three and also goes down in five waves instead of three, you're witnessing the beginning of a major bear market.

You will often see three clear waves up, although sometimes a move has more upwaves than three, as in Figure 2-3. The three-waves rule is only the model of how markets move, not a rigid orthodoxy.

Elliot Wave practitioners are the first to admit that calling corrective waves is tricky, much harder than seeing impulse waves. Experienced practitioners advise against straining to make a correction "fit" the Elliott Wave model. A correction often just keeps on going, too, whereupon it isn't a correction but a true reversal and thus a new trend in the opposite direction.

Counting waves can be an elaborate and time-consuming process, and miscounting as prices evolve can result in losses and having to start all over again. If the wave idea appeals to you, be prepared to devote a lot of time to it. If you choose not to count waves, you can still benefit from the observation that trends start with an impulse wave that then retraces in the opposite direction before the trend resumes. "Buy on the dip" isn't bad advice when you are sure that you have a trend.

Seeing too many retracements

Fans of the Fibonacci sequence assert that the 38 percent and 62 percent retracement levels occur more often than chance would allow, although I have never seen statistical proof. (Perhaps because any statistical studies would degenerate into squabbling over measurement criteria.)

Some traders embrace Gann's ideas, some embrace the Elliott Wave, some embrace Fibonacci numbers, and some embrace them all. If you were to put the main Gann retracement numbers (12.5, 25, 50, and 75 percent) and the main Fibonacci retracement numbers (23.5 percent, 38 percent, and 62 percent) on the same chart of a trend, you'd have so many lines that the next retracement would be bound to hit one of them or a level near one of them.

Some advisors who like all the ideas choose to display the retracements that did work while conveniently not mentioning all the others that could have been shown on the same chart. In other words, they're going to be right no matter how the retracement turns out. You may see advertisements and solicitations claiming that the seller has "objective" methods of forecasting securities prices, and these methods are often based on Gann or Fibonacci "scientific principles." Beware. By definition, all math is science. If you're going to follow an advisor, put your faith in a consistently winning track record rather than in claims of an inside track to universal truth.

Like all technical methods, applying Gann and Elliott Wave ideas is an art, and constant revision is necessary as prices evolve. Statisticians scoff at magic numbers, but in any particular market or security, if a majority of traders believe that a retracement will stop at 38 percent, 50 percent, or 62 percent after a peak, they can and do make it come about.

The sensible approach to Gann and Fibonacci retracement ideas is to be aware of their influence over some traders. You don't have to believe in cycles, the universal truth embedded in Fibonacci numbers, or that market prices follow a hidden system in order to take advantage of what the crowd is thinking.

Figure 2-3 shows a security with four waves and three corrections (69.2 percent, 35.7 percent, and 78 percent). Notice that none of the percentage retracements qualifies precisely as a Gann or Fibonacci number, although you might stretch the point and say that 68 percent isn't all that far from 62 percent (Fibonacci) and 78 percent is fairly close to 75 percent (Gann). Most traders acknowledge the wavelike movement of prices even if they don't try to count them according to the Elliott Wave principle.

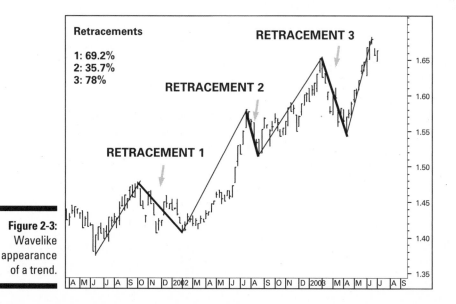

Figure 2-3:
Wavelike appearance of a trend.

Chapter 3

Going with the Flow: Market Sentiment

*Y*our goal as a technical trader is to identify what the crowd is doing and take advantage of it — without falling prey to the extremes of sentiment that can cause big losses when the market wakes up and realizes it has gone too far. When just about every trader is either bullish or bearish, you need to stop following the crowd. Acknowledging that the balance of buyers and sellers can tip violently, analysts have devised sentiment indicators and volume indicators to help identify crowd extremes. Sentiment indicators identify extreme situations so you can catch the next wave or get out of the way.

Sentiment and volume indicators operate on the principle that, "The trend is your friend — until the end," meaning that the crowd is wrong at price extremes. Some sentiment indicators apply to "the market" in its entirety, and others apply to individual securities. Volume directly represents the extent of trader participation and is a powerful indicator in its raw state, before you even manipulate the data to derive an indicator.

The word *indicator* refers to a statistic comprised of data about the price or volume of a security that has been reorganized or rearranged to provide analytical insight. You can use just about any market data that takes your fancy to create an indicator. Some indicators pertain to the entire market, like the day-to-day change in the volume on the New York Stock Exchange, and some indicators relate to specific securities, like IBM stock. The purpose of an indicator is exactly what its name suggests — to indicate the upcoming behavior of the price or volume. But remember, indicators only indicate; they do not dictate.

In this chapter, I discuss a few of the 100 or so sentiment and volume indicators commonly used. I can't possibly cover all of them, and besides, new sentiment indicators are invented every day. I also throw in a little guidance on the concept of probability, which is not as scary as it sounds. You need to have a basic understanding of probability to accept some of the inherent limitations of technical analysis and also to avoid getting cheated by sellers of technical programs.

Defining Market Sentiment

In technical analysis, sentiment comes in only two flavors — *bullish* (the price is going up) or *bearish* (the price is going down). At any moment in time, a bullish crowd can take a price upward, or a bearish crowd can take it downward. When the balance of sentiment shifts from bullish to bearish (or vice versa), a pivot point emerges. A *pivot point* is the point (or a region) where an up move ends and a down move begins (or the other way around). At the pivot point, the crowd itself realizes that it has gone to an extreme, and it reacts by heading in the opposite direction.

As far back as the early 1900s, traders observed that if they were patient and waited for a pivot point to develop, they could trade at the right psychological time — just as the crowd is beginning a new move. When the crowd is reaching an emotional extreme, the crowd is usually moving in the wrong direction. A reversal point is impending. You should do the opposite of what the crowd is doing, or at least get ready to.

Getting the Low-Down on Volume

You are more confident that a price move has staying power if you know that many traders are involved in a price move and not just one or two.

Volume is the term for the number of shares or contracts of a security traded in a period. Volume is the most powerful confirming indicator of a price move, and *confirmation* is a key concept in technical analysis. (See Chapter 16 for more on the confirmation concept.) When you look at price changes, you imagine buyers demanding more of the security at ever-higher prices or sellers offering a greater supply at ever-lower prices, which you can read about in Chapters 6, 7, and 8. But a price can move on a single large purchase or sale, especially if the market happens not to have many participants at that exact moment, a condition named *illiquidity*. (See Chapter 6 for a more-detailed description of liquidity.)

In technical trading, you use volume to measure the extent of trader participation. When a price rise is accompanied by rising volume, you have confirmation that the direction is associated with participation. You're no longer imagining demand as being behind the price rise, as when you perform bar analysis (see Chapter 6). Instead, you have outright, direct evidence of demand. Similarly, if you see a price fall by a large amount, but the change isn't accompanied by a change in volume, you can deduce that the price change was an aberration. Some trader made a mistake.

Volume tells us only the number of shares or contracts traded, not the number of participants. Obviously you can get a jump in volume that is due to only a handful of participants, and then you will be drawing the wrong inference from high volume.

In this section, you can turn up your use of volume in technical analysis by considering a few top-drawer indicators. These indicators tend to be among the most reliable in technical analysis.

Leading the way with spikes

Volume sometimes leads price. The most obvious situations are when volume spikes. A *spike* is a volume number that is double or more the size of volume on the preceding days. Say volume has been running at 100,000 shares per day for several days or weeks and suddenly it explodes to 500,000 shares. If the price had been in a downtrend, this wild increase in volume means that the crowd is throwing in the towel and exiting en masse.

When everyone has jumped off the bandwagon, get ready to jump back on. Nobody's left to propel the price lower. Conversely, the same advice is usually correct when you see a volume spike as the price is making new highs. The underlying principle is the same — the crowd has exhausted its supply of cash. Think about taking profit if you own the security. If you're considering a new position in a rising security that just had a volume spike, think again. Look at other indicators. Try to understand why so many people suddenly jumped on the bandwagon — does fresh news justify the increase in demand for the security, or is it just animal spirits?

A volume spike is one of the occasions when fundamental information is complementary to a technical observation. Beware a price making new highs coupled with a volume spike when there is no fresh news or fundamental information that attracted new buyers. Chances are that the top is in. If the security has new, legitimately exciting news and you can reasonably deduce that it attracted new buyers, you have a nontechnical reason to ignore the usual spike interpretation.

Tracking on-balance volume

On-balance volume (OBV) is a single number representing cumulative volume. A market technician named Joe Granville devised the OBV indicator to display volume adjusted as follows: To calculate OBV, you add volume on days that the close is higher than the day before and subtract the volume on days that the price is lower than the day before. You are assuming that when the price closes higher than the day before, demand was greater than supply at each price level. Buyers had to offer higher prices to get holders to part with their shares.

In OBV, you are attributing *all* the volume on a higher-close day to net buying and *all* the volume on a lower-close day to net selling. This assumption isn't realistic, but hang in there for another minute. See Figure 3-1, which shows IBM stock. Daily prices are in the top part, volume (in hundreds of thousands of shares) is the center of the chart, and the OBV indicator is in the bottom window of the chart.

OBV doesn't work all the time, but a change in the indicator often precedes a change in the price. You can see how to use the OBV indicator in two instances on the chart in Figure 3-1. Follow along:

- **The down move:** In the section of Figure 3-1 marked by the ellipse, notice how the price down move, already in progress, is suddenly accompanied by a big rise in volume. The increase in volume starts the day before the downward gap. I describe gaps in Chapter 7, but take my word for it: A falling price punctuated by a downward gap is a message that the price is going to fall farther. The OBV indicator forecasts the impending bottom, falling ahead of the volume spike and the gap.

  If you own the stock and see the OBV indicator start to decline and then you see spiky volume (like the area in the ellipse), you should sell. Holding on after the downward gap is to court a fat loss. In fact, the loss from the open on the gap-down day in Figure 3-1 to the close on the day of the lowest low is $7.22. If you had sold the stock on the very day that volume spiked, the day before the gap, you would have saved another $4.75, for a total of $11.97.

  Figure 3-1 shows that the stock did come back this time and put in higher highs a few months later. But you don't know that in advance. To hold on through the falling-price period would be to give up the chance to save as much as $11.97 in cash.

- **The up move:** OBV reaches its lowest levels about two weeks before Pivot Day 1, which features the lowest low in the series of lower lows, but a higher closing price and a gap upward the following day. (To refresh your understanding of the price bar components, see Chapter 6.) Notice on Figure 3-1 that OBV is already rising while the price is still falling, a divergence that is a critical clue to an impending change in the direction of the price.

The divergence of price and an indicator that normally move in tandem is a wake-up call. A change in volume often predicts a change in price. The indicator is telling you something you can't see with the naked eye — prices were putting in new lows but not consistently *closing* lower than the day before. Buying and selling pressure, or supply and demand, was reaching a balance.

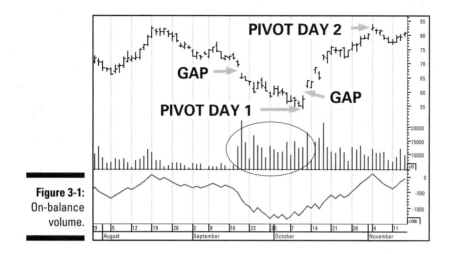

Figure 3-1:
On-balance
volume.

Your eye can see the price down move, but the indicator can detect the exhaustion of the sellers (supply).

The term *smart money* refers to traders who see the exhaustion of a price move ahead of the other traders. They are alert to the moment when the crowd suddenly realizes that it has taken a price too far — and reacts violently in the other direction. For example, down around the price lows in IBM stock in Figure 3-1, somebody had to be buying in order for the stock to close at higher levels than the day before (which is what changed the OBV indicator). These traders were the smart money.

Notice that after Pivot Day 1 in Figure 3-1 the price puts in several gap days upward. This message to the crowd is to buy, and they do, leading to Pivot Day 2 on Figure 3-1. If you had bought IBM at the close on Pivot Day 1 and sold it one day after Pivot Day 2 (when the OBV indicator turned downward), your profit and loss statement would look like Table 3-1.

Table 3-1	Profit and Loss Statement
Trades	*Amount*
Buy	$57.58
Sell	$81.68
Gain/Loss	$24.10

The raw percentage return is 42 percent for a holding period of a little over a month, or about 500 percent annualized. This ideal example in Table 3-1 illustrates exactly how using an indicator for buy/sell timing is supposed to work.

Truth to tell, though, no indicator works all the time, and this one doesn't, either. The OBV indicator didn't forecast Pivot Day 2 on Figure 3-1, although it did fall right afterward. Therefore, you'd have to say it was not leading this time, but rather *coincidental*. Even OBV inventor Granville famously missed a major bull market that started in 1982, and then persisted in saying it was a false bull for the next 14 years. However, OBV correctly predicted the crash of October, 1987 — in August, two months early. So you can see that Granville's personal woes with forecasting do not detract from the usefulness of his indicator, even if it can be tricky to apply.

Refining volume indicators

As noted in the section "Tracking on-balance volume" earlier in the chapter, the OBV indicator attributes *all* the day's volume to buying. This is not realistic. It makes more sense to attribute only a portion of the volume to the price rise, rather than the whole kit and caboodle.

A technical analyst named Marc Chaikin figured that a more representative amount would be the percentage equivalent of the price that is above the midpoint of the day. You calculate a *midpoint* as the high of the day plus the low of the day divided by two. Chaikin's version of accumulation and distribution is more refined than OBV.

If a security closes above its daily midpoint, bullish sentiment ruled. The close over the midpoint defines *accumulation*, referring to buyers being willing to pay higher prices to get sellers to part with the security. The closer the closing price is to the high, the more bullish it was. If the price closed right at the high, then you say that 100 percent of the volume can be attributed to bullish sentiment.

Conversely, *distribution* is the term for sellers willing to accept lower prices in order to induce buyers to buy. Lower prices imply bearish sentiment. Distribution is calculated the same way as accumulation — a close below the price midpoint means distribution. The closer the closing price is to the low, the more distribution existed. If the close is exactly at the midpoint, then the indicator has the same value as yesterday — and you have no reason to add or subtract volume from the running total.

Thinking Outside the Chart

You may have the inside scoop on the best stock ever, but if the entire market has a case of the collywobbles, your best-ever stock is likely to fall, too. Conversely, when the market is in a manic phase, even the worst of stocks gets a boost (hence the old saying, "A rising tide lifts all boats"). This ebb and flow isn't only because of individuals, but also because money flows into and out of mutual funds and other institutional players, like insurance companies and pension funds. All these institutions have latitude about how much money to keep in cash. In a mania, they get more fully invested, and in a panic, they pull funds out of the market and into cash.

Nobody knows for sure, but some percentage of any security's price move is attributable to changes in the market environment. Factors include not only the index to which it belongs, but also its size (large-cap or small-cap, for example) and sector (biotech, high-tech, no-tech). A guess is that about 25 percent of a price move in any single issue should be considered a function of what is going on in its index (or other benchmark to which the issue belongs).

To get a handle on possible market effects on your specific security, you want to measure overall market sentiment. You do this by looking at market statistics. Strictly speaking, market statistics are not *technical analysis,* which is the study of how specific prices behave. Nevertheless, sentiment measures can be helpful as a supplement and complement to your decision making.

In this section, you can combat the ups and downs of the market by gaining additional market tools to add to your chart tool belt. You are still looking for the supply-and-demand dynamics, just not for your own specific security.

Sampling information about sentiment

Most sentiment indicators look outside the price dynamics of a particular security or index of securities for information about whether the trading crowd is humming along with expectations of normalcy or is willing to jump ship. In technical trading, the key principle is to study what people *do* (price and volume), not what they *say.* You can do just that by following the suggestions in this section.

Monitoring investors: The Bull/Bear Ratio

Key reversals come when the majority of advisors (60 percent or more) are bullish or bearish. In other words, when everyone recognizes the trend bandwagon and has hopped on board, it's over. Investors Intelligence Service (started over 60 years ago) measures the balance of bullish sentiment against bearish sentiment (called the Bull/Bear Ratio) and claims an excellent track record in predicting turning points.

Note that other services have sprung up to measure bull and bear sentiment in general, in specialized sectors, and in mutual funds. You can find the Bull/Bear Ratio and other indicators on hundreds of Web sites and in business newspapers. To get a specific Bull/Bear Ratio from a specific vendor the minute it's published, you have to pay a subscription fee.

Following the money: Breadth indicators

Breadth indicators measure the degree of participation by traders in the overall market represented by an index, such as the Dow or S&P 500. You can track the breadth indicators to get a feel for market sentiment.

Breadth indicators include

- ✔ **Ratio of advancing to declining issues:** This indicator measures the mood of the market. Stocks that are reaching a higher price today than yesterday are called *advancing issues.* Stocks that are reaching lower prices are called *declining issues.* When advancers outnumber decliners, money is flowing into the market. Bulls are beating bears. Sentiment is favorable. When the rally starts getting tired, the number of advancing issues declines while the number of falling issues rises.

  If you subtract declining issues from advancing ones, you get the *advance/decline line.* In the same vein, if you divide advancing issues by declining issues, you get the *advance/decline ratio,* abbreviated A/D.

- ✔ **Difference between issues making new highs and new lows:** The logic is the same as in the advance/decline indicator. If more stocks in an index are closing at higher prices than the period before, bullishness is on the rise. When a higher number are putting in new lows, supply is overwhelming demand and the mood must be bearish.

Following the betting: Options

The Chicago Board Options Exchange (CBOE) is the venue for options trading in equity indices like the S&P and NASDAQ indices. The CBOE publishes the ratio of puts to calls. Here's what you need to know about puts and calls when gathering info about sentiment:

- ✔ **Put:** This term refers to the right to sell at a set price in the future. Traders who buy puts are bears (pessimists) who think the index won't reach their set price.

- ✔ **Call:** A call is the right to buy at a set price in the future. Traders who buy calls are bulls (optimists) who think they'll profit when the market rises to and beyond their set price.

Accordingly, the *put/call ratio* is an indicator of whether sentiment is bearish or bullish. A high put/call ratio means bears are winning. Recognize that an extreme of emotion like this is usually wrong, and marks a turning point. You should start planning to do the opposite. The same line of thinking holds true for a low put/call ratio: When emotions are running strongly optimistic, watch out for an opportunity to take advantage of a change.

Viewing volatility: The VIX

The volatility index (VIX) is among the most popular breadth indicators today. Theoretically, you can create a volatility index for any security in which options are traded, although it takes computational expertise. Its calculation is too complicated to get into here, but for information about volatility, see Chapter 14. For your purposes, know that when the crowd is jumpy and nervous, it projects that anxiety into the future and assumes that prices will be abnormal.

In other words, the crowd believes volatility will be high. When the price of VIX is high, options traders have been buying puts and selling calls on the index — they're bearish and think the market may fall. (For more on puts and calls, check out the section "Following the betting: Options," earlier in this chapter.) In actuality, what they really think is that the *risk* of a fall is high and worth spending some insurance money on. When VIX is low, the market is relaxed and confident — overly confident.

You can use VIX as a contrary indicator. When VIX is either abnormally high or abnormally low, you know it's getting to the right time to trade against the crowd. Start watching for reversal points in your own stable of securities. A high VIX value means exactly the opposite of what it seems to mean — the bottom isn't coming, it's already in! If VIX is low, the crowd is girding its loins for a big move. When VIX is low, traders are complacent. They're projecting the same price levels, or nearly the same levels, into the immediate future with little variation and therefore little risk.

Contrarians and cranks

A *contrarian* is someone who has a fundamental reason for thinking that a security is mispriced. In equities, one such reason could be insider info that an out-of-favor pharmaceutical company has secretly discovered the cure for some important disease and its price will shoot the moon on the announcement. In financial futures (stock indices, bonds, and currencies), a fundamental reason to judge a security mispriced may be a forecast of a central bank interest rate change that nobody else can see coming. A true contrarian is quite rare, although lots of people fancy themselves contrarians when they're just cranks. When a contrarian is right, he becomes a zillionaire and is called eccentric. When he is wrong, he stays poor and is called a crackpot.

In contrast, technical trading is by its very nature noncontrarian. You want to go with the crowd, not against it (most of the time). To identify when the crowd has gone too far isn't contrarian in the proper sense of the term. When you figure out that a pivot point is impending, you're a crowd leader. Confusion about the meaning of the word *contrarian* arises because some followers of sentiment indicators use it when talking about turning points predicted by indicator extremes. To recognize that at the top of a rally everyone is fully invested and no buyers are left is called *contrarian logic*. But to say that the crowd is wrong isn't contrarian — it's simply understanding crowd dynamics. A true contrarian has a fundamental reason to say that the crowd is wrong.

Following the earth's axis: Seasonality and calendar effects

You shouldn't be surprised to hear that heating oil futures go up as winter heads for Chicago. The prices of agricultural commodities rise and fall with the seasons. *Seasonality* is the term used for the natural rise and fall of prices according to the time of year.

Oddly — very oddly — equities and financial futures exhibit a similar effect: They change according to the time of year. The changes are regular and consistent enough to warrant your attention.

Defining seasonality and calendar effects

Seasonality used to be a word applied to agricultural prices, and *calendar effects* was a word applied to equities. Today they're used interchangeably. You can discover the seasonality characteristics of any given stock by using *seasonality trackers* on various Web sites, including the best-known seasonality tracker, Thomson Financial. Their Web site allows you to see a chart of any stock with its associated average returns by month, starting in 1986. You can also see a table of the months in which the stock rose or fell over the years.

You have probably heard the adage, "Sell in May and go away." This advice comes from work on calendar effects by Yale and Jeffrey Hirsch, who tested the correlation of stock indices with the time of year in their annual *Stock Trader's Almanac.* The sell in May rule is called the *best six months rule.*

Hirsch discovered that nearly all the gains in the S&P 500 are made between November 1 and April 30. This rule isn't true without exception, but it's true for most years since 1950. When April 30 rolls around, you sell all your stocks and put the money in U.S. government Treasuries. Come November 1, you reenter the stock market. If you'd followed this rule every year since 1950 and also modified the exact timing a little by applying the moving average convergence-divergence indicator (check out MACD in Chapter 12), a starting capital stake of $10,000 in 1952 would have ballooned to $1,472,790 by 2009. On average, you would've been invested only six and a half months each year — and remember, when you're not in the market, you're not taking market risk.

Other calendar effects include

> ✔ **January Barometer:** When the S&P 500 is up in January, it'll close the year higher than it opened. Since 1950, this rule has an accuracy reading of 90 percent.

- ✔ **President's Third Year:** Since 1939, the third year of a presidential term is always an up year for the Dow. In fact, the only big down year in the third year of a presidential term was 1931.

- ✔ **Presidential Election Cycle:** Wars, recessions, and bear markets tend to start in the first two years, while prosperity and bull markets tend to happen in the second two years. Since 1833, the last two years of a president's term produced a cumulative net gain in the Dow of 718.5 percent, while the first two years produced 262.1 percent.

Hirsch and others have discovered many other calendar effects. Hirsch's annual *Stock Traders Almanac* publishes the probability of any of the three major indices (Dow, S&P 500, and NASDAQ) rising or falling on any day of the year. The almanac bases this information on what has happened in those indexes on those dates since January 1953.

Using seasonality and calendar effects

Paying attention to calendar effects can help improve your market timing. When you're sitting down to make a trading or investment decision, you can avoid a costly mistake by consulting the calendar not only for the specific security, but also for the index to which it belongs.

Calendar effects are more than a curiosity, although a security on a wild rally isn't going to stop solely because it's May 1. But because so many traders and money managers know about calendar effects, they are to some degree a self-fulfilling prophecy.

Be aware that statisticians don't all agree on exactly how to measure seasonality effects. Seasonality statisticians quarrel with one another about matters big and small. If you have a talent for statistics and for judging among the available techniques, you can easily benefit by consulting seasonality studies or conducting your own.

Blindsiding the Crowd

You may find it comforting to think that you can find regularity and orderliness in charts, using the technical methods that take up most of this book, or the sentiment statistics pertaining to the market at large described in this chapter. But don't get too comfortable.

A big black hole in orderliness appears when markets puff up into manias and when they crash in panics. The art of technical analysis is to identify the crowd psychology underneath price moves. To the technical trader, just about any price move can be seen as a mini-mania or a mini-panic, which you can discover in Chapter 2. When the move is small, the mini-mania or mini-panic is forecastable and tradeable. But sometimes the market delivers a mania and an ensuing panic that are huge and all but define an era. Think of the Roaring 1920s and the crash of 1929, which took over 20 years to recover. This section gives you some comfort and guidance if you are unlucky enough to be fully invested when a panic arises.

Considering historic key reversals

An enduring mystery of market history is that big, key reversal points seem to come out of the blue. Seldom can you find a specific event that triggers a rally taking off or that can be named as the cause of a bubble bursting. Think back to the collapse of the United States equity markets in March 2000. Exactly what caused that fall? Experts can name a dozen contributing factors, but no one can put a finger on a single, defining factor. Technical indicators were very useful to exit not long after the bubble burst, but to be honest, this was a function of the risk management principles embedded in technical analysis far more than forecasting capability.

Many people give up on technical analysis at this point, but don't make the same mistake! You can trust your indicators up to a certain extent, but your overall survival as a trader depends on risk management, which I talk about in Chapter 5, and not on indicators themselves. Risk management is the only solution to giant random market effects. In the meanwhile, I have a useful way to think about randomness so that it won't overwhelm you. Check out the section "Enduring randomness" in this chapter for useful tips.

Take note that opinion is divided on whether historic key reversals or even *all* key reversals occur randomly. One camp says that news causes prices to change, and nobody can forecast the news. News is random. Therefore, prices must be random, too. But the other side notes that if prices were random, you wouldn't be able to see trends on a chart — and you clearly can. No amount of fancy theorizing can overcome the evidence of your eyes. If prices were random, prices wouldn't trend. But unmistakably, they do.

Any particular price may be random, but not *every* price can be random, or traders wouldn't be able to make a bid and an offer on the next price. The market would collapse — no trading would occur. Instead, traders remember preceding prices and put the current price into the context of those past prices. From past prices, you form an expectation of the future price. You will, of course, see inexplicable prices and it's fair to call them random.

So how can one or two random prices turn into a key reversal when other prices, whether random or on trend, don't? Nobody knows. But as a practical matter, if you follow your risk management principles, you don't need an answer to this question.

Enduring randomness

Technical traders acknowledge that random events can and do cause the occasional wild price departure from the norm, but the acknowledgement doesn't alter the expectation that prices will behave normally. For example, you sometimes see a price spike so big that you don't know how to interpret it (as you can see in Chapter 7). Often you never find out why such a bizarre price occurred.

A *price spike* is the equivalent of a tornado in weather forecasting. You know the conditions that cause tornadoes — you just don't know exactly when an actual tornado will develop.

Although nature may not be able to deliver a tornado in Alaska in January, the equivalent does happen in markets. Sudden cataclysmic events aren't as rare as you may imagine. Who would have thought that the S&P 500 could fall more than 20 percent in a single day? Most market observers used to say it was impossible. But that's exactly what happened on Black Monday, 1987. Most market tornadoes, like Black Monday, give plenty of technical warnings ahead of time. The problem is that traders often have those same warnings and don't get a Black Monday. This is an inconvenient fact of life that you have to accept.

Spikes are both a problem and an opportunity. If you know why a spike is occurring because you are well informed about world events and market chatter in response to the world events, you may chose to ride it out. But to exit on fear of randomness is okay, too. You take no risk when you are out of the market. Nowhere is it written that you must have a position in the market at all times.

Remembering the last price

Market panics and crashes on the scale of 1929, 1987, and 2000 are historic events outside the purview of the crowd's normal trading process. In normal trading, you can assume that a wildly erratic price has a low probability of occurring. But you can't attach a specific probability statistic to an event of historic proportions — partly because those events are so rare.

In weather forecasting, a low-probability event (like a tornado) that happens today doesn't change the probabilities of the usual high-probability events happening next week or next year. But in markets, a low-probability event does change the odds for the next period analysis because traders *remember*.

When you are performing technical analysis on your securities, you count on traders to remember the last prices and to form their trading plans on those prices. The next price is normally dependent on preceding prices, and most technical analysis programs allow you to project out a trendline (like a linear regression line, for example).

But one or two really big abnormal prices can sometimes upset the apple cart and determining which way the crowd will jump is sometimes just a coin toss. This analogy raises the issue of the reliability of indicators, which I describe in Chapter 4. They're essentially forecasting tools that depend on past behaviors to predict future behaviors, but they often fail near really big key reversals. Technical analysis is not science, as its inability to capture historic key reversals ahead of time demonstrates. In other words, having the best technical tools on the planet will not save you from a market tornado.

Thinking Scientifically

Even the best indicator fails to work all the time. In fact, some of the best indicators work less than 50 percent of the time, and that's when conditions are normal! Critics use this awful statistic to say that technical analysis is a waste of time. This harsh opinion results from a failure to appreciate the benefits of risk management embedded in the technical trading style.

You may think that it's overkill to discuss scientific method, but I can practically guarantee that this section will have a big payoff for you. That's because you're sure to see enticing advertisements for software or trading programs that are "scientific" and "objective." Well, all math is "scientific" and "objective" — but that doesn't mean you can use it to make money, and it certainly doesn't mean that using it will help you escape the next market tornado.

Conditions and contingencies

When you hear someone say, "Blue Widget has a 75 percent chance of rising," you can assume that three out of the last four times the technical method was applied, the security rose. The unspoken assumption is that conditions didn't change. But the market is not a laboratory. Of course conditions changed!

Your forecast needs to be qualified because of the thousands of factors that may come along and influence the price. *Contingencies* are things that are possible but not expected, or not expected in any great number at the same time. You know what a contingency is — like hitting every streetlight red on the way to the train station to catch the 6:09. If you hit the average number of red lights, you can make it on time to catch the train. If they're all red and you also have to slow down for construction, you miss your train.

When you hear a market maven predicting a price change with a 75 percent probability, chances are he's talking through his hat. He may have failed to incorporate all the reasonable contingencies, or he may have attributed too small a probability to any of them (or to all of them). Read financial history, and you find the ground littered with the corpses of traders who failed to include a key contingency in their calculations.

Most technical traders hate to attach a probability to a particular outcome, like "Blue Widget has a 75 percent change of rising." Reluctance to apply the term *probability* is due to a realistic assessment of the contingencies. In statistics, when you want to calculate the probability of two events happening simultaneously (called *joint probability*), you multiply their probabilities. If you have two remotely possible contingencies, each with a probability of 10 percent, the chances of both happening simultaneously is 10 percent times 10 percent, or 1 percent.

To calculate the effect of a 10 percent probability contingency on your trade, you take the reciprocal of the probability, or 90 percent, as the amount to modify the 75 percent. In arithmetic notation, it looks like this:

75 percent *times* 90 percent = 67.50 percent

Good grief — introducing one contingency reduced the probability of your outcome from 75 percent to 67.5 percent. It gets worse. If you have four contingencies and you attribute a 10 percent chance to each of them, the same process reduces your 75 percent odds to a mere 49.21 percent, which is less than 50-50.

Joint probabilities really stink, don't they? No wonder technical traders hate to declare a forecast! The more contingencies you admit, the lower the probability of the outcome.

Sample size

Statisticians say you need a minimum of 30 cases before you can say anything valid about the probability of history repeating itself. Scientists who do really serious science, like missiles and moon shots, demand a minimum of 200 cases. In setting up the Blue Widget example in the preceding section, I attributed a 75 percent chance of the price rising because three out of the last four times that conditions looked the same, that's what happened. But a sample size of four instances is hardly sufficient.

Your price data seldom presents you with 30 cases, let alone 200. Why should you accept less? The answer is that you're using a technical analysis method that works across a wide range of securities and time frames, even if you don't have enough cases in this specific security.

For example, when you have a support line (which I describe in Chapter 10) and your price breaks it to the downside, that's a sell signal. Over the past 100 years, technical analysts have used the break of a support line hundreds of thousands of times, maybe millions, and it worked. Using this method was the correct trading decision in the majority of a very large number of cases. Still, choosing to use the break of a support line as a signal doesn't work every time. A support line break is an example of a technical forecast that has a high probability in the context of many different contingencies and over many sets of conditions.

Other techniques are less reliable. You may think it would be wonderful to have a list of techniques with their *reliability quotient,* which is a ranking of how often they're right. Some writers and software vendors claim that their techniques are "over 75 percent correct." This lofty proclamation is hardly ever true. For one thing, the vendors aren't considering new contingencies and conditions. Markets are dynamic. Something that worked 75 percent of the time in the past may work only 65 percent of the time in the future, or some other percentage of the time, including zero — which is precisely what happens during manias and panics.

Part II

Preparing Your Mind for Technical Analysis

The 5th Wave — By Rich Tennant

Defining your investment risk with the: TOAST RETRIEVING RISK TOLERANCE TEST

LOW RISK | Waits for toast to pop up even though it's burning.

MODERATE RISK | Goes after toast with wooden toast prongs.

HIGH RISK | Goes after toast with all metal butter knife.

ULTRA HIGH RISK | Goes after toast with metal butter knife wearing a wet swim suit and a stainless steel colander on head.

In this part . . .

Trading has two components: The security's price and *you*. Start getting used to thinking about risk, because your own personal level of risk appetite or risk aversion affects how you analyze price movements. In this part, I show that none of the techniques for identifying and measuring market sentiment is 100 percent accurate, and so your choice of which technical methods to use is heavily colored by your perception of risk. Two people can agree entirely on what a technical indicator means and still make different — and equally valid — trading decisions.

Chapter 4

Using Indicators to Trade Systematically

*I*ndicators are a shorthand way to identify and measure market sentiment. They give you a platform for making rational trading decisions, bypassing greed, fear, and the other emotions that accompany trading.

In this chapter, I discuss using indicators to help you trade systematically. Technical traders believe that systematic trading has a sporting chance of making significant profits. But indicators don't always work, and I explain why in this chapter. To overcome the unreliability of indicators, a money management plan is necessary, which I cover in Chapter 5.

Trading is about money, and money arouses hot emotions. To speak of trading as involving only greed and fear, though, as most commentators do, is to shortchange the range of emotion in trading. Trading is also about personal success and failure. Traders feel remorse, shame, and despair as well as hope, joy, and satisfaction. Technical traders go to great lengths to remove emotion from trading decisions. The chief tool to squelch emotion is the indicator.

Introducing Indicators

An *indicator* is a calculation that you put on a chart to identify chart events, chiefly whether the price is trending, the degree of trendedness, and whether a trend turning point is being reached. The purpose of indicators is to clarify and enhance your perception of the price move.

Classifying indicators

Indicators aren't like ice cream with a million different flavors. You can classify your indicators easily, because they come in two varieties:

- ✓ **Judgment-based indicators:** This group includes visual pattern-recognition methods such as bar, line, and pattern analysis, as well as candlesticks (see Chapters 6 through 10). These indicators can be time consuming to master and to use. They're also hard to translate into software formulations so that you can backtest them to see how they would've worked over the price history of your security.

- ✓ **Math-based indicators:** The math group includes moving averages, regression, momentum, and other types of calculations (see Chapters 10 through 15). Expressing chart events in mathematical terms allows you to backtest the event over historical data to discover how well it predicts the next price action.

You may prefer to jump straight to math-based indicators because they're faster, cleaner, and "scientific." But math-based indicators do the same job as judgment indicators — they display price data in a specific format to assist you in making a trading decision. Just because they're based on math doesn't mean that they aren't subjective. _You_ determine the specifications of math-based indicators in the first place (such as how many days are in a moving average). Visual recognition and math-based techniques are equally valid and useful. Some traders use only visual-recognition techniques, some use only math-based indicators, and some use both.

If math isn't your cup of tea, don't worry. The math involved in most technical analysis isn't all that difficult (except up in the stratosphere of advanced technical analysis). You can apply math-based techniques without understanding the math behind them as long as you understand the crowd behavior the indicator is identifying and how to apply the indicator. Think of it as knowing how to drive a car without being able to build a carburetor.

Understanding what indicators identify

In Chapters 1 and 2, I point out that securities prices are sometimes _trending_ — they have a strong directional bias — and that trends are punctuated by _retracements,_ or small moves in the opposite direction before the trend resumes. At other times, prices go sideways, called _range-trading,_ which can be considered a trend in its own right. Finally, trends end, and after they end, they may reverse to the opposite direction. So indicators identify five conditions; note that in this list, I put some suggestions next to each condition, but someone else could name other, equally valid, indicators:

- ✓ A trend is beginning (moving average crossover or pattern breakout).

- ✓ A trend is strong or weak (slope of linear regression or moving average).

- ✓ A trend is retracing but will likely resume (relative strength index).

- ✓ A trend is ending and may reverse (momentum, moving average crossover, or pattern breakout).

- ✓ A price is range-trading (slope of linear regression or moving average).

Each indicator works best in one situation and less well in others. Technical traders argue the merits and drawbacks of indicators in each situation, and if you ask ten technical traders to list their top indicator for each task, you'll get ten entirely different lists. To a certain extent, the indicator you choose for each task depends on the security and also on the analytical time frame.

Choosing your trading style

Unless you're trading setups, which I describe in Chapter 16, the trend is always the focus. In a perfect world, you first determine whether your security is trending or range-trading sideways, and then you apply the appropriate indicator. In practice, you can't always classify price moves as trending or not trending in a neat and tidy way. Besides, prices usually have an identifiable range, whether they're trending or not. In addition, retracements always create doubt — you find yourself wondering, "Is it a momentary correction or a reversal?"

Generally, traders tend to have one of the following two personal trading styles and the style dictates the holding period:

- ✓ **Trend-followers:** Traders who like to identify trends may wait out retracements and sideways range-trading situations until they resolve back into a trend. Other trend followers use information from momentum indicators to modify their positions, for instance by taking some profit when the security becomes overbought or oversold even though the trend is just pausing. They expect it to continue. (See Chapter 2 for a definition of overbought and oversold and Chapter 13 for overbought and oversold indicators.) Figure 4-1 illustrates a trend, complete with minor retracements, and shows how a trend-following trader makes decisions.

- ✓ **Swing traders:** These folks operate whether a trend is present or not. *Swing trading* is buying at relative lows and selling at relative highs, regardless of whether the price is trending. Swing trading is more flexible than trend-following, because you can apply the techniques under different market conditions. However, the drawback to swing trading is that it requires more frequent trading and the profit on each leg of the trade tends to be smaller than in a single trend-following trade.

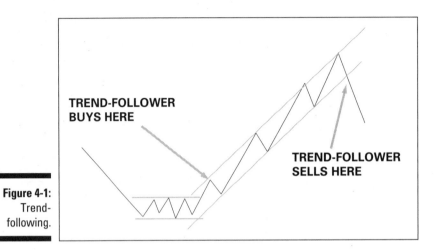

**TREND-FOLLOWER
BUYS HERE**

**TREND-FOLLOWER
SELLS HERE**

Figure 4-1:
Trend-
following.

A swing trader may know that a price is downtrending, for example, but he's still willing to buy it for a short-term profit opportunity when a momentum indicator says it's temporarily oversold and likely to enjoy a bounce upward. Figure 4-2 shows how the swing trader tries to capture every move, including the retracements. (I use the same chart as in Figure 4-1.)

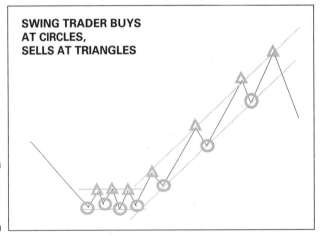

**SWING TRADER BUYS
AT CIRCLES,
SELLS AT TRIANGLES**

Figure 4-2:
Swing
trading.

If you mix trend-following and swing-trading indicators, you may get confused. One may tell you to stay long when the other one says sell. One example of this is when a downtrending price becomes temporarily oversold and then bounces upward. You may engage in a little wishful thinking that you see a trend reversal, and you become a buyer of what you think is a new uptrend.

Fading the trend

Prices move two steps forward and one step back. Sometimes you see a pause in an uptrend arriving, and you know that early buyers are about to take profit, setting off a domino effect of falling prices. You know that the uptrend is well established, but instead of waiting for the trend to end, you sell your position and also go short today with the intention of exploiting just this one small retracement down move. Selling into an uptrend sounds counterintuitive. But in practice, retracements are fairly reliable. Trading the retracement is called *fading the trend,* and it has become very popular in recent years, especially in futures. Fading the trend works best if the countertrend trade is very short term (such as hours or days).

When you fade the trend, you break a cardinal rule of technical trading — to trade with the trend, which is based on the Dow principle that once a trend is established, the probability is high that it will continue. Therefore, to fade the trend is a purely opportunistic action based on an understanding of crowd psychology. Fading the trend also illustrates that the frame of reference of technical trading isn't the security and its fundamentals, but crowd behavior. Just remember, swing trading against the trend requires lightning speed, total concentration, and nerves of steel.

To try to avoid making this mistake, you need to choose a core guiding principle, either trend-following or swing trading (see Chapter 16).

If you choose trend-following, you choose to suffer through the downward bounce in an uptrend (or the upward bounce in a downtrend). And if you have correctly identified the trend, your patience pays off and the trend resumes. If you choose swing trading, you need courage, because sometimes you're trading against the trend. Remember that your choice of trending or swing-trading indicators determines your holding period. Trending indicators generally keep you in a trade for longer than swing-trading indicators.

The best guiding principles are the ones that relate directly to the supply and demand dynamics that *you* can see on the chart. Simple, old-fashioned techniques, such as bar reading and pattern identification, are powerful. Math-based indicators are powerful, too, but if you find that you can't describe market sentiment — what the crowd is feeling — from a math-based indicator, don't use it. Remember that using just *one* indicator-based rule to guide your trading (whether judgment- or math-based), such as buying when your security breaks a resistance line or selling when it falls below a moving average, can make or save you a bundle.

Examining How Indicators Work

Indicators aren't inherently tied to particular time frames, nor do they have a single correct interpretation. For example, the standard momentum indicator

I describe in Chapter 13 uses 12 days, and the standard interpretation is that you buy when the indicator is over zero and you sell when the indicator is under zero. But you could use five days or any other number of periods for the indicator, and you could also sell when the indicator turns downward even if the value is still above zero.

In the sections that follow, I describe the general way indicators work, but be aware that technical traders are mavericks and use indicators in an infinite variety of ways.

Finding relevant time frames

Most indicators measure price and volume changes relative to previous prices and volume over a specific *lookback* period, such as 12 days or 21 days. If you compare the trend-following chart in Figure 4-1 with the swing-trading chart in Figure 4-2, you can easily deduce that trend-following uses indicators with a relatively longer time frame than swing-trading indicators.

Most indicators have a range of time in which research shows they work best. Most charting software incorporates this info and comes with preformatted indicators with default parameters, such as 12 periods for the momentum indicator.

A default parameter is only a starting point, and if 12 periods doesn't work for you as a momentum indicator, you're welcome to use a different number of periods. Twelve periods is the default because researchers found it the best number over many thousands of price series. To adopt the default parameter does *not* mean that you must trade every 12 days if you use the momentum indicator to guide you. It means that *looking back* 12 periods from today tends to give you useful information. See Chapter 13 for more on momentum.

Most indicators and patterns can stretch from a few minutes to several days or even many months, with a few exceptions. You wouldn't use momentum, for example, on a monthly chart but you could use it on 12-minute bars. Support and resistance lines can be drawn on a chart of any time frame, and you can often see patterns like a head-and-shoulders on 60-minute bars as well as a chart containing a year of data. Technology offers the ability to put an indicator on the screen that traditionally used (say) 12 days — but today it can be 12 periods, and the period could be 15-minute bars. (See Chapter 6 for a discussion of intraday time frames.)

The ability to apply an indicator over any time frame reflects the *fractal* quality of prices — the weird and wonderful fact that without a label, a price series of 15-minute bars often can't be distinguished from a month's worth of daily bars. Intraday bars are like microcosms of daily bars, and daily bars are like microcosms of weekly or monthly bars. Traders respond to price changes in regular, consistent, and repetitive ways no matter the time frame.

To pick indicators to go with your time frame, get rid of the idea that you already know your time frame. You may think you're a long-term trader but then discover a real affinity for an indicator that works stunningly on your favorite securities at 20 days. You don't want to miss out on an indicator that "belongs" to a different time frame just because you've already boxed yourself in. The indicator may be more flexible than you first think. You can use short-term indicators to make long-term trades and the other way around. Thousands of technical traders all vover the world are inventing new twists and tweaks on indicators all the time.

Heeding indicator signals

Indicators are designed to give buy and sell signals, although in many instances, the signal is more like a warning and doesn't have a black-and-white embedded decision rule. Indicators generate signals in three ways as I describe in the sections that follow — crossovers, meeting a range limit, and convergence and divergence.

Crossovers

The term *crossover* refers to one line crossing another line. Crossovers in technical analysis and trading include

- ✔ **The price crossing a fixed historic benchmark.** (See the "Establishing Benchmark Levels" section, later in the chapter.)

- ✔ **The indicator crossing the price or the price crossing the indicator.** (See Chapters 10 and 13 for support and resistance lines and moving averages).

- ✔ **One line of a two-line indicator crossing the other.** (See information on the moving average convergence/divergence indicator in Chapter 12.)

In most instances — but not all — the price crossing an indicator is named a *breakout,* one of the most important concepts in technical analysis. When a price rises above a long-standing resistance line, for example, technical traders say it "broke out" of its previous trading range and now the sky's the limit — until the new range is established. Usually, you want to scrupulously observe and measure a breakout. If the indicator line is at 10 and the price goes to 12, it's a breakout. If the price goes to 10.05, it's also a breakout.

The word *breakout* itself tells you the crowd psychology behind the price move. In an upside breakout, bullish sentiment triumphed. The bulls broke out of the enclosure and are cavorting in the pasture. When bearish sentiment wins, the bears have broken down the fence and are eating your prize roses. A breakout doesn't necessarily imply a trend reversal, though; sometimes a breakout is a confirming factor that the existing trend is gathering new momentum or passing new benchmarks.

Range limits

Oscillators describe where today's price stands relative to its recent trading range, as I describe in Chapter 13. Oscillators are usually based on 100, so they range from zero to 100, or minus 100 to plus 100, or some other variation using the number 100.

In practice, traders find that usually the scope of the price range falls well under the outer limits and doesn't vary by more than 20 percent to 80 percent of the total possible range, so they draw a line at 20 percent of the maximum range and another at 80 percent (or 10 percent and 90 percent, or some other variation). When the indicator approaches one of the lines, the price is nearing an extreme of its recent range. This is a warning of an overbought or oversold condition and thus a potential retracement or reversal. Depending on whether you're a trend-follower or a swing trader, you may alter the amount of your position or alter your stop (see Chapter 5). If you're a swing trader, you may use an actual crossover of the range lines as a buy/sell signal.

Convergence and divergence

Convergence refers to two indicator lines coming closer to one another, such as when a support line and a resistance line converge to form a triangle (see Chapter 9) or two moving averages get closer together (see Chapter 13), indicating less difference between their numerical values. Convergence is most often seen in indicators on the price chart, and generally means that the price action is starting to go sideways or has a narrower high-low range, or both. A sideways move, in turn, generally leads to a breakout. Convergence does not have an embedded trading rule and is more often used as a warning that a change in direction or the strength of a trend is changing.

Divergence refers to two indicator lines moving farther apart, such as when the spread between two moving averages widens. Divergence also refers to an indicator and the price going in different directions, and this is the most common and useful application of the observation. Momentum indicators, in particular, reshuffle the components of the price bar to come up with a price's rate of change, so that the slope of the indicator is a sophisticated measure of the strength of a trend. When the price is still rising (making new highs) as the momentum indicator starts to fall (making progressively lower highs), the price and indicator are diverging.

Divergence is one of the few leading indicators in technical analysis and something you should note as a warning of a possible trend change, although it, like convergence, doesn't have an embedded trading rule.

Establishing Benchmark Levels

Some price chart characteristics are inherent to the chart and not deliberately placed indicators. Every price series has absolute highs and lows in its history. Technically, these characteristics aren't indicators, and yet they may serve to indicate future price action. You've probably heard the phrases "52-week high" or "52-week low," meaning the security is reaching a one-year high or low. A new one-year high or low has no analytical value to the technical trader — unless it's also a historic high or low. A *historic* high or low is an absolute level that becomes a benchmark.

Examples of historical highs are the all-time high in the S&P 500 at 1553.11 in March 2000 that was not bested until October 2007 at 1565.42. Another example is the all-time high in spot gold at $850 in January 1980, not surpassed until 2010.

As in these cases, when a price makes a new historic high or low and then retreats in the other direction, years can pass before the benchmark is matched again. In the meantime, intermediate highs and lows emerge and become benchmarks in their own right. At the time they occur, they seem "historic." After a bounce up off a new low, traders hesitate to break it, but after they do, the price accelerates to the next low. The same thing happens on the way up to new highs. Profit taking after a high causes the price to dip, and traders hesitate to breach the new "historic" high. Historic levels are magnetic — they attract some traders to try to break them — but they are also barriers. Hesitation ahead of the breach of a benchmark price can be prolonged, demonstrating that traders are fully aware of "historic levels."

 Historic levels are a cause and an effect of strange indicator behavior. If an uptrending indicator like the moving average flattens out mysteriously, widen the time frame on your chart to see whether the price is near a historic level. The market is going to test the old high. If the test fails, expect a retracement and maybe a reversal. If the price passes the test and makes a new high, you expect the price to accelerate with high momentum and deliver a juicy profit. See the discussion on momentum in Chapter 13.

Choosing Indicators

The good news is that everything works, at least some of the time. Moving average indicators work (see Chapter 12). Channel breakouts work (take a peek at Chapter 11). Trading in a three-to-five-day time frame with candlestick analysis works (see Chapter 8). But indicators only *indicate.* They don't *dictate* the next price move.

All newcomers to technical analysis (and many old hands as well) tend to lose sight of the limitations of indicators. Folklore says that technical traders are always seeking the Holy Grail, or the perfect indicator or combination of indicators that is right 100 percent of the time. It doesn't exist. One of the reasons it doesn't exist is that *you* are different from the next guy. Equally important, *you* change over time. The ideal indicator that delivered great profits ten years ago is one that you now avoid as carrying too much risk. In other words, an indicator is only what you make of it — how you apply it.

The old joke has it, "Give 12 technical traders a new indicator, and a year later you have 12 different track records." How you use an indicator isn't set by the indicator itself, but by the trading rules you use. Indicators and trading rules have a chicken-and-egg relationship. The process of selecting and using indicators involves not only the characteristics of the indicator, but also a consideration of the trading rules you must employ to make the indicator work properly for you.

For example, you may like an indicator but find it generates too many trades in a fixed period, so you don't execute every single signal. Someone else may use the identical indicator, but instead of overriding indicator signals with personal judgment like you, he modifies the exact timing of trades by using a second indicator. I talk about combining indicators in Chapter 16.

Modifying indicators with trading rules is *always* better than overriding them. To override your indicator haphazardly is self-defeating. You're letting emotion back in. Plus, you won't get the expected result from the indicator — and then you'll blame the indicator. Fortunately, most indicators are fairly flexible. They can be adapted to fit the trading style you prefer, such as the frequency of your trades. Indicators are about price-move measurement. Trading rules are about you and your tolerance for risk. Trading rules must be appropriate to the indicators you choose. In short, don't pick indicators that you can't follow, like a momentum indicator that gives ten trading signals per month when you don't have the time or inclination to trade that often.

Optimizing: Putting Indicators to the Test

The first step in seeing whether a given indicator can work for you is to test how it would have worked in the past. You expect price patterns to repeat, because crowd psychology doesn't change much. *Optimization* is the process of testing a hypothesis on historical data (backtesting) to discover which parameter would've worked best. In practice, the terms *backtesting* and *optimization* are used interchangeably.

Optimization is a necessary evil because when you're starting out to trade a new security, you don't know which indicators to use or which parameters to put into the indicators. In keeping with the empirical approach, try various indicators and different parameters in the indicators to see what works.

I say that optimization is evil because common sense tells you that conditions are never exactly the same and what worked on historical data may not work in the future. Backtests to find good indicators and optimum parameters give you a sense of accuracy and reliability that is almost always misleading. Keep reading for more on optimization.

Constructing a backtest optimization

Backtesting is a valuable exercise that delivers a measure of how well an indicator parameter might work — in a situation where you have no other evidence that the indicator will work at all. Backtesting is better than eyeballing multiple versions of the indicator on a chart.

A popular place to start backtesting indicators on your security is the simple moving average crossover. The goal of the backtest is to find x, which is the number of days in the moving average that would generate the best profit by using a crossover rule (See Chapter 12). Here's the formal hypothesis: "If you buy XYZ stock every time the price crosses above the x-day moving average and sell it every time the price crosses below the x-day moving average, it'll consistently and reliably be a profitable trading rule."

Just about every software package allows you to search for the optimum moving average and will deliver the results in minutes. In this case, I ordered the software to test every moving average from 10 to 50 days over the past 1,000 days to see which moving average would have delivered the most profit on XYZ stock (the name is withheld to protect the innocent). I also ordered a buy-only strategy, although you can also test for additional gains from going short (to sell today without owning the security and buy it back later after the price has fallen). You can see the top-three best results in Table 4-1.

Table 4-1	Results of Simple Moving Average Crossover Backtest on XYZ Stock		
Number of Days in Moving Average	**Average Profit/Loss**	**Percent Gain**	**Number of Trades**
10	$1.56	68.60%	178
31	$3.02	59.34%	32
35	$3.32	61.69%	47

The Table 4-1 test results shows that if you had been willing to trade 178 times in 1,000 days, or roughly every 2 weeks, you would have made 68.6 percent by using a 10-day moving average crossover of the price. Is that a good number? One way to judge is to compare it to buy-and-hold; in other words, buying on Day 1 and selling on Day 1,000. In this case, the software calculated the buy-and-hold return as 43.4 percent, so for all that trading work, you made an additional 25.2 percent. On a $10,000 starting capital stake, that's $2,520. Or did you? I didn't include brokerage and other costs in this calculation.

Always look at an indicator backtest *after* slippage. *Slippage* is the reduction in trading profits that arises from the cost of trading. It includes not getting the exact price on your screen, having to trade on the opening price because your indicator didn't give you the signal until yesterday's close was in, the bid-offer spread, commissions, and fees. Checking the indicator's performance after slippage can make all the difference between a profitable trading rule and an unprofitable one.

In Table 4-2, factoring in the cost of slippage now makes the 31-day version of the simple moving average the better choice.

Table 4-2	Results of Simple Moving Average Crossover Backtest on XYZ Stock Incorporating $10 Per-Trade Slippage		
Number of Days in Moving Average	**Average Profit/Loss**	**Percent Gain**	**Number of Trades**
10	$0.36	28.60%	178
31	$2.70	49.34%	32
35	$2.10	31.69%	47

Refining a backtest

In the simple moving average crossover tests in Tables 4-1 and 4-2, I used one criterion for selecting the optimum moving average — percent gain. But percent gain is not the only goal. If percent gain were the only goal, you could find yourself accepting a trading regime that delivers 100 losing trades for every 10 winning trades. The ten winners must each be a home run to make up for all those losses. But you are looking for systematic trading, not a few home runs that may not repeat in the next 1,000 days. Therefore you also care about the number of winning trades versus losing trades and about the average win-loss ratio. You want as few losing trades as possible and you want to get more profit from the average winning trade than you lose on the average losing trade.

This time, I asked the program to show the top most profitable combinations of the two moving average crossover trading rule. Here is the hypothesis I seek to prove: "If you buy XYZ stock every time the shorter-term moving average price crosses above the longer-term moving average and sell it every time the shorter-term moving average crosses below the longer-term moving average, it'll consistently and reliably be a profitable trading rule."

As in the first two tests (Table 4-1 and 4-2), I told the program to buy only and tested over the past 1,000 days every short-term moving average from 1 to 20 days against every long-term moving average from 21 to 100 days. I also stipulated a $10 slippage cost of each trade. Table 4-3 shows two of the results.

Table 4-3	**Results of Two Moving Average Crossover Backtests on XYZ Stock**			
Short-term Moving Average/ Long-term Moving Average	**Percent Gain**	**Total Trades**	**Total Winning Trades/Total Losing Trades**	**Average Gain/Loss**
Version 1: 10/73	58.60	8	6/2	1.75
Version 2: 5/10	63.48	147	47/100	0.56

The average gain-loss column indicates that Version 1 makes less profit than Version 2, but takes only eight trades over the 1,000 days. Version 1 also has a much higher number of winning trades than losing trades and a higher gain-loss ratio. Most traders will zoom in on that win-loss ratio and pick the top combination for the lower number of trades and the higher average gain-loss ratio, even at the expense of some profit.

Backtesting never delivers a single, no-brainer parameter. Even after factoring in brokerage and slippage costs, you still have to choose between the parameter that calls for more trades over one that calls for fewer trades, and between one that delivers more winning trades than losing trades, and the one that delivers a better win-loss ratio. You hardly ever find a parameter for your indicator that meets all three criteria.

Fixing the indicator

The two moving average crossover backtest results in Table 4-3 highlight some of the common problems you encounter when you begin backtesting indicators. I go into more detail about these issues in the following sections.

Overtrading

Some indicator parameters call for more-frequent trading than you can spare time for. You therefore need to find adjustments to the indicator to reduce the number of trades without damaging the returns from the winning trades. One solution is to filter the buy/sell signals by specifying that you want the software to generate a buy/sell signal only if the price is x percent above or below the moving average or has been above or below the moving average by y amount of time. Most indicators can be filtered in this way.

Losing trades

The single best way to reduce your losing trades is to add a confirmation requirement, such as one of the momentum indicators. In fact, in my own experience, adding 12-day momentum as an additional requirement can reduce the number of trades by 30 to 50 percent without sacrificing much profit. And because the trades being eliminated by momentum confirmation are generally losing trades, the gain-loss ratio improves, too.

Applying the indicator again

After choosing your indicator parameter, your job isn't finished. Backtests are hypothetical. You didn't actually make those trades. To get a more-realistic idea of how an indicator-based trading rule works, backtest the rule on his- torical price data and then apply it to out-of-sample data. In the XYZ case in Table 4-1 and 4-2, for example, I backtested on 1,000 days of data. Now I should backtest it on the next 500 days of data. If the results are about the same on the fresh data, you consider your rule to be *robust,* meaning it works across a wide range of conditions.

Evaluating the risks of backtesting

The flaw in optimization is that the ideal parameter for an indicator is ideal only for the past. Critics of backtesting point out that even if your indicator is robust on the next 500 days of out-of-sample data, after you actually add that 500 days to the backtest, the perfect parameter is now some other number. You can go mad backtesting until you are blue in the face, and you will never find the optimum parameter that stays the same over time.

The unreliability factor gets worse if you fiddle with the indicator with filters. This is named *curve-fitting,* or making the indicator perfect for the past. The probability of that indicator being perfect for the future is low, because the market is dynamic and changes.

Don't count on finding a magic number to put into your indicators. In fact, you can use the default parameters that you find in books and software without harm to your performance — if you have good indicators for the security and apply your trading rules with care and consistency.

Chapter 5

Managing the Trade

*I*n technical trading, you use indicators that help you identify what the price is doing — trending, going sideways, making a peak or a bottom, and so on. Indicators give you useful information about price dynamics, but it's up to you to build trading rules around them. Indicators are about price changes. Trading rules are about you and your money.

In this chapter, I talk about developing trading rules that match up with your indicator skills, your appetite for risk, and your choice of time frame. Special emphasis is on stop-loss rules — don't leave home without one.

Talking about managing the trade before I talk about indicators may seem a little strange, but I have a very good reason for it. You may see ads or get e-mails touting "the one indicator that will make you 89 percent in the next three weeks" or "the dirty little secret that guarantees 92 percent profits in a year." Of course you know better than to believe these silly promotions (don't you?). Well, all through this book, I show you every single one of these "hidden secrets" and magic flash point indicators. Some of them actually perform as well as advertised, at least sometimes. But they don't do you a lick of good unless you prepare your mind ahead of time to take a new kind of responsibility — the responsibility of planning each trade.

Building Trading Rules

To plan and manage your trades, you need trading rules. A *trading rule* is the specific action you take when certain conditions are met. At the most basic, a trading rule instructs you to buy or sell when an indicator meets a preset criterion (like the moving average crossover in the case in Chapter 4). Most indicators have a buy/sell trading rule already embedded in them, as I describe in each of the chapters about indicators (see Chapters 6 through 17).

But technical trading is a mindset that goes beyond using indicators. Trading rules improve your trading performance by refining the buy/sell signals you get from indicators. Trading rules tend to be more complex and contain more conditions than raw indicators, such as "buy after the first 45 minutes if x and y also occur" or "sell half the position when z occurs."

Your overall goal should be to get the highest return for the lowest risk. How can you accomplish this? You start with a plan.

Your trading plan outline

You may think that you can do it the easy way, by having a technical expert send you a newsletter or a password to a technical Web site that gives you the magic trade of the day. The expert may even explain and illustrate the technique. But when it fails — and they always fail at some point — you end up poorer and probably pretty mad at the charlatan who sold you a trading program based on MACD, the stochastic oscillator, or something else you could have done yourself without paying a big subscription fee. You may even walk away saying technical analysis is hokum.

The fault lies not in the "magic" indicator but in the trader, or rather the trader's lack of a trading plan. Good trading isn't about the securities you trade or about indicators. It's about planning the trade in full ahead of time and following the plan. Strictly speaking, managing the trade isn't exclusive to technical analysis. But all successful technical traders manage their trades.

At each step you have to decide which indicators or combinations of indicators to follow, and your exact specifications for them. Here's what your indicators and rules need to do:

1. Determine the current trend.
2. Establish the rules for opening a position.
3. Manage the money at risk by scaling up or down.
4. Establish the rules for closing a position — set stops and targets.
5. Establish a reentry rule after being stopped or after the target is hit.

The technical trader plans the trade from entry to exit. This is the opposite of traditional investing, where you buy a security for an indefinite period of time and seldom establish in advance the level at which you will sell. But if you want to increase your stake or preserve capital, it's when you sell that counts. You sell for one of three reasons — you met a profit target, you met a loss limit, or you chose to increase or decrease the risk of the trade.

Step 4 is the most important step. If you do the other steps but neglect Step 4, you will not succeed in trading. The paramount rule in technical trading is to control losses. You can pick so-so securities and apply so-so indicators to them, and if you're trading systematically, you can still make a decent net gain if you only control losses.

Common questions and concerns

The overall subject of money management is a big one, and I can't hope to cover more than some basics here. However, I address some of the most frequent queries about technical trading in this section:

- **How much should I put into technical trading? Ten percent of my capital? Fifty percent?** No single correct answer exists. You have to decide this one on your own. You might start out with 10 percent and move it up to a higher proportion as you gain expertise and confidence. One thing is for sure: You should never start technical trading with a stop that costs more than you can bear. Van Tharp, the author of the book *Definitive Guide to Position Sizing*, offers a sensible methodology that keeps us away, mostly, from the horrors of fancy mathematics.

- **How much risk should I take?** Before you enter a new position, you should define your *initial risk*, which is the dollar amount you are willing to lose if the trade goes bad. If your security is priced at $8, you could set your initial risk at $2. Tharp calls this number R and notes that if differs from the usual definition of financial risk that involves variance as measured by the standard deviation. (See Chapter 14 for some digestible information about the standard deviation.)

  The amount of loss you embed in your stop-loss should be limited to R or a *fraction* of R. In this example, that means your stop-loss would entail losing less than $2, say $1.50. Your expected gain should be a *multiple* of R, meaning you would risk a loss of $1.50 only to make more than $2. Okay, how much more? Let's say you are willing to risk losing $1.50 only if you can make twice R, or $4. This level of risk ensures that on average, your gains are bigger than your losses.

  Now you examine your security in the context of a possible $5.50 price swing over your expected holding period. If the maximum high-low range of your security is $3, you have no chance of making $4 (unless volatility changes), but you still have a chance of seeing your $1.50 stop get hit. You need to modify your expected gain to no more than $3. Now your risk-reward ratio is 2:1, meaning that you should make $2 for every $1 you lose over the course of many trades in this one security.

- **How many securities should I trade?** As a general rule, you want more than one security as a form of diversification (which reduces the risk of losing it all in a single event), but less than 20 securities (which would require too much analysis even for a full-time trader). Three to five securities are about right, especially for a newcomer.

✔ **Which securities?** This question is trickier. Again according to Tharp, you can add up the *R* values for each of your securities and average them, giving you the expected return. If you are not happy with this number, you can alter the portfolio to include securities with a higher or lower *R* to shift the average. Similarly, you can take the square root of the mean *R* of the portfolio to measure its variance, and if that is a number that is too high or low for you, you can alter the composition of the portfolio.

✔ **How do you allocate your capital among the securities you're trading?** You can divide it up equally, or you can allocate a higher percentage to the security getting the most winning trades over the past 30, 60, or 90 days. You can also allocate according to the volatility of the security (check out Chapter 14 for more on volatility).

Finally, you can apply *fixed fractional position sizing*, popularized by Ralph Vince, which calls for allocation as a function of total possible loss as a fixed percentage of total capital. Say you have $10,000 in capital and you want to buy Blue Widget stock at $40 per share. You set your stop at $2, meaning you will sell if it reaches $38. At the same time, you want to limit the possible loss on Blue Widget to 2.5 percent of your total portfolio, or $250. Therefore, you can buy no more than 6.3 shares of Blue Widget.

Buying only 6 shares (an odd-lot, where a standard lot is 100 shares) can be done but at a high commission cost. You need to pick a lower-priced stock, reduce your stop, or raise the percentage of your portfolio dedicated to a single security. Even if you plan not to use fixed fractional position sizing, remember that this example embodies the spirit of managing the trade.

Taking Money off the Table: Establishing the Profit Target

When you have a gain in a trade, how much is enough? How do you know when to take profits? Unfortunately, few gurus offer guidance on how to design a take-profit rule. You never know at the beginning of a trend how long it will last, or how far it will go. The central issue in managing the trade is that you can have control over the size of your losses (via stop-losses), but very little control over the size of the gains. You can buy a stock at $5 and make sure that you only lose $2, but you cannot force the stock to go to $9.

In practice, each individual trader develops his own technique that is a combination of risk analysis and indicator readings. The optimum way to take profit is, in fact, one of the great, unexplored frontiers of technical trading. Here are some choices for selecting a profit target:

✔ **Name a dollar amount.** Logically, you are compensated by an amount that is a multiple of the risk you are taking. This is the Tharp approach I mention in the section, "Common questions and concerns." You set your initial risk at $2 and are willing to accept a loss of a fraction of that, or $1.50. Your profit target is double initial risk, or $4. Because the security initially costs $8, you seek a 50 percent return. This expected gain may or may not be realistic depending on your holding period, changes in volatility, and other factors. After you have made the 50 percent, however, you obey the target and exit the trade when it reaches $12. The problem with this approach, of course, is that the price may keep on rising and then you have an opportunity loss if it reaches (say) $20.

✔ **Set a true-range amount.** Your security, historically, has an average high-low range of $10 over 20 periods, your expected holding period. You want to capture 75 percent of the range, or $7.50. Because you use indicators to time your entry, you assume that you are entering at the low end of the range; therefore, 75 percent is realistic. When the price reaches your target, you take profit.

The problem with this approach is twofold: The range can widen or narrow. If it widens, you aimed too low and if it narrows, your original target is too ambitious. Second, how do you sit through a pullback? You may have met the goal of entering at a low only to have an aberrant pullback take the price down 30 percent rather than up 75 percent. This movement was not enough to hit your stop but now your profit target is $10.50 away from the current price. Because you know the average range is $10, the probability of meeting your $7.50 target within your holding period just went out the window.

✔ **Rely on indicators.** Instead of formulating take-profit rules, most technical traders rely on indicators to signal when a move has ended — the signal is the *de facto* take-profit rule. Relying on indicators is "winging it" and actually requires more market monitoring than the fixed dollar amount or average true-range methods, which deliver a number you can convert into a standing order with your broker.

Controlling Losses

Your level of risk seeking or risk aversion is personal. Therefore, nobody can design rules for you. You must do it for yourself. Ask yourself whether you'd faithfully follow every buy/sell signal generated by a given indicator when the backtest of the indicator predicts that you will have some individual trades that entail a loss of 50 percent of your trading capital. No?

Well, how much of your trading capital *are* you prepared to lose? This is not an idle question. Your answer is critical to whether you succeed in technical trading. If you say you can accept no losses at all, forget technical trading. You *will* take losses in technical trading. If you say that you're willing to lose 50 percent in a single trade — whoa, Nellie! That's too much. Three or four losing trades in a row and you would not have enough capital left to do any trades. I offer some help in deducing your personal number in the following sections.

Experienced traders ask themselves, "How much will I lose today?" when they wake up every morning. They expect loss on some level. In contrast, beginners find losses almost impossible to contemplate. Yet if you don't control losses, the question is not whether you go broke, but *when* you go broke (as a famous trader named W.D. Gann wrote on the very first page of one of his books).

Exiting a losing trade is the single hardest thing to do in trading. For one thing, exiting means that your indicator let you down. Accept that your indicators have shortcomings and that your job is to overcome those shortcomings by using money-management rules.

A bigger problem may be your bruised ego. To sell a losing position means that you failed, and the standard response to a loss is denial. "It will come back!" you cry. In the long run, maybe it will come back. But by then, you may be broke and unable to take advantage of it. Flip back a few pages and look at Table 1-1 in Chapter 1 that shows the percentage gain that you need to recover a loss. To recover a 50 percent loss, you need to make a 100 percent gain.

Every top trader admits to taking bigger losses than they planned. Many go out of business for a period of time, only to come back later with essentially the same indicators — and better ways to manage the trade. In fact, some investors say that the best time to place money with a professional trader is right after he has taken a fat loss — because then he's a better trader. Note that such investors aren't predicting he will be a better indicator analyst, but a better *trader*.

Using the First Line of Defense: Stop-Loss Orders

You use a stop-loss order to overcome the unreliability of indicators as well as your own emotional response to losses. A *stop-loss order* is an order you give your broker to exit a trade if it goes against you by some amount. For a buyer, the stop-loss order is a sell order. For a seller, it's a buy order.

If market conditions are choppy (high volatility), you may want to widen your stop even though your own particular security is behaving nicely. In this instance, you fear an overflow effect from the general market to your particular security. You may switch from a money-based trailing stop like the 2 percent rule to a volatility or pattern type of stop.

To know when to put on the brakes with a stop-loss order, keep reading. You absolutely need to understand stops to trade successfully.

Mental stops are hogwash

You should enter your stop-loss order at the same time you enter the position. In fact, you need to know the stop in order to calculate how big a position to take in the first place, if you're using any risk-management rule. Why some traders don't do this is a mystery. Many traders say they keep a mental stop in their heads, but this "method" is a delusion. The trader is conning himself into thinking that he'll be watching the price every minute the market is open and will have the gumption to sell at a loss if the limit is reached. But no one can watch the market every minute, and in practice, most traders with mental stops sit hopelessly by as the trade goes further and further against them.

Other traders say that their security isn't suitable for stops because it's too volatile. Or the trader is so big that the market would find out where his stops are and maliciously target them. Another rationalization is that the trader's stops get hit, and often, only for the price to move back in the original direction right afterwards. This excuse isn't a reason to avoid using stop-losses. It's a reason to reset the stop to a better level.

To pretend that you have a mental stop or to refuse to place stops is to avoid accepting the reality of trading — it's a business, and setbacks happen in business. Setting a stop-loss order is like buying insurance in case the store burns down. Not to take out insurance is to treat trading as a hobby and view the amount at stake as play money rather than as risk capital.

Sorting out the types of stops

Technical traders have developed many stop-loss principles. Each concept is either a fixed trading rule or a self-adjusting one. Stops relate to indicators, money, or to time, and often these three don't line up neatly to give you an easy decision. You have to choose the type of stop that works best for you.

The 2 percent stop rule

Probably the most famous stop-loss rule is the fixed 2 percent rule that was employed by a trading group named the Turtles. The *2 percent rule* states that you should stop a loss when it reaches 2 percent of starting equity. If you're trading risk capital of $10,000, you can afford to lose no more than $200 on any single trade if you expect to stay in business for a long period of time. The 2 percent rule is an example of a *money stop,* which names the amount of money you're willing to lose in a single trade.

Two hundred dollars may sound like a tiny number to you, but in the context of active trading, this figure is quite large. You need only 50 losing trades in a row to go broke. And 50 trades may sound like a lot of trades, but you find that many valid indicators have you trading that often, depending on your time frame. If you're trading 15-minute or 60-minute bars, you could easily have more than 100 trades in a month.

Although your indicators should be better than to have 50 consecutive losses in a single security, if you're trading several securities, 50 is no longer a large number. If you're trading five securities, for example, you go broke after ten consecutive losses per security.

Risk-reward money stops

The *risk-reward ratio* puts the amount of expected gain in direct relationship to the amount of expected loss, as in the Tharp approach I mention in the "Common questions and concerns" section in this chapter. The higher the risk-reward ratio, the more desirable the trade. Say, for example, that you're buying Blue Widget stock at $5 and your indicators tell you that the potential gain is $10, which means that the stock could go to $15. You could set your initial stop at $2.50, or 50 percent of your capital stake, for the chance to make $10. That gives you a risk-reward ratio of 10:2.5, or 4:1. (Strangely, the amount of the gain, the *reward,* is always placed first in the ratio, even though it comes second in the name.)

But consider the premise from this example — your ending capital triples your initial stake. But gee, expecting a 300 percent return is going a bit far, isn't it? Well, it depends on your skills. If you consistently forecast and get 300 percent gains, good for you. You may be able to accept a higher initial stop-loss level than other mere mortals.

To apply the risk-reward ratio in a conservative and prudent manner, turn it upside down. Instead of calculating it with your best-case expected gain, use a realistic worst-case estimate of the gain. Your worst-case gain should be higher than your worst-case loss. For example, say you're prepared to lose $2 for the chance to make $4. Your risk-reward ratio is 4:2, or 2:1. If you practice this exercise on every trade, the risk-reward ratio becomes a filter that winnows out trades that may be high probability but with excessive risk.

Calculating the risk-reward ratio and using it to set a stop has its own dangers. In the Blue Widget case above, you're willing to lose 50 percent of your capital. If you lose, you can take only a few such trades before you run out of money. Moreover, you can start out with a fixed risk-reward money stop but then change it to an adjustable stop as you modify your idea of how much the trade could potentially gain. Say the price falls from $5, your original entry, to $3.50. But the average range is widening and still telling you the potential high price is $15. If you buy more at $3.50 and the $15 is indeed reached, your gain is even bigger in percentage terms. Using the risk-reward ratio this way is how traders trick themselves into adding to losing positions, the blackest of cardinal sins in trading.

Analyzing risk-reward ratios is a complex task requiring knowledge of statistics and probability — a sophisticated task and beyond the scope of this chapter. But just remember that in technical trading, the general rule is to take small losses and aim for bigger gains, not to take big losses and aim for gigantic gains.

Maximum adverse excursion

John Sweeney developed the concept of *maximum adverse excursion,* which is the statistically determined worst-case loss that may occur during the course of your trade. Using this method, you calculate the biggest change in the high-low range over a fixed period (say 30 days) that's equivalent to your usual holding period. Actually, you need to calculate the maximum range from the entry levels you would've used. Because you know your entry rules, you can backtest to find the maximum range that was prevalent at each entry.

For example, if the security never changes from high to low by more than $10 over the period, you could set your stop at $11. You should see a regular pattern between the maximum adverse excursion and your winning and losing trades over time. In fact, you can use the inverse of the adverse excursion, the *maximum favorable excursion,* to select trades in the first place. See Chapter 14 on volatility.

Trailing stops

Trailing stops use a dynamic process that follows the price: You raise the stop as the trade makes profits. A trailing stop is set on a money basis — you maintain the loss you can tolerate at a constant dollar amount or percentage basis. You could, for example, say that you want to keep 20 percent of each day's gain, so every day you'd raise the stop day to include 80 percent of the day's gain. This method means calling the broker or reentering the stop electronically every day. The important point is to keep the stop updated to protect gains and guard against losses at the same time.

Trailing stops are highly protective, but you risk being stopped out on an arbitrary price event that isn't really related to the overall price trend. Some traders object to the trailing stop on the grounds that the normal average daily trading range almost certainly encompasses the trailing stop level on many occasions. A random event can cause a small spike, for example.

Indicator-based stops

Indicator-based stops depend on the price action and the indicators you use to capture it. Indicator stops can be either fixed or self-adjusting. I mention them at various places throughout the book; here are some important ones:

- ✔ **Last-three-days rule:** The most basic of stop-loss rules is to exit the position if the price surpasses the lowest low (or highest high if you're going short) of the preceding three days. This idea sounds a little corny. However, it jibes well with another piece of trading lore that says a trade should turn profitable right away if you've done the analysis right and you're actually buying right after a low or selling right after a peak. If the price first rises for a day or two but can't hold on to the gain, the up move that you think you've identified is probably a false one. Consider the crowd dynamics (see Chapter 2) and how they play out on the price bar (covered in Chapter 6). You need a series of higher highs *and* higher lows to name an uptrend. If you get a lower low in the first three days, the probability is good that the trade is going south.

✔ **Pattern stops:** Pattern stops relate directly to market sentiment and are very handy. Most are of the fixed variety. I list a few below:

- The break of a support or resistance line is a powerful stop level, chiefly because so many other traders are drawing the same lines.

- The last notable high or low (the *historic* level; see Chapter 4) or the high or low of an important time period, like a year, are noteworthy.

- You can infer stops from other pattern indicators, such as the center confirmation point of the W in a double bottom or the M in a double top (see Chapter 9). When the confirmation point is surpassed, the probability is high that the move continues in the expected direction. If you're positioned the wrong way when the pattern appears, the pattern confirmation is also your stop level.

✔ **Moving-average stop:** You can also use a separate indicator that isn't part of your buy/sell repertoire to set a stop, such as a moving average (see Chapter 12). You may not use a moving average because of its lagging nature, but many traders use a breakout beyond the 10-day moving average as a warning to reduce a position, and the 20-day moving average as a stop. You may find it interesting how often a retracement will penetrate a 10-day moving average but halt just short of crossing the 20-day moving average. A moving-average stop is clearly of the self-adjusting variety.

Volatility stops are the most complex of the indicator-based, self-adjusting stops to figure out and to apply, but they're also the most in tune with market action. Many variations are available. Here are three of particular interest:

✔ **Parabolic stop-and-reverse model:** Invented by Welles Wilder, the parabolic concept is easy to illustrate and hard to describe. The principle is to create an indicator that rises by a factor of the average true range (see Chapter 7) as new highs are being recorded, so that the indicator accelerates as ever-higher highs are met and decelerates as less-high highs come in. In an uptrend, the indicator is plotted just below the price line. It diverges from the price line in a hot rally, and converges to the price line as the rally loses speed. See Figure 5-1. The parabolic stop is both self-adjusting *and* trailing — a rare combination.

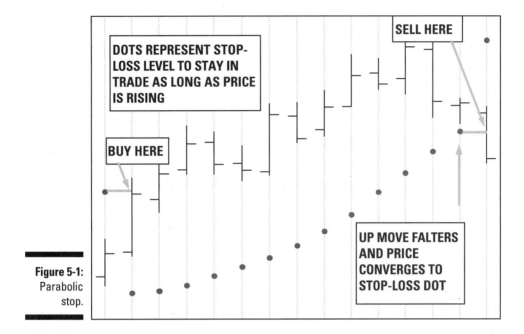

DOTS REPRESENT STOP-LOSS LEVEL TO STAY IN TRADE AS LONG AS PRICE IS RISING

BUY HERE

SELL HERE

UP MOVE FALTERS AND PRICE CONVERGES TO STOP-LOSS DOT

Figure 5-1:
Parabolic
stop.

✔ **Average true-range stop:** This stop is set just beyond the maximum normal range limits. The average true-range channel is described in Chapter 14. You take the average daily high-low range of the price bars, adjusted for gaps, and expand it by adding on a constant, like 25 percent of the range. Say your average daily trading range is $3. If the price goes more than 25 percent beyond the $3 high-low range, you consider it an extreme price and the signal to exit. The average true-range stop has the virtue of being self-adjusting, but it also has the drawback of setting a stop that has nothing to do with your entry.

✔ **Chandelier exit:** This stop solves the entry-level issue. Invented by Chuck LeBeau, the chandelier exit sets the stop at a level below the highest high or the highest close *since your entry.* You set the level as a function of the average true range. The logic is that you're willing to lose only one range worth (or two or three) from the best price that occurred since you put on the trade. Like the parabolic stop, the chandelier is both self-adjusting and trailing.

Indicator stops usually entail taking a loss greater than the 2 percent benchmark rule (see "The 2 percent stop rule" section on this topic). This factor hands you a hard decision. If you take the 2 percent rule, you have to live with the remorse of exiting trades only to see the price move your way later on, the dreaded whipsaw. If you take an indicator rule that entails losses greater than 2 percent of your capital, but have a series of losing trades early in your trading career, you could lose a lot of money before you figure out how to adapt and apply indicators.

Time stops

Time stops acknowledge that money tied up in a trade that's going nowhere can be put to better use in a different trade. Say you're holding a position that starts going sideways. It is reasonable to exit the trade and find a different security that is moving. Remember, the purpose of trading is to make money.

Clock and calendar stops

Clock and calendar stops pertain to a price event happening (or not happening) considering the time of day, week, month, or year. Clock-based rules abound. Some technical traders advise against trading during the first hour in the U.S. stock market, because buy- or sell-on-open orders are being executed then (see Chapter 6). Others say that more gain can be had from the first hour than any other hour of the trading day if you can figure out which way the crowd is trading. As I describe in Chapter 16, one setup technique is to buy or sell the direction of an opening gap — and be done in an hour.

In foreign exchange, you often see prices retrace at the end of the European trading day — about 11 a.m. in New York — as traders there close positions. Not only is this a swell entry place when you're sure that you know the trend, but it's also a benchmark for the U.S. trading day. If the price fails to close higher or lower than the European close, it means that American traders are having second thoughts about the trend.

Adjusting Positions

Stops are the first line of defense against indicator failures and market catastrophes. But to exit a position is an extreme response when your uncertainty isn't high. A stop is a blunt instrument when more delicacy may be called for. (For more on stops, see the earlier section, "Using the First Line of Defense: Stop-Loss Orders.")

Most indicators are black and white. You should either buy or sell. They lack nuance. Similarly, stops are a one-way proposition. But often when you're using multiple indicators, you don't get a clear-cut trading decision, or as the trade progresses, one of your confirming indicators weakens and is no longer offering the comfort of full confirmation. Perhaps a pattern spells doom to your position. You don't use patterns and perhaps you don't like patterns, but it's a nagging worry.

Another reason to adjust positions gradually instead of betting the ranch on day one is to follow the confirmation principle (see Chapter 16). You can start a new position by placing the first trade for one-quarter or one-third the amount of money you plan to place in that specific security and add to it as confirming indicators come in. Likewise, you can reduce the size of your position as warnings arrive from indicators (such as momentum indicators like the stochastic oscillator; see Chapter 13).

Position sizing can add or subtract from your bottom line by as much or more than your choice of securities or indicators. When you get an itch to change position size, consider whether it's because your appetite has changed, or variance has changed. Appetite may change because you just got a big bonus and are putting it all into your trading account. Now you're willing to take a bigger loss per trade. Or perhaps one of your securities makes a giant breakout, and the trend gathers steam in a straight line for an abnormally long period of time (with low volatility). Risk is (temporarily) lower.

In the fixed fractional allocation system I describe, you allocate capital among securities according to potential loss as a percentage of total capital. Therefore, scaling in or scaling out of each security by simply changing the amount of loss you are willing to take on any single security is very easy. Willingness to increase the loss you may take automatically (and conveniently) changes the number of shares or contracts you should be holding.

To increase the size of a position is called *scaling in* and to reduce the amount you have at risk is *scaling out*. In the sections that follow, I go into more detail on these terms and concepts.

Reducing positions

The safest way to reduce the risk of loss is to reduce exposure to it — start scaling out. If you've bought on an indicator-based signal but you think you know of a fundamental reason why it's not going to be a good trade, the two conflicting ideas may cancel each other out. Similarly, you may have a nicely trending security and get a surprise stop hit that you don't trust, because you think you can identify the cause as an anomaly. Instead of being paralyzed or not trading at all, you have a few options:

- ✔ Delay following the indicator signal until the nontechnical event risk is past. Some traders advise reducing (or exiting) positions ahead of known event risks, such as central bank meetings, earnings announcements, and national elections.

- ✔ Stay in the trade, but reduce the amount of money you allocate to it (and perhaps tighten the stop). You can also hedge the risk in the options market or by taking the opposite position in a correlated security, but on the whole, scaling out is the most direct and efficient method.

Adding to positions

You can add to a position, or scale in, when your existing position is highly profitable. Statisticians debate whether you should add to winning positions by using unrealized profits from the existing trade, called *pyramiding*. To *pyramid* is to use hypothetical profits to enlarge your position. Say you started with $1,000 and the trade has now generated another $1,000 in paper profits.

Why not borrow against that extra $1,000 to buy some more of this high-performing security? The answer is that if a catastrophe strikes and the trade goes against you, your risk of loss can become huge — more than your original stake if your stop fails (or, heaven forbid, you didn't place one). Be aware that if you engage in pyramiding, you're taking a higher risk than if you don't. Pyramiding without proper stops has probably caused more traders to go broke than any other cause.

In addition to the fixed fractional rule I describe in an earlier section called "Common questions and concerns" in this chapter, other techniques for scaling in and out include:

- If you're using a 2 percent stop rule (see section on this topic), when the existing position has gained a profit that is greater than the 2 percent of starting capital you would have lost if the stop had been triggered, you add the amount of the surplus profit to the position with its own 2 percent stop. The problem, of course, is that it's awkward to trade in odd lots, and odd lots don't even exist in futures.

- If you're using *margin* (where the trader puts down only a fraction of the value of the contract being traded), one rule of thumb is to add to the position when the existing trade has earned the cost of the minimum initial margin of a second position. If you're trading on a 50 percent margin, you add to the position when the existing position has racked up enough paper gain to fund the new position.

    This rule is especially valuable in the futures market, in which the trader puts down only a small fraction of the value of the contract being traded. For example, if the initial margin required by the exchange and your broker is $2,500, you don't add a second contract to your position until the first contract has a profit of $2,500. By then, you figure that the move is well in place. But remember, you have to have one stop-loss order on the first contract and a different one on the second trade.

Applying stops to adjusted positions

If you're using an indicator stop and it signals that the price rise is over, doesn't that mean you want to exit all positions at the same level as soon as possible? The answer from statisticians is "maybe." It depends on whether you're thinking in chart terms or money-management terms. If you're using a breakout concept to set your stop, for example, the price crossing a support line (see Chapter 10) is a sell signal that would apply equally to all positions.

If you're using a 2 percent or other rule (like the chandelier exit I mention in this chapter) that is calculated specifically with reference to your starting point, you exit each trade according to the rule. This method has benefits and drawbacks. The benefit is that you're still in the trade if the stop was triggered for one trade but the price retracement is only a minor, temporary one. You still have other positions left and if the price makes a big jump your way, you're correctly positioned to take advantage of it. The drawback is that a well-set stop may really identify a change in overall price behavior. If it's a catastrophic price move, you may not get good execution of your stops and may end up losing more than the amount you planned.

Part III
Observing Market Behavior

The 5th Wave   By Rich Tennant

In this part . . .

The key to understanding technical analysis is to understand the price bar. Everything in technical analysis, even the most sophisticated indicator, arises out of the price bar and its components. When you look closely at the price bar and at small series of price bars, you can understand what the trading crowd really thinks of the security.

Chapter 6

Reading Basic Bars: Showing How Security Prices Move

*W*hen you start looking at charts, you may see what looks like a bunch of unrelated dots. It may take a little practice to see, but inside each dot on the chart lies a world of information. The "dot" is really a price bar, which graphically represents all the transactions done in the security, revealing supply and demand at each point.

In this chapter, I define each component of the price bar. I demonstrate how to transform the numbers on the price bar from abstract dollar amounts into the market sentiment of the participants in that security, either optimistic or pessimistic. You know the phrase "Actions speak louder than words"? Reading price bars is the perfect application of that saying. Traders may *say* that they feel optimistic about the price of the security going up, but the price bar tells you what they really think by showing you what action they took. Reading price bars is about being a detective examining the hard evidence — and disregarding witness accounts.

Building Basic Bars

The price bar is the basic building block of technical analysis. After you have a grip on the price bar, almost nothing in technical analysis can confuse you for long. Honest. Resist the temptation to skim over the bar chart material to get to the more glamorous-sounding techniques. You can't grasp the principle of most indicators without first understanding the price bar because most indicators are nothing more than an arithmetic manipulation of the four price bar components.

The price bar is also your touchstone for identifying trendedness and critical changes in trendedness. Prices change from day to day in numerous ways, but seldom in random or meaningless ways. Every major trend starts with a change in the price bar on a single day or over only a few days, and the earlier you get in a new trend, the more profit you make. In Chapters 8 and 15, I describe two other ways of displaying price information, but right now, focus on getting the components of the standard bar down cold.

I start off here with a brief overview of the price bar and then detail each piece of it at length in the sections that follow.

Getting in on the action: The price bar in brief

The *price bar* describes and defines the trading action in a security for a given period. *Trading action* means all the real-money transactions conducted during the period. The price bar measures actual deals done with cold, hard cash, not what somebody wished, imagined, or contemplated. For the sake of simplicity, this chapter refers to a daily price bar because most of the time, you're working with daily price information. As I explain later in this chapter, a price bar can encompass different periods — anything from a minute to a month. But the scope of the period doesn't change the price bar dynamics I describe in this chapter.

Check out the standard price bar in Figure 6-1. Like all bars, it consists of four components:

- ✔ **Open:** The little horizontal line on the left is the opening price.
- ✔ **High:** The top of the vertical line defines the high of the day.
- ✔ **Low:** The bottom of the vertical line defines the low of the day.
- ✔ **Close:** The little horizontal line on the right is the closing price.

This Open-High-Low-Close component set of the price bar is often abbreviated OHLC.

The two little horizontal lines on the price bar are called *tick marks*. In trading parlance, a *tick* represents a single trade at a single price, so the tick mark representing the open or the close refers literally to a single transaction or to a batch of transactions all at the same price and at the same time. The high and the low don't need a tick mark because the end of the bar conveys that information.

The daily price bar shows the effects of every price factor in the market for that day, including the overall environment, the fundamentals of the security, and the collective emotional condition of the traders in the security that day.

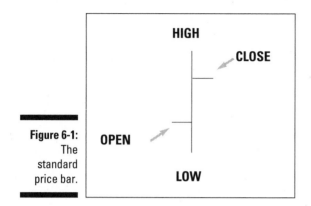

HIGH

CLOSE

OPEN

LOW

Figure 6-1:
The
standard
price bar.

The price bar tells you the outcome of the battle between the buyers (bulls) and the sellers (bears). Hidden in every price bar are a winning group and a losing group. If the price opened at the low and closed at the high, the winners that day were the buyers. If the price opened at the high and closed at the low, the winners that day were the sellers. You almost always have to take into consideration the price action embedded in the bar the day before in order to make the winner-loser judgment. For example, you can have an opening gap down from the day before that still delivers a close at the high of the new bar — but that close at the high is still lower than the close the day before. Who is the winner on this day? Well, anyone who bought at today's low (not the poor guy who had bought the previous day).

But back to the single bar. Each bar reflects a very real contest — and you measure the outcome in money. If the bar is very tall, encompassing a $10 range when the normal bar for this security is only $3, the trading was a Titanic battle. If the bar is very short, say $1, it was a pillow fight. On every single trade, one party wins and the other party loses. That is why trading — like war — is called a zero sum game.

The relationship between prices and volume is important in judging the bar. *Volume* is the number of shares or contracts traded during the period that your bar encompasses. Everything that you infer about the state of mind of the market participants is subject to confirmation by volume. For example, if the price bar is three times the usual size, you would want to verify that a large number of traders were active that day by looking at volume. It would be wrong to see a trading battle if only one trade was done at the $10 high. In that case, the $10 price is an anomaly. Somebody made a mistake — either the buyer at $10 or the data collection department at the exchange.

When you get befuddled by a tangle of patterns and indicators on your chart, return to the basics — a clean chart that contains only the price bars — and ask yourself "What are these bars saying?" Chances are they are singing quite a tune. Price bars are the raw material of indicators, so when indicators are giving you conflicting or confusing signals, go back to the source. Observing the characteristics of the price bar and interpreting changes correctly can save your hide. In fact, many traders make all their decisions on the price bar alone. See Chapter 16.

Setting the tone: The opening price

The *opening price* is the very first trade done between a buyer and a seller on the trading day. It reflects the new day's hopes and fears. The meaning of the open, like all the price bar components, comes from its relationship to the other components of the bar as they develop and to the components of the bars that had come before, especially the close.

Sometimes the opening price means nothing at all. Market prices are sometimes random because people make decisions about their money that have nothing to do with the price, but rather with their personal needs. Maybe Uncle Herbert got up this morning and said to himself, "I think I'll sell my Blue Widget shares at the open today and go on a cruise." Randomness can also affect the other parts of the price bar, not just the open, of course.

In U.S. stocks, the exchanges decided years ago to stop recording the first trade. When you see the open in a newspaper or most data services, that numbers is often not actually the first trade of the day, but a synthetic price (like an average of the first five trades) devised by the *data collector* (the exchange where the security is traded or a private data vendor like Reuters). This is why the opening price varies from one data source to another. Not having accurate data drives some technical analysts wild because the opening price sets the tone and if somebody made it up, it doesn't matter how reasonable the calculation process — it's not literally the first price of the day. This problem is now compounded by the existence of several exchanges trading the same equity securities and related options.

Some equity analysts say that they never look at the open because it's not strictly accurate. And although in futures trading the open is the real McCoy, in many instances (such as equity index futures and foreign exchange), trading has been going on in the overnight Globex market, so the actual open on the U.S. exchange floor is hardly ever a surprise.

So should you heed the open? Yes. In equities, any particular opening price may not be accurate, but over a series of days, the open adequately represents the sentiment at the beginning of the day. Heed the opening price in futures, too, including equity index futures. The open is your benchmark for evaluating the price action over the course of the day.

The opening price's most important relationship is to the close of the day before. Whether the open is up or down, you can figure out how to evaluate the opening price in the following sections. (For more on the close, see the section "Summarizing sentiment: The closing price," in this chapter.)

When the open is up

If the open is up from the close the day before, you imagine that the first trader of the day spotted overnight news favorable to the security, or is expecting favorable news, or has some other reason to think his purchase will return a gain. If you, too, want to be a buyer today, his action reinforces your feeling. The first trade sets the tone.

Sometimes a good opening is due to a practice named *buy on open*. You can't automatically attribute optimism or hopefulness to an opening bounce, because

✔ Mutual fund and other professional managers have preset allocations to specific securities. When fresh money comes in the night before, these managers are going to distribute a certain percentage of it to all the securities in the fund selected by the new customer. To buy on open is the easiest way to top up a fund, but this action is not necessarily a judgment on that security that day.

✔ Fund managers want to clean out stops from the day before. A *stop* is a preset sell order usually designed to prevent losses or otherwise exit the trade; see Chapter 5. A stop placed significantly beneath the close from the day before may be hit merely because all the market makers have not refreshed their bids at the time the market opens. This type of buying an open occurs particularly with more lightly traded issues, not the big names trading millions of shares a day.

Fund managers and other professionals control far larger sums than individuals do, and you don't know what proportion of opening trades are due to genuine research-based enthusiasm and what proportion is due to the mechanical buy-on-open effect. The market can take up to an hour to get down to new business.

How do you know whether an opening bounce is due to fresh enthusiasm or just the mechanical buy-on-open effect? You have to study each security to see whether it normally displays the effect. Heavily traded, big-name securities (such as IBM stock) are less susceptible to an opening bounce than specialized securities with a narrower trader base (like cocoa futures).

When the open is down

If the opening price is below the close of the day before, look out! Maybe bad news came out after the close last night. The bad news may pertain to a political event, a change in interest rates, a bankruptcy in the same industry, or a zillion other factors (see the discussion of events in the sidebar "Current events: Buy on the rumor; sell on the news," in this chapter).

Some traders may have executed a *sell on open,* although to sell on the open is not a common practice. A *sell-on-open order* is just what it sounds like — an order given the night before to exit the trade at whatever the price happens to be, although hunting for stops at the open is widespread and can create either a buying or a selling surge (for more on stops, see the section, "When the open is up").

Summarizing sentiment: The closing price

The *closing price* is literally the last price at which a buyer bought and a seller sold before the closing bell. The close is the most important part of the price bar. In fact, if you were to draw a chart by using only one of the bar components, you'd usually pick the close. A set of closes over a small number of days is an indicator in its own right. The close remains the most important price bar component even though after-the-bell trading was introduced to the retail market in the early 2000s.

The close is the most important part of the price bar because it summarizes what traders feel about the security. They've watched this price all day, and by the end of the day, they have a sense of how popular it was near the lows (lots of buying going on) or how unpopular near the highs (lots of selling going on). Remember, they're also looking at volume to confirm these impressions. As the close approaches, traders have to decide whether to hold the security overnight, a course of action they take only if they think it's going up farther tomorrow and they won't be able to get it more cheaply than they already have.

Note also that the close is what brokers use to value your portfolio at the end of an accounting period, and the close is used to calculate the "mark-to-market" value of a futures position. Professionals whose job performance depends on end-of-period accounting care passionately about the close and you may sometimes see them engineering a higher close in the last few minutes of trading.

After-hours trading creates a problem in evaluating the close. How do you treat the close when your security makes a new high or new low in after-hours trading — only ten minutes after the close? The answer is that you don't adjust the close. In terms of managing your data, the open and close are associated with the trading hours of the primary exchange where the security is listed — the New York Stock Exchange, the Tokyo Stock Exchange, the Chicago Mercantile Exchange, and so on. If the security trades wildly higher or lower from the "official" close, the new information is included in the price data for the next day. This can result in some peculiar outcomes, such as the price opening at $5 and closing at $7 on its primary exchange during the exchange's regular hours, but both the high and the low occurring in after-hours trading — and reaching (say) $4 at the low and $9 at the high. The new high and low gets incorporated in the next day's data.

As with all price bar components, what's important is the relationship of the close to other bar components, especially the open today and the close yesterday. Don't dismiss the daily bar because your trading style is for a multi-day period. Over time, the cumulative relationship of the close to the close the day before gives you a good impression of directional bias.

You often hear "it's up on the day" or "it's down on the day," referring to the closing price relative to the close the day before. Here's the skinny on these technical trading terms:

- ✔ An *up day* is one where the close is higher than the close the day before.
- ✔ A *down day* refers to a day on which the close is lower than the close the day before.

I go into more detail on these concepts in the following sections.

When the close is up

If today's close is consistently higher than yesterday's close, day after day, buyers are demanding more and more of the security and are willing to pay an ever-higher price to get it. In other words, the close is up. See Figure 6-2. With the exception of Day 4, every close is higher than the close the previous day.

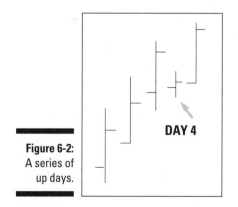

DAY 4

Figure 6-2:
A series of
up days.

If you see an up-day trend like the one shown in Figure 6-2, you want to join the crowd and buy into the trend.

When the close is down

In Figure 6-3, you can see that Day 3 starts a series in which each close is lower than the day before. Here the sellers are willing to take ever-lower prices to get rid of the security. The market assumes that those holding an inventory of the security are willing to sell at lower and lower prices in order to get buyers to demand it. This action is the same as your auto dealer putting last year's cars on sale just before the new models come in. By lowering the price, he creates demand. When you see a down move like the one in Figure 6-3, you should join the crowd and be a seller.

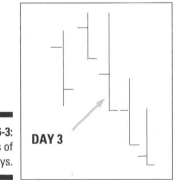

Figure 6-3:
A series of down days.

DAY 3

Hope, fear, and risk management at the close

On an up day, you hear that "today the bulls won" or on a down day, "today the bears won." This talk of bulls and bears acknowledges the emotional aspect of trading — *bulls* are buyers who are hopeful of higher prices later that they can sell for a profit, and *bears* are pessimists who foresee prices falling. You can also say that the bulls are motivated by greed and the bears are motivated by fear. However, greed and fear aren't the only emotions traders feel, and some even find the use of the word *greed* offensive. Traders also make buy/sell decisions to manage risk, a nonemotional reason.

Just as some traders buy on the open as a standard practice, some traders sell on the close, chiefly to eliminate the risk of loss if something were to happen overnight that would cause the price to fall. Institutions as well as individuals use his simple risk-management tactic. Should you? Only if you're trading without a stop or you fear the market could gap over your stop.

Because so many people exit on the close, the close is seldom the high of the day. And when the close *is* at the exact high of the day, that's useful information. It means people who do hold overnight positions are buying right up to the last minute, offsetting the usual end-of-day sales.

Current events: Buy on the rumor; sell on the news

New highs and lows are often the seed of a new trend, and usually arise directly from a specific piece of news. Fresh news that causes a new high or a new low is an *event*. The risk that a new high or low will ensue from the news is *event risk*. It may seem odd, but most events are not surprises, but rather scheduled, such as

✔ News or a rumor pertaining to the security itself, such as a company's earnings announcement

✔ Market-related events such as options expiration dates or the end of a calendar or tax period

✔ Scheduled releases (such as the Fed's interest rate statement or any of a dozen economic reports)

Event risk also refers to unexpected developments:

✔ Acts of terrorism and war.

✔ Natural disasters.

✔ Correlation of a stock to the performance of the major indices. Even if your stock is doing well, for example, it can open down from the close the night before as a side effect of a drop in the index or sector to which it belongs.

✔ Previous technical levels, such as a round number (like 10,000 on the Dow) or a historic high or low (see Chapter 4).

Traders treat forecasts prepared by economists and analysts as though the event had already happened precisely as predicted. In other words,

they "build in" the forecast to the price, creating the very high on the price bar that the news is supposed to produce. This practice is named *buy on the rumor,* where rumor refers to the forecast.

The rest of the phrase is *sell on the news*. The news is the event itself. You sometimes get the seeming paradox of a price reaching a new high *before* the event and falling lower immediately *after* the event, even when the news matches the forecast. The lower price comes about because the early birds take profit on the up move that they themselves engineered. The new low is usually short lived. After all, the forecast was for good news and the good news occurred, so the news was properly built in and the new high is the appropriate price.

If the news is much better than forecast, though, traders don't take profit because better-than-expected news draws in new players and sends the price higher still. Then the early birds are positioned to make even better profits. Should the news fail to match expectations, traders and investors alike sell, and the dip may turn into a longer-lasting price drop. Either way, to buy on the rumor pays off for the short-term trader who keeps his finger on the trigger. Evaluating forecasts and being mentally ready to buy or sell at the moment of impact of the news is a difficult and risky business. It's no wonder risk-averse traders get out of the market altogether around scheduled event dates. Buy on the rumor, sell on the news is a primary cause of technical price developments, and in many instances, the only "technical analysis" that commentators mention (along with the 200-day moving average — see Chapter 12).

Going up: The high

The *high* of the price bar is literally the highest point of the bar. It's the highest price at which a buyer and seller made an exchange of cash for the security. The buyer obviously thought he was getting a bargain or good value and thinks that the price will rise some more. The seller holds the opposite view, that the price will likely fall.

The high of the day has meaning only in the context of its relationship to other parts of the same bar, especially the close (see earlier section), and to the high the day before.

When the price closes at the high of the day, traders are extremely optimistic of more gains to come (bullish). When the high is at the open and it's all downhill for the rest of the day, traders are pessimistic (bearish).

Getting to the bottom of it: The low

The *low* of the day is the cheapest price at which the buyer and seller exchange cash for the security. The buyer thinks he's getting a good value and that the price will rise. The seller believes the price is going to fall or is already falling.

As with the high of the day, the low has meaning only in the context of its relationship to other parts of the price bar and the bars that precede it. When the low is lower than the open, it probably means that some fresh news has come out after the opening bell that offsets any buy-on-open orders or initial sentiment. When the close is at the low, it means that bad news or negative sentiment ruled for the day.

You can judge the power of fresh negative news by checking whether it inspired traders to produce not only a close at or near the low, but also a low that is lower than the low the day before.

Putting It All Together: Using Bars to Identify Trends

In the previous sections, I talk about interpreting market sentiment from the relationship of the price bar components to one another largely *within* a single bar. When you look at the components *across* a series of bars, you get even more information. In fact, you get so much information that you risk information overload. Interpretation — figuring out supply and demand from the bars — becomes a lot more complex.

Some charts or parts of a chart are such a chaotic mess that no regularity or pattern exists at all. But a security whose price jumps around all over the place without rhyme or reason would soon run out of people to trade it. As I discuss in Chapter 2, the law of supply and demand states that for every security, you can find some price that persuades suppliers to part with it or buyers to purchase it. After a price is established through the execution of a real cash trade, traders have a baseline from which to track prices. *Any* transaction may occur at a random price, but not *every* transaction can occur randomly, or the market in that security would collapse.

The central observation of technical analysis is that the price bar embodies all the supply-demand dynamics of the day and that a series of bars on a chart shows the evolution of the supply-demand dynamics over time. Some percentage of the time, the evolution is visible in the form of a trend. In this section, I describe how to use combinations of bars to help identify a trend.

Identifying an uptrend

The textbook-perfect *uptrend* is a series of up-day price bars (close higher than the close yesterday) that have higher highs *and* higher lows in a majority of the bars:

- ✔ **Higher high:** When the high today is higher than the high yesterday or higher than the high of the past few days, you have a *higher high.* Higher highs refers to visible peaks, not a higher high every single day. A series of higher highs often signals that the market is feeling enthusiastic about the security. But you usually don't know at the time whether a new high or a small series of new highs is the beginning of a trend.

- ✔ **Higher low:** You need to qualify the higher high as truly indicating that a trend may be forming. What you want is an additional confirming condition — you can specify that you must also have *higher lows.*

Now you have two pieces of evidence that bulls outnumber bears. A series of higher highs together with higher lows hints that a trend is forming. After two days, you aren't yet sure what is happening, but you're starting to get excited. After all, your goal in identifying a trend is to buy near the beginning of the trend. As I describe in Chapter 1, your key assumption is that a trend, once formed, will continue. If you have two higher highs with two higher lows, can you assume that Day 3 will also deliver a higher high and a higher low?

Not necessarily. Alas, prices don't move in straight lines. You often see a series of two or three higher highs interrupted by one or two lower highs. This happens for several reasons:

- ✔ Traders already in the security are taking an early profit.

- ✔ The market is reconsidering whether the new high is really justified.

- ✔ The higher highs were just a random accident.

You seldom see an unbroken series of higher highs on every single day. Go to Figure 6-2. You see a series of days on which the close is higher than the close the day before. At the same time, the price is making a fresh high nearly every day, but not every day without fail. See the bar marked "Day 4." On that day, the close was higher than the open and the low was higher than the day before, but the high of the day was not higher than the day before. Oh, oh. What does that mean? Remember, you don't know yet what Day 5 is going to bring at the time you're looking this chart.

Most analysts tell you not to worry about this particular configuration of bars. It's an uptrend, all right, and you know this because you have an unbroken series of higher *lows*. Day 4 is a disappointment — it doesn't deliver a higher high — but the low is higher than all the previous lows. By considering the additional factor of higher lows, you confirm that the probability is pretty good of getting a higher high and a higher close on Day 5.

Pinpointing a downtrend

A *downtrend* is a series of down-day bars (a close lower than yesterday) characterized by lower lows and lower highs in a preponderance of the bars. For example: Look at the down days in Figure 6-3. After the first day, each of these bars has a close lower than the close the day before. Day 3 has the same high as the day before, but a lower low. On Day 3, you start to get the idea that this may be the beginning of a downtrend.

When identifying a downtrend, a series of lower highs is a good confirming indicator to the series of lower lows. The same psychology applies as when an uptrend starts, only in reverse. Sellers see that new lows are occurring — somebody must know something negative about the security. Traders aren't willing to hold a falling asset, and they unload it at ever-lower prices. Meanwhile, fans of the security can't give it support at yesterday's low — selling pressure is too great.

Wading through Murky Bar Waters

Reading bar charts isn't always a clear-cut process. In bar terms, a trend has two identifiers — a series of higher highs (or lower lows) and a series of up days (or down days). (See previous sections in this chapter.) Technical analysis doesn't offer a hard-and-fast rule on which identifier is more important. Traditional technical analysis emphasizes that you need higher lows to confirm the higher highs in an uptrend, but candlestick analysis, which I cover in Chapter 8, says that the position of the close trumps every other factor, including a new high or low.

In practice, you find that the weight you place on the position of the close is a direct function of how far out in time you want to extend your forecast. Traditional bar chart reading generally has a longer forecasting time frame than candlestick chart reading and a longer expected holding period over which you plan to own the security. In traditional bar analysis, you may accept two, three, or even more days of *countervailing bars* (bars that don't confirm the trend). In other words, in a long-term time frame, you can have several down days in a valid uptrend. In candlestick analysis, you may accept only one day or none because the trading style associated with candlestick analysis is very short term.

So how should you approach bar reading to break through the muck? In this section, I suggest sticking to attributing supply-and-demand analysis to the high and low of the bar.

Paying heed to bar series

Most of the time, a series of higher highs with higher lows or a series of lower lows with lower highs does mean that a trend is emerging, even if the close is not yet in the right position to confirm it. Higher closes are the logical outcome of new highs if they persist in a series, just as lower closes are the outcome of a series of lower lows. The mind of the market isn't hard to read. Market players start wondering why new highs or lows are occurring. They know a new high or a new low can occur only if some trader decides to buy or sell there — so what does he know that other traders don't know?

New highs and lows arouse emotions in the following ways:

- ✔ A new high or low makes market participants nervous. A sufficiently large number of new highs triggers greed — better buy now so you don't miss out, even if you don't know why the new high is occurring. The result is a higher close as buyers pile in near the end of the day.

- ✔ New lows scare just enough traders that they sell their positions, even in the absence of any fresh news that would justify it. Sellers are unwilling to hold a falling asset and so sell, causing a lower close.

But sometimes it's the other way around — you get a series of up days without getting a series of higher highs. In other words, the close today is higher than the close yesterday, but the high today isn't higher than the high yesterday. Pay attention anyway because new highs may start to appear. These new highs may happen solely because so many people are aware of the meaning of up days and down days. In other words, so many people look at technical indicators — and a series of up days or down days is a basic indicator — that they *anticipate* higher highs or lower lows. By acting on that expectation — buying or selling ahead of the actual appearance of a higher high or lower low — they make it happen. You can observe this type of self-fulfilling prophecy often in technical analysis.

Understanding relativity

The textbook uptrend is a series of up-day price bars (close higher than yesterday) that have higher highs *and* higher lows in a preponderance of the bars. A downtrend is a series of down-day bars characterized by lower lows and lower highs in most of the bars. Your task is to define when a lower low from the day before is relatively harmless and when a higher high is relatively significant. But markets are not neat and tidy, and not every bar is going to qualify on all three criteria.

See Figure 6-4. This chart depicts an uptrend — even though not every bar qualifies as belonging to an uptrend. You see lower lows as well as several days on which the bar is a down day. Down days are colored black, and up days are gray. This figure demonstrates two points where textbook definitions of trends are relative.

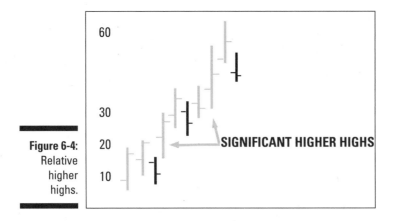

Figure 6-4:
Relative
higher
highs.

What is relatively harmless or significant is a subjective judgment. Try to make the effort to think about what highs and lows are saying about immediate supply and demand for the security:

  ✔ **Significance:** What is a significant high? You determine the answer to that question. You can judge significance by eyeing the chart, or you can specify rules, such as "a significant high is one that is *x* percent higher than the average of the past *y* highs." You can use software to develop a "filter" that defines criteria like a "significant high." In Figure 6-4, two significant higher highs stand out. They each represent a 50 percent gain from the previous up day high. Note also that every high is higher than the day before, but every significant high is higher than the highs that came before.

🖋 **Preponderance:** In addition to revealing that some bars in an uptrend can be net down days, Figure 6-4 illustrates that not every high in an uptrend has to be higher than the one before. You just need to identify a preponderance of higher highs and a preponderance of higher lows. *Preponderance* generally means "majority." For example, a preponderance of higher highs may mean a simple majority, say six of ten bars, accompanied by six of ten higher lows. However, determining a preponderance is your call. Maybe you like seven out of ten. You can eyeball it or use software to develop a precise definition and backtest it on historical data.

If you use charting software to look at charts, turn on the feature that lets you visually differentiate between up days and down days. A standard practice is to make up days green and down days red. It takes no practice to see where a trend is interrupted by bars that don't qualify.

Avoiding misinterpretation

A series of price bars isn't always trended, of course, but sometimes you can misinterpret what you're seeing if you aren't careful. You may see a series of higher highs but forget to make sure that each bar has a higher low and is an up day. Or you see a series of lower lows but forget to check that the high is lower or that the bars are all down days.

You may see a price series where every day brings a new high but every day also brings a close lower than the day before and a low that is lower than the lows on preceding days. This situation is shown in Figure 6-5.

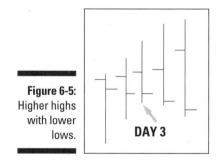

Figure 6-5:
Higher highs
with lower
lows.

DAY 3

Figure 6-5 reminds you that it's not enough to have a series of higher highs in an uptrend — you also have to have higher lows. This set of bars is a series of down days (the close is lower than the close the day before). It's hard to swallow, but this figure displays a downtrend emerging at the third bar. Your eye may want to see an uptrend, but when you look more closely and analyze the bars for all three conditions, you have only one uptrend condition (higher highs) that is more than offset by the two downtrend conditions (lower lows and lower closes). Appearances can be deceiving.

You may never know for sure why such a strange series of bars develops. However, here are a few theories:

- ✔ Some traders plan to exit at the end of the day no matter what (I describe the exit-on-close strategy earlier in the chapter). This is a risk-management decision, not a commentary on the price.

- ✔ Some group in the market wants to see this security make higher highs, and so they buy near the highs, hoping that a new high will "create demand," as in an auction. Such buyers may be insiders or option traders trying to trigger a specific price level.

- ✔ A trader may be trying to test a support or a resistance line (which I describe in Chapter 10).

Knowing when bar reading doesn't work

Some price series are unreadable. You can't figure out what the market is thinking because the market is changing its mind just about every other day. Figure 6-6 is such a chart. The series of gray up days is a minor uptrend and the following series of black down days is a minor downtrend — but then things fall apart. You see higher highs followed by lower lows and no consistency in the placement of the close (up day or down day).

What do you do in a case like this? Nothing — at least not anything based on interpretation of the bars. When bars are in a chaotic mess like in Figure 6-6, the probability of picking the right direction (up or down) is very low. You'd just be guessing. And although you have to accept imperfection and a certain amount of ambiguity in bar-chart analysis, the whole purpose of technical analysis is to obtain a higher probability of making the right decision. Guessing defeats the purpose.

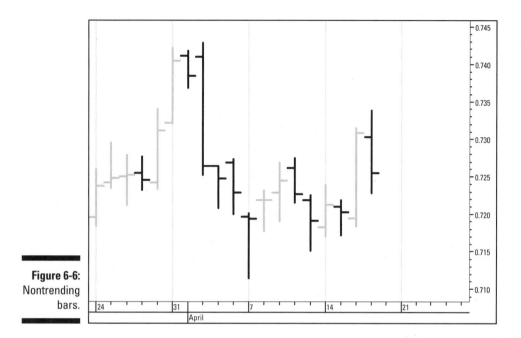

Figure 6-6:
Nontrending
bars.

Looking at Data in Different Time Frames

In preceding sections, I talk about the price bar as a daily bar. In practice, you find that looking at data in a different time frame is often useful when you are facing a trading decision. You can zoom out to a higher time frame (such as weekly) or zoom in to a shorter time frame (hourly).

Price bars are fractal, meaning you can't tell by looking at a chart what time frame the bars represent. A chart of 15-minute price bars can't be distinguished from a chart showing daily bars. They both show the same bar components acting in the same ways. If a chart isn't labeled, you can usually assume that the bars are daily bars. No matter what time frame you select, everything in this book (including the following sections) about the price bar and its components is valid.

Using daily data

Most beginners start with the daily price bar. Daily data is widely available and free or cheap. Daily data is the standard because

✔ Most of the commentary in newspapers, magazines, and Web sites refers to daily bars. It's the "base case."

✔ Embracing daily price bars puts you on the same page with the majority of people in the market.

✔ Even people who use intraday data (such as hourly bars) also look at the daily price bars.

Technical analysis writers are sensitive to the increased use of intraday data, and today usually speak of *periods* rather than *days*. Changing the vocabulary has the unfortunate effect of making some technical analysis writing sound formal or pompous — but it's more accurate.

Zooming out to a higher time frame

You can display prices in a weekly or monthly format. Mutual fund bars containing all the components are available only weekly. Quarterly and annual charts are seen less often. The universality of standard bar notation isn't hard to understand — after all, a week has an opening price (the first trade on Monday morning) and a closing price (the last trade on Friday afternoon), with a high and a low somewhere in between. The weekly close is a summary of the sentiment of the majority of market participants for the week, just as the daily closing price summarizes sentiment for the day.

You can often see trends and patterns over longer time frames that are hard to see on a daily chart. If you're using charting software, make the habit of toggling the chart from a daily time frame to the weekly and monthly time frames to see whether anything pops out at you. In addition, you can use, say, a weekly chart to confirm a new trend that you discover on a daily chart.

Zooming in to a shorter time frame

Many traders today track and trade prices on shorter time intervals, like the 60-minute bar. The following sections outline how you, too, can get your hands on the data and select the best interval after you have the numbers.

Getting the data

Live, real-time data used to be too expensive for the little guy and only big firms could afford to buy it for their professional traders. Now anyone can buy it for a few hundred dollars per year. With a 10- or 15-minute time delay, you can get intraday price bars for free on many Web sites. Most brokers give you free live data in return for your opening an account.

When you subscribe to a data service, you can organize intraday data in any interval you like — 5-minute bars, 15-minute bars, 60-minute bars, and so on. You could have 7-minute bars or 73-minute bars, if you really wanted to. The notation is the same as in daily bars, though. The opening price is the price of the first trade during the period, and the closing price is the last trade done during the period, and so on. You can also see *tick bars,* a somewhat weird way of looking at prices in which a bar is created every 20 or 50 ticks no matter how much time it takes.

Choosing an interval

If you start using intraday price bars, how do you select the interval? Experts are reluctant to give advice on this point. Leading data vendor eSignal offers standard intervals of 1, 3, 5, 10, 13, 15, 30, and 60 minutes, as well as daily, weekly, monthly, or custom intervals of your choice. (You have to wonder why users told eSignal they wanted the 13-minute interval.) In foreign exchange, you may often see traders use bars covering 240 minutes (four hours) or 360 minutes (six hours), a tidy way of keeping track in a 24-hour market as it travels around the globe.

The only logical way to select an interval is to treat it like a new pair of jeans. Try them all on your favorite security and see how they look. Selecting the interval to use in displaying bars is subjective. Sometimes you may want to use an odd number of minutes (like 13 or 73) because those bars regularly show patterns that give you insights. Remember, bar reading is a visual art. Other times you may prefer to look at what everyone else is looking at, on the principle that following the crowd is usually the right way to forecast.

You want an interval that accurately represents activity in the security and suits your needs at the same time. If you're trading an equity that has trading volume of only 10,000 shares during the day and all of that is done in 5 trades, spacing your bars at 3-minute or 15-minute intervals is silly. Your result would be a chart that is mostly blank, and every trade looks like it gapped from the one before. (For an explanation of gaps, see Chapter 7.)

If you're watching a traditionally heavily traded security, such as IBM, though, you get a complete bar for every 1-minute interval, and each bar contains the open, high, low, and close of that minute. Be careful not to sabotage your analysis by selecting a time frame that's out of sync with the normal flow of trading in the selected security.

The key to selecting the right interval is the liquidity of the security you're trading. *Liquidity* refers to potential volume in this context — kind of like a bench of buyers waiting around for their chance at bat, meaning a price that pleases them, with an opposing bench of sellers willing to throw balls until somebody takes a swing. A liquid security has lots of buyers and sellers, with some of them active at all times. Liquidity results in real trades that are measured as volume. A security with only one or two interested parties is not liquid, as you may have discovered if you ever tried to sell a thinly traded penny stock.

Select intraday bar intervals that are proportional to the minimum volume of the security being charted. How do you judge what is proportional? You match the interval to your purpose. If you're trading on a daily time frame in which you make two decisions per day, one to buy and one to sell, you want to see bars that have enough substance to convey real information. If a 1-minute or 3-minute bar chart produces just a dot, you need to increase the interval. If 15-minute bars are big enough to read, perhaps you can stop there. But try the 30-minute and 60-minute bars while you are at it. You may like them better.

Chapter 7

Reading Special Bar Combinations: Small Patterns

*T*he price bar is the basic building block of technical analysis, and a series of price bars on a chart is your basic workspace. (For the basics of the price bar, see Chapter 6.) Charts contain endless combinations of bar configurations, and you can't possibly memorize all the combinations and permutations. Being able to identify a few special cases, however, is useful because you see these cases often enough that they serve as signposts to guide your interpretation of what the price is going to do next.

"Special bars" are a small series of two to five bars — called *combinations* or *configurations* — that stand out on a chart. You can see them immediately, and so can everyone else. All the special bars and configurations are either trend-confirmation or trend-reversal patterns. Over the years, traders have interpreted these special bar combinations in specific ways, which I describe in this chapter. Knowing how other traders feel toward specific bar configurations can help you make your own trading decisions.

As a general rule, you want to "go with the flow" — trade with the conventional wisdom about the meaning of the configurations. If you're a very short-term trader (three to five days), a good time frame to trade when you're new to technical analysis, the special-case configurations literally tell you how to trade. If you're a longer-term trend trader, the earlier you use these configurations to identify a new trend, continuation of the trend, or the end of an existing trend, the more profit you make. Check out the following sections in this chapter for more details on configurations.

Finding Clues to Trader Sentiment

You use price bar combinations to determine whether your security is start-ing a trend, staying on a trend, or losing its grip on the trend. The start of a new trend is sometimes the end of an old one, called a *reversal*. In this sec-tion, you can figure out how these price bar combinations give you clues about general market sentiment in order to anticipate your next move.

Tick and bar placement

REMEMBER

In Chapter 6, I define an *uptrend* as a series of bars featuring higher highs together with higher lows, and a *downtrend* as a series of lower lows together with lower highs. An uptrend also features bars that have a close higher than the day before — up days. A downtrend contains mostly down days (closes lower than the day before). A fourth factor you want to consider is whether the close is above the open (or below the open in the case of a downtrend).

You hardly ever see a series of bars where every single one of these factors confirms the trend. Because prices never move entirely in a straight line, you have to accept that some bars in a trend don't fall into line with all the trend criteria. You may have one or two bars in an uptrend that don't have higher highs or a few bars where the close is lower than the day before. Such varia-tions in *tick placement* (the horizontal line marking the open and close) and *bar placement* (position of a price bar relative to the bars that precede it) are normal in even the best-behaved trend.

Some bars are just a little out of line, but sometimes you see bars that really stand out. It takes almost no practice at all to differentiate ordinary out-of-line bars from special configurations that traders consider to be associated with specific interpretations.

In a series of three bars, each having four components, you can get any one of 2,463 permutations of configuration. When you specify joint conditions, such as higher high together with higher low, the number of combinations reaches into the millions — and that's just with three bars! So, when you see the special cases, you know that you've got a valuable clue to upcoming price behavior. This is why, by the way, we can dismiss charges that technical analysis is not "proven" scientifically. The computational power to prove the validity of any single bar configuration does not yet exist. That doesn't mean that the majority of human beings do not respond the same way to the same patterns on a chart in the year 2020 as in the year 1920.

Even so, the interpretation guidelines aren't 100 percent right at all times. In fact, nobody can tell you even roughly what percentage of the time the standard interpretation is correct, because it may be correct all the time in one security but only 10 percent of the time in another, or correct 75 percent of the time in one year but only 50 percent in another.

A bar component or even the placement of the entire bar can be random. Random highs and lows, and even a few random bars, are caused by a "greater fool" making a trade at a sucker price or a whole batch of traders mistakenly believing a false rumor. Often you never know the reason for some weird bar configuration. Some securities have a high number of known configurations, and some are prone to out-of-whack (meaningless) configurations. The orderliness and regularity (or lack of regularity) is a function of the crowd that trades each security, and should be a consideration when you're choosing what securities to trade. See Chapter 14 on volatility.

Types of configurations

Just like patterns (see Chapter 9), when you spot a special small-bar configuration, you're looking for either trend confirmation or a signal that the trend is at risk of ending. Here are two types of configurations:

- ✔ **Continuation patterns:** The trend is continuing. The direction and pace of the trend are about the same as they were before. Relax. The more confirmation you can get, the safer you feel. You see hard evidence of the trend continuing, such as a preponderance of higher highs and higher lows marking bullish sentiment on the part of the trading crowd.

- ✔ **Reversal patterns:** The trend is switching direction. When the trend shifts from down to up or up to down, the configuration of the bar components and their placement across a series of price bars often shout, "The trend is changing!" from the rooftop. Listen up. If you have a position in the security, a reversal pattern tells you to exit. If you hold on to the position anyway, your risk of loss is much higher.

  A reversal pattern is not only a warning to exit when you're invested in the security, it's also advance notice that a good entry place may be coming up. For example, when a downtrend ends, you may see one of the very specific reversal patterns that is a reliable precursor to a buy signal.

Trading range

In every instance of special bars in this chapter, the size of the daily high-low range is a key factor. The *daily trading range* is the difference between the high and the low of the day. You can also say that the range defines the emotional extremes of the day:

✔ If you have a bar with a small range in a sea of larger bars, the market is indecisive. Indecisiveness isn't the same thing as indifference. Indecisiveness can be dangerous — nobody wanted to buy at a higher high, so perhaps buyers are getting tired of that security at current prices. A change in sentiment may be brewing, such as deceleration in a price rise that precedes the end of the trend.

✔ When it's one very large bar in a sea of smaller ones, pay attention. Something happened. Traders are willing to pay a *lot* more for a rising security, or they want to dump a falling one so badly that they'll accept an abnormally low price.

Note that if you include gaps, covered later in this chapter, the true range of a series of small-range bars suddenly gets a lot bigger.

Identifying Common Special Bars

Special bars almost always mean the same thing, and in turn you can focus on a few of the common special bars with confidence in their reliability. In this section, you can get a feel for these common special bars, pictured in Figure 7-1, and figure out how to identify them with ease. Look carefully at Figure 7-1, because this section refers to it often.

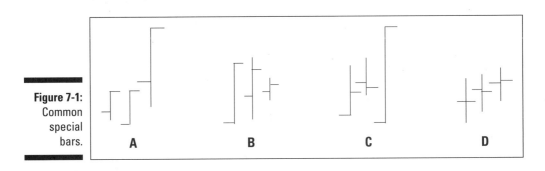

Figure 7-1:
Common special bars.

A   B   C   D

Use logic and common sense when you're looking at special bars. You are trying to understand what buyers and sellers might be thinking — which I cover in Chapter 6 and in this chapter — so keep it simple. Don't think that you've found a zebra when you're looking at a horse.

Closing on a high note

It's wildly bullish when the price closes at the high over several days. A series of *closes at the high* — and its downtrending counterpart, *closes at the low* — indicate that the existing trend is likely to continue. In Figure 7-1, Configuration A illustrates closes at the high. The price has closed at the high of the day for three days running, and the third bar is much longer than the others, which means the high-low range is wider than the previous two days. So, what's happening?

The first two bars show the close at the high at about the same level. On the second bar, the low of the day was lower than the low the day before, meaning that sellers came out of the woodwork. But the bulls fought back, buying more and more, so that the close was still at the high, trumping the lower low. Day three delivers a whopping gain — and a third close at the high. By now you may be ready to bet the ranch on this configuration.

Your instincts are right, with one caution: A big gain is often followed by *profit-taking* by active traders. Three days isn't enough to call this configuration a *trend,* so traders call it a *move.* It doesn't matter whether the closes-at-high occur at the start of a trend or while the trend is in progress — a fat gain always inspires some traders to take profit. Profit-taking doesn't change a trend, but can dent performance the next day. You may see a lower high or a lower close.

You can use your imagination (or turn the book upside down) to envision the parallel configuration on Configuration A of Figure 7-1 — closes at the low. As you may expect, a series of closes at the low imply that a downtrend is forming or worsening.

Spending the day inside

Configuration B in Figure 7-1 shows the inside day. An *inside day* refers to a price bar that meets two criteria:

- ✔ The high is lower than the previous day's high.
- ✔ The low is higher than the previous day's low.

Testing folklore

An inside day signals that the market is having second thoughts about a security. Some analysts say that an inside day is always a continuation bar. Others, notably candlestick chartists (see Chapter 8), see an inside day (named a *harami*) as a warning of a possible trend reversal. Which interpretation is correct?

No one can give you a definitive answer. Trading Systems Analysis Group (TSAG) examined the data of 60 equities over four years — over 60,000 price bars — and found 2,000 instances of inside days. About half the time in an existing uptrend, the bar after an inside day delivered a higher high (a continuation) and about half the time it didn't. For existing downtrends, the percentage was the same — about

half the time the inside day was followed the next day by a lower low. Actually, there was a tendency to continue the existing trend on the day after the inside day — a higher high in an uptrend and a lower low in a downtrend — but it was so small as to be right on the edge of the margin of error.

The inside day is still useful to signal that sentiment *may* be ready to change. Also, keep in mind that the TSAG study is limited to the exact question asked — what happened the next day? This doesn't address what happened two days later, or three days. View the inside day as a signal alerting you to watch for a breakout, however minor, without telling you the direction.

An inside day is a bar "inside" the previous day's high-low range. It reflects indecision. Buyers didn't feel strongly enough about this security to buy more. Sellers weren't particularly inspired to sell, either. The inside day doesn't suggest what's going to happen the following day. But it does warn that the market is starting to reconsider what it feels about this security.

Getting outside for the day

Check out Configuration C in Figure 7-1, which is the outside day. On an *outside day*, the high-low range of the bar is outside the range of the preceding bar. The open and close ticks can appear anywhere on the outside day bar, but two variations stand out:

- ✔ **The open is at the low, and the close is at the high.** This configuration suggests that something new has happened to inspire bullish buying right up to the end of the day.

- ✔ **The open is at the high, and close is at the low.** You can deduce the opposite supply-demand setup here. Sentiment turned bearish and sellers overwhelmed buyers, right to the end of the day.

Although the size of an outside day bar gets your attention, its appearance alone doesn't tell you much. After considering where the open and close are located on the bar, take a look at what else is going on in the market, especially the configuration of the preceding bars. Here is what you can see:

- **No trend exists.** The outside day alerts you to a possible trend beginning.

- **A trend is in place.** The outside day may suggest a reversal or a continuation, depending on where the open and close are and which direction the security is trending. The outside day has a higher high by definition, but a higher close as well implies continuation in an uptrend and reversal in a downtrend, especially if the close is exactly at the high. Similarly, the outside day has a lower low by definition, so it confirms continuation in a downtrend, especially if the close is at the low.

Finding the close at the open

Configuration D in Figure 7-1 shows a series of bars where the close is at or near the open. As you can guess, a close at or near the open reflects indecision among market participants. Trader opinion is divided as to whether this bar generally signifies a continuation or reversal pattern. Consider it a clue to look at what else is going on, such as trading volume.

However, in specific instances, the interpretive process gets a bit more definite: When the open and close are at (or almost at) the same price, *and* they're at the high or low of the day, you have a greater chance of determining whether the trend will continue or reverse. Which way the cookie crumbles depends on what was happening before:

- **In an uptrend:** If the open and close are near the high, look for the uptrend to accelerate (continuation with gusto). If they are near the low, look for a reversal.

- **In a downtrend:** If the open and close are near the low, expect more of the same. If they are near the high, think about a reversal.

Decoding Spikes

While the inside day and the outside day I depict in Figure 7-1 have high-low ranges noticeably different from the preceding bars, they don't make your hair stand on end. Sometimes, though, the market delivers an exceptionally big bar with a wildly out-of-whack high or low. Figure 7-2 shows two of these uncommon price bars, called spikes.

A *spike* is a bar that encompasses a much wider high-low range than the bars immediately preceding it. Do spikes matter? Yes, although sometimes they're just randomly generated by rumors and market silliness.

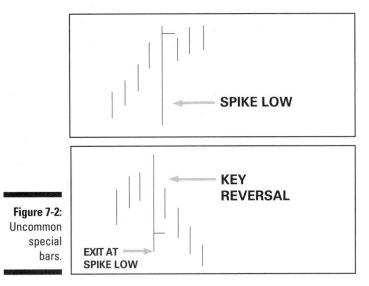

Figure 7-2:
Uncommon
special
bars.

In some cases, a spike turns out to be an anomaly. The top example in Figure 7-2 shows such a case. The spike low suggests that some people panicked and were selling so much and at such a frantic pace that buyers got a bargain at abnormally low prices. But panic was misplaced. The next day, the price resumed its uptrend and its same "normal" high-low range. The spike was just an oddity — a random move. Maybe the panicked sellers believed a rumor that the buyers didn't hear or knew was false. Or perhaps the sellers were deliberately trying to break a support line, as I describe in Chapter 10.

The bottom spike example in Figure 7-2 is, in contrast, an important bar named a *key reversal* because on the next few days, the price proceeded to make lower highs and lower lows — this bar marks a trend reversal. Key reversals can be ordinary bars and aren't always spikes, but when you see a spike, always ask yourself whether it qualifies as a reversal.

As the spike is occurring, you don't know where the low is going to come until after the bar is completed, and obviously you can't exit the trade until then (in other words, in the next trading session). You still don't know what bars will ensue, but you can make note of the spike low after it forms and keep it in mind as a benchmark for a stop, even if the bars that follow the spike retrace some of the down move, as they do in Figure 7-2. You seldom know whether a spike is random or meaningful on the day that it happens. Only hindsight can tell you that.

Though hindsight has the final say on the meaning of a spike, you can still use spikes for the following immediate analytical purposes:

- ✔ **Investigate the environment.** Sometimes you *do* know when a spike is a key reversal, because you can determine what shock caused it and use your judgment in interpreting that the news or event is sound.

- ✔ **Trust the close.** As a general rule, you're safe assuming that the close is the most important part of the bar because it sums up the sentiment for the day. To see the usefulness of the close, take a look at the two examples in Figure 7-2:

    - **Continuation spike:** In the top chart showing a spike low, the close is near the high. The wider high-low range and the lower low are a worry, to be sure, but the position of the close near the high trumps those worries.

    - **Key reversal day:** The bottom chart in Figure 7-2 shows three components to worry about — not only the wide high-low range but also the lower low and close near the low.

A key reversal bar is also called a swing bar, although not all swing bars are spikes. A *swing bar* is any bar that is the final and lowest low in a series of lower lows or the final and highest high in a series of higher highs, as in the bottom chart in Figure 7-2. You can see a spike bar at the end of the day after the close, but you can't identify it as a swing bar until after two additional closes.

A conservative trading tactic is to order your broker to sell the security if the price falls below the low of the spike day over the next two or three days. This method is plain old crowd following. Everybody can see the same spike low and many will have sell orders at that level, and you should, too. The bar following a spike is often an inside day. Other times the following bar has a new higher high only a few pennies above the spike high and a close lower than the spike bar close. Neither bar is helpful. They're simply inconclusive, and you have to wait for additional evidence to get guidance on how to trade.

Grasping Gaps

A gap is one of the most important special bar configurations. A *gap* is a major, visible discontinuity between two price bars on a chart. Because every bar encompasses all the transactions made during a specific period, a gap marks the absence of any transactions at the prices covered by the gap. In this section, I give you pointers to identify gaps and how to use them.

Pinpointing a gap

The gap is a void — no supply is offered at the prices the gap encompasses. Check out the gap in Figure 7-3. Prices had to shift upward in order for supply and demand to meet again and for both buyers and sellers to be satisfied. On daily charts, you can often see an opening gap when the opening price today diverges dramatically from yesterday's high or low, although you can also see gaps between bars on intraday charts.

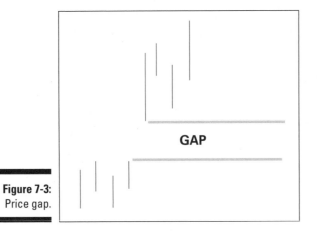

GAP

Figure 7-3:
Price gap.

You can *identify* a gap at the open of the bar but you can't *measure* a gap until the day's trading is over. Then you measure it from yesterday's high to today's low (for an upside gap) or from yesterday's low to today's high (for a downside gap). The gap is between the bars, not between the opens and closes. If the security opens on a gap but then the gap is filled during the day, the gap doesn't show up on a daily chart. The same thing is true if a security gaps during the day on an hourly chart — the daily bar doesn't show it.

Gaps are usually triggered by news, like earnings or some other event, whether true or invented (rumors). Events are the source of most key price moves, especially gaps. Prices don't, on the whole, move randomly — traders have reasons, right or wrong, to buy and sell. Even the strongest trend can be broken by a piece of fresh news contrary to the trend direction. Authentically big news trumps the chart (nearly) every time.

That's why gaps are such a valuable pattern — you know instantly how the market is interpreting the news. The reason to read bars is to get an accurate assessment of whether news is big or merely ordinary. Some news is easy to interpret. News will start a new uptrend if it's wildly favorable or halt an uptrend dead in its tracks if it's wildly unfavorable. But much of the time, you don't know how to interpret news — and there is so much news! — until you see how the market treats it in the form of the bar on the chart. Traders often get the bit between their teeth on news and this is especially clear with gaps.

Consider how a gap develops. Say that Blue Widget stock closes on Monday at $15 per share. After the closing bell, it announces bad news — the book-keeper embezzled several million dollars and ran off to Rio. (You've probably noticed how companies always wait, if they can, until after the market closes to deliver bad news. Presumably they hope that what looks just awful at 5 p.m. won't look so bad the next morning.) However, in this case, the market is unforgiving and the next day, Blue Widget opens gap down at $10. Most people deduce that the opening gap down implies further price drops, and they proceed to sell — in droves.

The total gap for the day may not be $5, though. During the course of the day, Blue Widget may trade as high as $12, making the net gap a $3 gap. If the price of Blue Widget normally trades in a $2 high-low range, $3 is still a sig-nificant number — 50 percent higher than normal. Gaps are significant when they're proportionally large compared to the trading range (see the "Kicking things off: Breakaway gaps" section in this chapter).

Gaps occur with good news, too. If Blue Widget announces a fabulous new discovery, the opening price on the following day may be a gap up, like the one in Figure 7-3. You may deduce from this gap that some traders (including well-paid professional analysts) had a whole night to evaluate the news, and *they* bought the stock at the open, so you should buy it, too. The gap implies buyers anticipate the stock rising throughout the day from the opening price, and you want to jump (if not leap) on this bandwagon.

Using primary gaps to your advantage

Gaps are, indeed, a wonderful trading opportunity if you can differentiate between a common gap and uncommon gaps. In the following sections, I describe the main types of gaps and how to use them.

Lacking opportunity: Common gaps

A *common gap* is one that appears out of nowhere for no particular reason (no fresh news). Common gaps can occur in trending and nontrending prices. If the price is trending, it fails to change the trend. If the price isn't trending, it fails to initiate a trend. Common gaps are generally insignificant.

What causes a common gap? Simple error. Common gaps often occur when liquidity is low, meaning few players are in the market. Some trader sees a price offered that's a gap away from the last price posted and decides to buy. The offer may have been a mistake, too, or the offering trader could be trying to break a trendline or have some other hidden agenda. But because the market doesn't have many participants and the fresh news is minor, if there's any at all, the effort fizzles.

A common gap tends to have low volume on the gap day. To judge an opening gap, consult volume. If volume is low or normal, traders aren't jumping on the bandwagon, and it's probably a common gap. If volume is abnormally high, traders are jumping on the bandwagon, and the gap will probably lead to a big rise or fall in the coming days.

A security that normally has low volume tends to have more gaps than heavily traded securities. A low-volume security is described as *thinly traded,* meaning few market participants. Don't try to interpret gaps in thinly traded securities. These gaps are usually just common gaps and mean nothing at all.

Kicking things off: Breakaway gaps

A *breakaway gap* is an important event because it almost always marks the start of a new trend. Not only do you get the gap and a new trend, but you also get a major change in the appearance of the chart, such as a widening of the normal high-low daily trading range, an increase in day-to-day volatility, and much higher volume. All these changes occur because the breakaway gaps draw in new traders. A breakaway gap is event driven, usually on some news about the security itself. Figure 7-4 illustrates a breakaway gap.

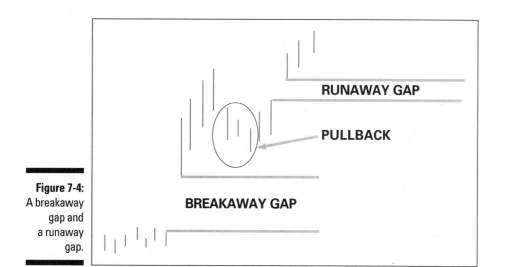

RUNAWAY GAP

PULLBACK

BREAKAWAY GAP

Figure 7-4:
A breakaway
gap and
a runaway
gap.

To qualify as a breakaway gap, the gap has to

- ✔ **Be proportionately big to the usual trading range:** If the security normally trades in a $3 range between the daily high and low, and the gap is $15 between the preceding day's high and the gap-day open, you can instantly recognize that "something big happened."

- ✔ **Occur when a price is either slightly trending or moving sideways:** Nothing much is going on in the chart, and then bam! Fresh news creates new supply-and-demand conditions and ignites a trend.

You interpret a breakaway gap depending on whether it's upward or downward, according to supply and demand, in the following way:

- ✔ **Upside breakaway gap:** Good news creates demand. New buyers want to own the security and are willing to pay ever-higher prices to get it. Volume is noticeably higher than usual.

- ✔ **Downside breakaway gap:** Traders can't wait to get rid of their holdings and accept ever-lower prices to achieve that goal. Volume may or may not be abnormally high.

Continuing the push: Runaway gaps

A *runaway gap* occurs after a security is already moving in a trended way and fresh news comes out that promotes the existing trend. See the second gap in Figure 7-4. What's the difference between a breakaway gap and a runaway gap? A breakaway gap starts a trend. A runaway gap continues a trend. In both cases, buyers become exuberant and offer higher and higher prices. Sometimes fresh good news bursts forth, sometimes traders make up fresh good news, and sometimes the buying frenzy is just feeding on itself in the absence of any news at all.

Notice on Figure 7-4 that after making new highs following the runaway gap, the price fell a little. A falling price after a dramatic move up is called a *pullback*. The security stops making new higher highs and may make some lower lows, but doesn't go as far as the low on the breakaway day. A pullback after a dramatic price move represents profit-taking by the early birds and is very common. In fact, professionals count on the pullback to "buy on the dip." If they get really enthusiastic, reentering professional traders often supply the energy for a runaway gap that follows a breakaway gap.

Calling it quits: Exhaustion gaps

Exhaustion gaps occur at the end of a trend, signaling that the party's over. Volume is usually low. What's exhausted is the news that propelled the security up in the first place and the energy of the early buyers. An exhaustion gap is usually followed by a reversal.

Here's how it works. This example is an exhaustion gap at the end of an uptrend, but the mechanics are similar for a downtrend exhaustion gap as well. When you see a gap up in an existing uptrend *and* volume is low on that day, you have to wonder why the gap appeared. Volume tells you that buyers aren't pounding on the sellers' doors to get the security.

Presumably some greedy seller is out there, along with one last fool who's willing to pay a gap-worth more than the last trade. The buying frenzy is over, but the buyer doesn't realize it. He fails to see that there are a lot of offers and few bids. In short, everybody who wanted to buy has already done so. But somebody has to be the last buyer, and this particular one got taken to the cleaners — in the form of the gap. When he turns around and tries to unload his recent purchase, he finds no buyers, at least no buyers at a profit to him, and has to dump the security at a loss.

You can distinguish an exhaustion gap from a runaway gap by looking at volume, which is usually low at an exhaustion gap. Anytime you see wild new highs (or lows) that aren't accompanied by wild new high volume, be suspicious of the staying power of the move. You can exit altogether or move up your stop-loss order.

Scoring big: Island reversals

Sometimes an exhaustion gap is followed immediately by a breakaway gap going in the other direction (see previous sections for details on exhaustion and breakaway gaps). This occurrence is how an island reversal forms. An *island reversal* is a single, isolated price bar with a gap up on one side and a gap down on the other. It looks like an island in a sea of price bars and is almost always an unusually long bar — a wide high-low range.

Take a look at Figure 7-5. You see a series of higher highs, including a minor gap up, but then the last buyers realize that they are all alone on top of the mountain. They start to sell in a panic and are willing to accept a much lower price. Now the price takes off in the opposite direction on a breakaway gap. Remember, a breakaway gap tends to have high volume.

Watching volume can get a little tricky. The island reversal bar has a higher high but is accompanied by low volume. This combination is the warning. The next day, as the breakaway gap develops, it has unusually high volume. High volume in combination with the downward gap is an indication that early selling is strong and prices later in the day aren't going to go back and fill that gap.

Now consider this case in reverse order. Everyone and his brother has been dumping the security, and it's been gapping downward as it trends downward. This time the frenzy is a selling frenzy. At some point, Trader Bruce realizes that the selling has gone on long enough and maybe the price is now too low — a bargain. Trader Jane agrees and buys it from him, and offers it on in the market at a gapping price — and wins. Turn Figure 7-5 upside down and you can see how an island reversal at the bottom looks.

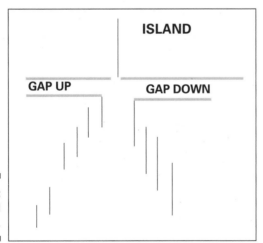

Figure 7-5:
Island
reversal.

Examine price bars, and you can see a lot of gaps. Seldom, though, do you see an island reversal. But when you do see it, here's how you can act:

✔ An island reversal at the bottom: Buy.

✔ An island reversal at the top: Sell.

Despite its rarity, chances are good that a large number of other people will identify the makings of an island, too, and cause the expected reaction — the self-fulfilling prophecy aspect of technical analysis.

Although you can't know for a day or two after the second gap that you have an island reversal, many commentators speculate that an island is forming when they see the *first* gap. Close your ears when you hear market chatter like this. Form your own judgment. "Is an island reversal forming?" is the second most-asked question that market technicians hear and one that can't be answered on a technical basis until a day or two *after* the second gap. ("Is it a head-and-shoulders pattern?" is the most-often asked. See Chapter 9 for a discussion of head-and-shoulders patterns.)

Filling That Gap

You may hear that a gap *must* be filled. This emphasis on filling the gap is usually nonsense uttered by people who are trying to sound worldly and wise, but really don't know what type of gap they're dealing with. *Filling the gap* means that prices return to the level they occupied before the gap. Figure 7-6 illustrates filling the gap.

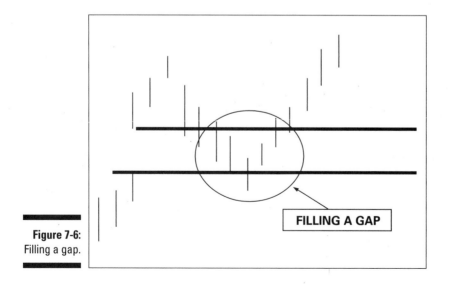

FILLING A GAP

Figure 7-6:
Filling a gap.

If a security takes off on a breakaway gap, sometimes the price doesn't return to fill the gap for many months or even years — if ever. Stop and think about it: When the fundamentals of a security change dramatically, why would market participants sell it back down to the level it was before the big event? Conditions have changed permanently and so has the price of the security. If a company has invented some new must-have product, the new higher stock prices may not be the right price, but the old prices based on the old conditions aren't right either.

A runaway gap or common gap is another matter. Demand for the stock is normal and not under the influence of news or changing conditions, so the gap may be filled by bargain hunters. Sometimes a gap gets filled because the chatter about "filling the gap" makes it a self-fulfilling prophecy.

How do you know whether a gap will be filled? If it's a breakaway gap, it probably won't be filled, at least not in the near future. If it's a common or runaway gap, it might get filled or it might not. You need to look at other indicators (such as momentum in Chapter 13 to confirm whether a price move is at risk of going backward to fill a gap).

Using the Trading Range to Deal with Change Effectively

The length of the price bar, the *trading range,* plays a role in the special bar configurations, spikes, and gaps I discuss in this chapter. But the trading range has meaning in its own right, which you can discover here. As I define in the "Trading range" section earlier in this chapter, the trading range is the difference between the high and the low. It measures the maximum distance that the price traveled that period. If you see a security that has been averaging a $3 high-low range and suddenly it starts trading consistently in a $5 range, something happened — no matter where the opens and closes are.

Paying attention to a changing range

Market prices are seldom boring. Events unfold, information leaks, and stories break. When conditions change, the average trading range is sometimes the first aspect of price behavior to change.

A change in the high-low range, which you can see in Figure 7-7, usually precedes or accompanies a change in the direction or slope of a trend. Take note — it's often a leading indicator. Take a look at Figure 7-7 and note the following terms:

✔ *Range expansion* is a lengthening of the price bars over time — the high-low range is getting wider (visible in Chart A of Figure 7-7) — and usually suggests a continuation pattern.

✔ *Range contraction* is a shortening of the price bars — the high-low range is getting narrower (check out Chart B in Figure 7-7) — and suggests that a trend reversal may be coming soon.

A change in the size of the bars — range expansion or contraction — doesn't tell you anything about the *existing* direction of the price move. The range can expand or contract in both uptrends or downtrends.

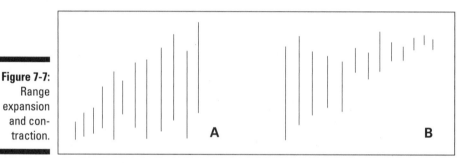

Figure 7-7:
Range expansion and contraction.

Determining the meaning of a range change

As a general rule, an expanding range is a continuation pattern and a contracting range suggests that a trend reversal is impending. Sometimes your only clue to a shift in market sentiment about your security is a change in the high-low range, but check for these confirming conditions as well:

✔ **Volume:** Look to see whether the volume is rising or shrinking.

• **Rising volume:** More people are trading the security, or existing traders are taking bigger positions. This rising volume usually accompanies range expansion and is an excellent indication of an accelerating trend. The acceleration can be in either direction, up or down. If you see an expansion of the range and it fails to have an accompanying rise in volume, you have a mystery and need to look at some other indicators, like momentum (see Chapter 13).

• **Shrinking volume:** Fewer people are in the market for this security, or existing traders are reducing their allocations to this security. Falling volume often accompanies range contraction.

✔ **Open-close position:** Here's an outline of the four possible open-close combos and what they likely mean:

- **Expanding range, higher closes:** Buyers are excited about the prospect of the price going higher still.

- **Expanding range, lower closes:** Sellers are ever more anxious to unload the security.

- **Contracting range, higher closes:** In all range contractions, traders start to feel uneasy about the direction that the security has been trending. But a higher close can offset some of the negative sentiment inherent in a contracting range.

- **Contracting range, lower closes:** This combination is doubly negative. Traders may not be causing lower lows, but they are unloading at or near the close, forcing it lower. Range contraction usually means that activity is drying up and volume is low — so if you see high volume and a lower close in a contracting range, you probably want to get out of Dodge (exit the security).

Looking at the average trading range

The trading range is a valuable analytical tool. But you want to capture a change in the range in some more-efficient way than eyeballing a bunch of bars and trying to figure out whether they're getting bigger or smaller. You can calculate the average high-low range on a piece of paper, a spreadsheet, or by using charting software.

The *average trading range* is the average distance between the high and the low over a specified period of time. You know what an average is — you measure ten of something, add up the measurements, and divide by ten. If you have ten days' worth of high-low ranges that add up to 32, you know that the average daily trading range for the ten-day period was $3.20.

The average trading range is one of the best tools you have for keeping your sanity and perspective. If you know that the average daily trading range is $3.20, the most you can expect to make on this security in a single day is $3.20, and that's assuming that you could buy at the exact low and sell at the exact high — and assuming that it's an average day.

When your broker, your brother-in-law, or an e-mail solicitation says you can make $500 in the next month in a specific security, you know that it's hardly likely. If the security moved up by its average range every day with no pullbacks for the entire 22 days in a trading month, your most likely gain would be $70.40. Unless your informant has certain knowledge of some news or event that is going to change things, his forecast is silly. Under normal, average conditions, you can expect the average trading range to persist.

In practice, forecasts of abnormally big gains are usually based on forecasts of a breakout and the expectations that the breakout will incorporate a gap on the expected fabulous news. So, how do you incorporate gaps into average range analysis? Keep reading the following sections.

Checking out the gaps

Whether you're evaluating a potential gap-making event or just looking at ranges for clues to market sentiment, you need guidance on how to take gaps into account. In the earlier forecasting a $500 gain in a month example, it would take more than one gap to deliver this outcome. Gaps almost never come in multiples. In other words, the trader promising this type of gain is in the grip of a delusion — don't join him there!

In regular bar work, say that you are merrily averaging your daily high-low ranges and suddenly you have a gap. You need to account for that gap or you will be literally missing something. Figure 7-8 displays the problem. On Day 1, the high-low range is $2. The next day, the price opens gap up, but the daily range is the same $2. Therefore, the average range for the two days is also $2. Looking at the average range alone, without inspecting every bar and every space on the chart, you wouldn't know that the gap occurred. Well, so what? Maybe the gap is just a common old gap that doesn't mean anything (see the "Lacking opportunity: Common gaps" section in this chapter). If it were an important gap, like a breakaway gap (see the "Kicking things off: Breakaway gaps" section in this chapter), you'd see the range expanding (plus a rise in volume), and the whole issue would be moot, right?

The reason you need to account for the gap is that it often precedes a longer-term change in the range, which is what you're looking for. If you measure each day separately and average those numbers, the range looks the same from day to day. For the first two days in Figure 7-8, though, the range is actually from the low on Day 1 at $1 to the high on Day 2 at $7 — or a $6 range. In short, the range doubled but the averaging process doesn't capture this change. In fact, if the range on Day 2 had been smaller, say $1.50, the average would be less than $2. Just looking at the average range on a numerical basis, you would think that the range had contracted — exactly the opposite of what really happened.

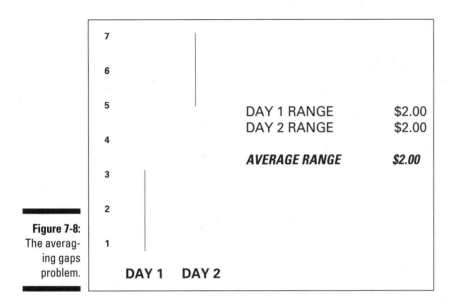

DAY 1 RANGE	$2.00
DAY 2 RANGE	$2.00
AVERAGE RANGE	*$2.00*

DAY 1   DAY 2

Figure 7-8:
The averag-
ing gaps
problem.

Discovering the average "true" range

If you want to make a trading decision based on a change in the average trading range, you need to adjust the averaging process to account for possible gaps. You do this by starting at the most important component of the price bar: The close. As a rule, to calculate the true range today after a gap, you start from the close on the day before and end at today's high. You are substituting the first day's close for the second day's *open* in order to incorporate the gap.

In Figure 7-8, Day 1's range was ordinary. The gap happened afterward. Why not use Day 1's high rather than the close? Aren't you double-counting by including the space between the high and the close from Day 1? No, because in range work you don't really care about the gap itself — you care about the total range of prices *today*. The close was the end of trading yesterday, and you're now considering it the start of trading today. Because the close is the most important part of the bar, traders are hypersensitive to an opening gap away from yesterday's close.

Figure 7-9 shows this new measurement. Pretend that the close on Day 1 was $3, or $2 over the open at $1. Subtracting that close from the high on Day 2 at $7, you get a true range of $4. Averaging that with the original Day 1 range of $2, you get $3, the average true range. If Day 2's price bar gaps downward, you incorporate the gap by measuring from the close on Day 1 to the low on Day 2.

Why the word *true?* Because the inventor of the idea, J. Welles Wilder, Jr., selected this word. The average true range is sometimes called *Wilder's average true range,* or simply ATR.

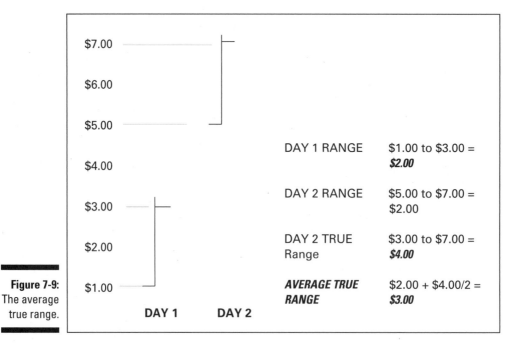

DAY 1 RANGE	$1.00 to $3.00 = *$2.00*
DAY 2 RANGE	$5.00 to $7.00 = $2.00
DAY 2 TRUE Range	$3.00 to $7.00 = *$4.00*
AVERAGE TRUE RANGE	$2.00 + $4.00/2 = *$3.00*

Figure 7-9: The average true range.

The bigger the shift in the size of the range, the bigger the trading opportunity (or warning to exit). You judge a shift in average true range the same way as in a regular high-low range (see the section "Determining the meaning of a range change" in this chapter), but with greater confidence that you're measuring and not just eyeballing. If your security normally trades in a daily range of $10 and then it starts trading at $6, $4 and $2, something is happening. Go find out what.

In Figure 7-10, for example, you see a price in the bottom window on an uptrend, but the average true range in the top window is falling. It reaches a low level just as the trend is ending (note the circle). Notice that after the trend reversal, you get a big-bar down day and corresponding rise in ATR.

The ATR can be hard to use, in part because the ATR line can be choppy, it doesn't track the trend slope, and it in fact can diverge from it, as it does in Figure 7-10. Plus, the ATR requires bar reading to get it right. By the time you get the big-bar down day, you already know this trend is ending. But do not neglect ATR as a warning indicator — sometimes it's the only warning you get.

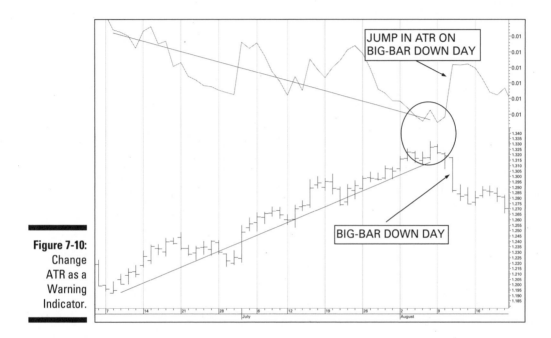

Figure 7-10:
Change
ATR as a
Warning
Indicator.

Chapter 8

Redrawing the Price Bar: Japanese Candlesticks

In This Chapter

▶ Introducing candlesticks

▶ Going over a few specific patterns

▶ Using candlesticks with other market tools

Candlestick charting displays the price bar in a graphically different way from the standard bars described in Chapters 6 and 7. Candlestick charting was developed in Japan at least 150 years ago, where traders applied it to prices in the rice market.

A trader named Steve Nison brought candlesticks to the attention of western traders in 1990. Candlestick patterns became instantly popular because they embody the principle of imputing trader sentiment to the bars, as in "shaven top," where the close is at the high. As I say in Chapter 6, close at the high means strong bullish sentiment. Today you can buy software that identify candlesticks by name and give guidance on interpreting them.

In this chapter, I break down the components of a candlestick and explain why candlesticks are so useful. Note that in some instances, a stand-alone candlestick is a "pattern" in its own right, and such candlesticks always have a name. (For more on patterns, check out Chapter 9.) Named candlesticks and small series of candlestick patterns number in the dozens, and I can't cover all of them in this chapter. I select a few candlesticks and combinations that stand out. If candlestick charting appeals to you, check out *Candlestick Charting For Dummies* by Russell Rhoads (Wiley).

Appreciating the Candlestick Advantage

Candlesticks are visually compelling. You can quickly and easily figure out how to identify a handful of the top candlestick patterns. Here are some of the advantages you can expect:

- ✔ Many candlesticks are simple to use and interpret, making it a splendid place for a beginner to start figuring out bar analysis — as well as for old hands to achieve new insights. Your eye adapts almost immediately to the information in the bar notation.

- ✔ Candlesticks and candlestick patterns have delightfully descriptive and memorable names — charming and sometimes alarming — that contain the seeds of interpretation. The names help you remember what the pattern means. Among the colorful names are "abandoned baby," "dark cloud cover," and "spinning top."

- ✔ Candlestick bar patterns and their interpretation are widely known, so you can expect other participants in the market to respond in a specific way to specific patterns.

- ✔ You can use candlesticks on any chart, with any other indicators, just like standard bars.

- ✔ Candlestick shapes can be dramatic, so they can often bring your attention to a trend change earlier than standard bars do. As I describe in Chapter 7, some exceptional bar patterns embody a forecast that's usually correct, such as the breakaway gap and the island reversal. Standard bar analysis offers very few such patterns, but candlestick analysis offers dozens.

- ✔ Candlestick patterns excel in identifying strategic market turning points — reversals from an uptrend to a downtrend or a downtrend to an uptrend.

Dissecting the Anatomy of a Candlestick

Ready to dive into the components of the candlestick? The first thing you notice is that the candlestick form emphasizes the open and the close. See Figure 8-1, the open and the close mark at the top and bottom of the box, named the *real body*. A thin vertical line at the top and bottom of the real body, named the *shadow*, shows the high and the low. (See Chapter 6 for a discussion of the basic bar components — open, close, high, and low.)

I present some more details on the candlestick bar components in the following sections.

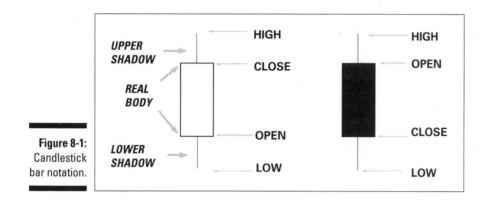

Figure 8-1:
Candlestick
bar notation.

Drawing the real body

The *real body* encompasses the range between the open and the close. The color of the real body tells you how the daily struggle between the bulls and the bears played out. Here's what the colors mean:

- **White real body:** The close is higher than the open. A white body is bullish, and the longer the body, the more bullish it is. A long candlestick indicates that the close was far above the open, implying aggressive buying. In the daily battle of bulls and bears, the bulls won.

- **Black real body:** The close is lower than the open. A black body is bearish, and the longer the body, the more bearish it is. A long black candlestick indicates a preponderance of sellers throughout the session. In the daily battle of bulls and bears, the bears won.

The two candlestick bars in Figure 8-1 show the identical open and close, but coloring one of them black creates the optical illusion that it is bigger. That black bar demands your attention, which is one reason candlestick charting is appealing — and effective. (For more appealing aspects, see the section "Appreciating the Candlestick Advantage" in this chapter.)

Don't confuse candlestick charting with standard bar notation when it comes to color interpretation. In standard bar notation, which I discuss in Chapter 6, a bar is colored to denote an up day if the close is higher than the close the day before. A down day is when the close is lower than the day before. In candlestick notation, only today's open and today's close, without reference to yesterday's prices, determines the color of the bar.

As in all bar analyses, *context* is crucial. Although you may sometimes use a single candlestick bar as an indicator in its own right, most of the time you use it in relation to the bars that precede it. One small white-body bar in a sea of black bars, for example, may mean the bulls won that day, but it was a minor event. The one white bar may signal that the bears are losing power, but you wouldn't use it all by itself to call the end of a black-bar downtrend.

Doing without a real body: The doji

A candlestick that has no real body or only a very small one is named a *doji.* In a doji, the open and the close are at the same or near the same level. See Figure 8-2 for three types of dojis. On its own, a doji doesn't tell you much about market sentiment. You interpret a doji bar in the context of the pattern of the preceding bars. A doji implies that sentiment is in a transitional phase. It's a neutral bar, neither bullish nor bearish, that gains meaning from its placement within a set of bars.

When you see a doji after a prolonged uptrend, the doji may mean that the buyers are coming to the end of their bullish enthusiasm. (In Chapter 7, I discuss that when the close is at or near the open, market participants are indecisive.) A doji coming immediately after a very long white bar in an uptrend shows that the market is tired. This particular doji is named a bearish doji star. A bullish doji star is a mirror image — it comes after a big black bar in a downtrend. In other cases, it signals an impending reversal.

The doji form contains important information, regardless of the shadows, although shadows have their own additional meaning and are covered in a later section. Always take notice of a doji or series of dojis after a trend has been in place for a while. It's a transitional bar and you should always be on the lookout for any transition that can affect your trade.

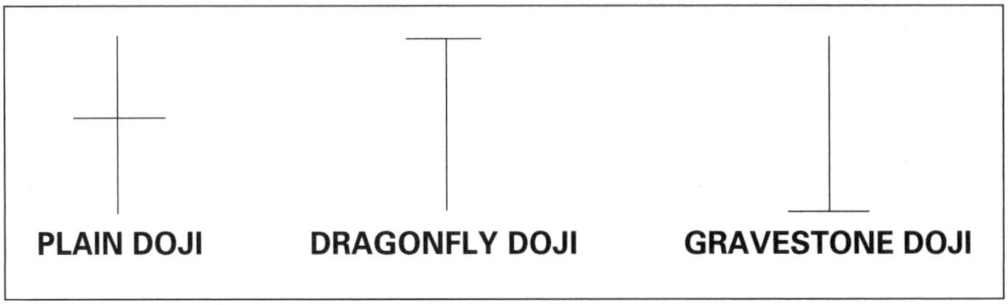

Figure 8-2:
Doji
candlestick
patterns.

PLAIN DOJI   **DRAGONFLY DOJI**   **GRAVESTONE DOJI**

Catching the shadow

The high and the low prices are shown in the *shadows,* which you can think of as a candlewick (on the top) or a tail (on the bottom). Although the shadow is secondary to the real body in importance, shadows contribute useful information about market psychology, too, and modify your interpretation of the body. Shadows offer special interpretive clues in three instances:

✔ The real body is a doji.

✔ The shadow is missing.

✔ The shadow is extremely long.

Want to know more about interpreting shadows in these three situations? Keep reading.

Shadows in the doji bar

In many instances, the doji is just a plain one with ordinary, same-size shadows, as shown in Figure 8-2. However, the two most useful types of doji bars, also shown in Figure 8-2, are the following:

✔ **Dragonfly doji:** Look for the long, lower shadow that means the open, high, and close were the same or nearly the same. Sellers were trying to push the price down and succeeded in making a low — but they didn't succeed in getting it to close there. Because the close was back up at or near the open, buyers must have emerged before the end of trading and bought enough to move the close to the high or nearly to the high.

How you interpret the dragonfly depends on what bar patterns precede it. Your options include the following:

- If the price move is a downtrend, the dragonfly may mean that buyers are emerging and the downtrend may be ending.

- If the dragonfly appears after a series of uptrending bars, buyers failed to push the price over the open to a new high while sellers succeeded in getting a low, so the uptrend may be in trouble.

✔ **Gravestone doji:** Take a look at that long upper shadow in Figure 8-2. This bar, the exact opposite of the dragonfly, is formed when the open, low, and close are the same or nearly the same, but a high creates a long upper shadow. Although buyers succeeded in pushing the price to a high over the open, by the end of the day the bears were fighting back and pushed the price back to close near the open and the low. This push is a failed effort at a rally, but you can interpret the bar best in the context of the other bars that precede it:

- If the gravestone bar appears after a series of uptrending bars, buyers failed to get the close at the high. Sellers dominated and the uptrend is at risk of ending.

- If the price move is a downtrend, the gravestone doji may mean that buyers are emerging and the downtrend may be ending.

Missing shadows

The absence of a shadow at one end is called a *shaven top* or a *shaven bottom.* To get a shaven top or bottom, the open or close must be exactly at the high or the low, as you can see in Figure 8-3. These candlestick bar notations are called *marubozu candles*, and you can classify the types of candles by using the following descriptions:

Figure 8-3:
Missing
shadows.

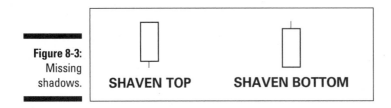

SHAVEN TOP   **SHAVEN BOTTOM**

> ✓ **Shaven top:** No upper shadow exists when the open or close is at the high. A shaven top can be black or white, and come about in two ways:
>
>   • If the open is at the high, the day's trading was all downhill from there. Not only is it a black candlestick, bearish to begin with, but it's also doubly bearish that no net new buying occurred after the open.
>
>   • If the close is at the high, the net of the day's trading was at higher prices, which is bullish. The candlestick is also (by definition) white — a bullish sign.
>
> ✓ **Shaven bottom:** No lower shadow exists when the open or the close is at the low of the day. A shaven bottom can come in two ways:
>
>   • If the open is at the low, bulls dominated all the day's trading.
>
>   • If the close is at the low, all the day's trading points to bearish sentiment.

Really long shadows

When the shadow is as long as the real body, or longer (see Figure 8-4), traders are expressing a sentiment extreme. They may or may not follow through the next day by pushing the *close* to the high or low breaking point, though. Evaluating a long shadow can therefore be tricky.

As a general rule, judge a long shadow by its placement on the chart (relative to preceding bars), such as the following:

✔ **Long upper shadow:** The high of the day came well above both the open and the close, whether the real body is black or white. Here's how you can interpret a really long upper shadow:

- If the price series is in an uptrend, the long upper shadow is a failure to close near the high. If the uptrend is nearing a resistance level (see Chapter 10 for a discussion of resistance), the long upper shadow may signal a weakening of the uptrend. If a long upper shadow follows a doji bar indicating indecisiveness, you should worry that the uptrend may be over.

- If the price series is on a downtrend, the long upper shadow suggests that some market participants are buying at higher levels. Especially if a long upper shadow follows a doji bar, you should wonder if the downtrend might be ending.

✔ **Long lower shadow:** A long lower shadow means that the low of the day came well under both the open and the close, whether the real body is black or white. Here's what that means in the technical analysis world:

- If the price series is trending down, the long lower shadow is a failure to close near the low. If the downtrend is nearing a support level (see Chapter 10), the long lower shadow may signal a weakening or an end of the downtrend.

- If the price series is trending up, the long lower shadow suggests that traders were not willing to keep buying at the high levels right up to the close. They were exiting under the high, and therefore think that new highs are not warranted. This signal can be a warning sign of the trend decelerating or ending.

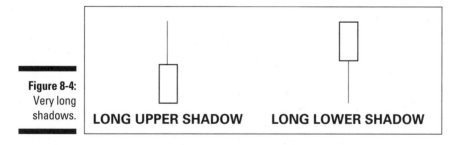

Figure 8-4:
Very long
shadows.

LONG UPPER SHADOW   **LONG LOWER SHADOW**

Sizing Up Emotions

Identifying when traders are reaching the end of their emotional tether is one of the primary goals of candlestick charting. And a change in the size of the bar is one of the best indicators of this. The candlestick technique sensitizes you to spot extremes of emotion, which is why it is a valuable tool for marking possible support and resistance at overbought or oversold levels (which I discuss in Chapter 2). You can also easily spot range expansion or contraction (see Chapter 7).

For example, at the beginning of the "Dissecting the Anatomy of a Candlestick" section, I discuss the idea that the longer the bar, the more bullish or bearish it is. If you're looking at a series of medium-sized bars and suddenly see one relatively long bar (as you can see in Figure 8-5), it may be telling you that support or resistance has been reached. Support marks an extreme level where buyers perceive that the price is relatively cheap, and resistance marks an extreme level where sellers perceive that the price is relatively high, inspiring profit-taking or least an end to accumulation. (See Chapter 10 for all the details.)

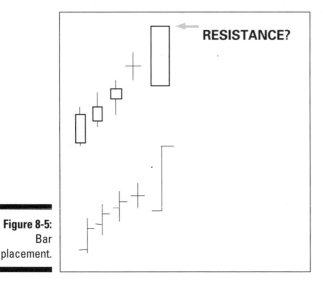

Figure 8-5:
Bar
placement.

In the top illustration in Figure 8-5, you see a series of three white bars making higher opens and higher closes, followed by a doji and an exceptionally long white bar. If you look at this chart in standard bar notation, as shown in the bottom illustration of Figure 8-5, you might say to yourself, "Higher high, higher lows, higher closes, trend okay." But the unusually tall bar stands out more prominently in candlestick mode — especially following the transitional doji — and alerts you to the possibility that all the buyers who were going to buy have just done so in one last burst, and the price may have formed a resistance level at the top of the bar (the close, in this case).

If the long bar were a black bar, denoting that the close was lower than the open, you would find it easy to deduce that the up move might be ending. A long black bar implies panic selling. But to interpret the white bar as an ending burst in an uptrend is more subtle. In fact, an expert in reading standard bars would see the same thing. Candlesticks just make it easier, especially for traders just starting our or who prefer simplicity.

Identifying Special "Emotional Extreme" Candlestick Patterns

Dozens of possible bar placement combinations and permutations are possible. In this section, I cover several of the most popular patterns and how you can tell the difference between them. These special "emotional extreme" candlestick patterns are unique to candlestick analysis and do not appear in the standard bar pattern analysis I discuss in Chapter 9.

Interpreting candlestick patterns

Two similar candlesticks or candlestick patterns often have the exact opposite interpretation, depending on where they fall in a series. You have to memorize the exact patterns to avoid getting confused. I selected just two of the many candlestick patterns to illustrate how tricky some candlestick interpretation can get.

Hammer and hanging man

Both of these candlestick types have a small real body and only one shadow — a long lower shadow. While similar, noticing their differences is crucial to your interpretation. The long shadow of the hammer extends to the downside off a white body, while the long shadow of the hanging man extends to the downside off a body that is either black or white. See Figure 8-6 for an exact image. How can it be a hanging man if the body is white? You can tell from the placement among the rising and then falling bars on either side.

You'd think that the white-body version would automatically be a bullish indicator and the black-body version a bearish one, but interpreting this candlestick depends on its placement on the chart, regardless of the real-body color. If the candlestick appears in a downtrend, for example, it marks the likely end of the trend even if the real body is white.

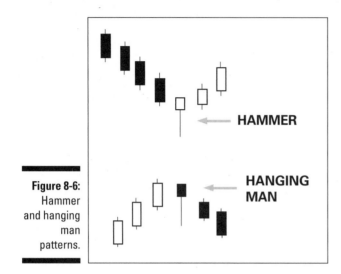

Figure 8-6:
Hammer
and hanging
man
patterns.

HAMMER

HANGING
MAN

You may see a hammer in many other contexts, but when it has a white body and comes after a series of black downtrending bars, it implies a reversal. Note that the close is higher than the previous close, too. In this context, the long lower shadow means the sellers were able to achieve a new low, but buyers emerged at some point during the day and the close was higher than the open, indicating last-minute buying.

The hanging man looks the same except it usually has a black body coming after a series of white uptrending bars. The long lower shadow marks the bulls' failure to prevent the bears making a new low and also from keeping the close below the open. You may see this bar in other places within a series of bars, but when you see it at the top of an uptrending series, consider that the trend is probably over. The wise course is to take your profit and run.

Harami

A small real-body candlestick that comes after a bigger one is called a *harami,* which means pregnant in Japanese. A harami (see Figure 8-7) implies that a change in sentiment is impending. Technically, the harami pattern requires two bars, so it doesn't stand alone. On this chart, I show the shadows of the harami bar as also inside the scope of the first big bar, although this isn't essential to identifying the pattern.

A harami can be white or black, and in fact, it can even be a doji. The smaller the real body, the more powerful the implication that a reversal is impending. In Figure 8-7, the white bars are seemingly downtrending — already a confusing combination. You also see a large white bar in Figure 8-7.

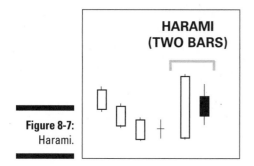

Figure 8-7:
Harami.

As I discuss in the section "Sizing Up Emotions" in this chapter, the size of the bar is important. Both the exceptionally small harami and the exceptionally big bar preceding it express extreme emotion. The big bar means a bullish "let's-buy" emotion. Seeing just the big white bar after a series of smaller ones that are downtrending, you may think that the bulls finally got the upper hand, and this movement is the start of an uptrend — especially because you have an indecision doji just ahead of it. But then the small black harami following the big white bar should disillusion you. If an uptrend was forming, the harami just put the kibosh on it.

Turning to reversal patterns

Reversal patterns number at least 40, and identifying reversals is the main application of candlesticks. The following are some of the most popular and easily identified candlestick reversal patterns.

Bearish engulfing candlestick

An *engulfing pattern* signals the reversal of a trend. The word *engulfing* refers to the open and close of the bar encompassing a wider range than the open and close of the day before. In Figure 8-8, the engulfing nature is the dominant characteristic so that the lower close pops out at you even though the bar also has a higher open. When a bar starts out at a higher open but then closes at a lower level, the bears won that day. Not shown in Figure 8-8 is a *bullish engulfing candlestick,* which is white. The higher close is visually compelling because the real body is so big. Like the harami, the engulfing candlesticks require two bars.

Shooting star

You can characterize the *shooting star* pattern by a small real body and a long upper shadow, as you can see in Figure 8-8. As I discuss in a section "Really long shadows" in this chapter, the long upper shadow in an uptrend implies a failure of the trend — a failure to close near the high. The addition of the doji bar indicates traders were already becoming indecisive the day before.

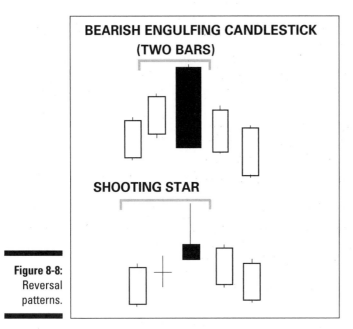

Figure 8-8:
Reversal
patterns.

Continuation patterns

Candlestick patterns are most often used to identify reversals (see preceding section), but continuation patterns do exist. As the name suggests, a continuation pattern gives you confirmation that the trend in place will likely continue. This section covers three continuation patterns you may see while candlestick charting.

Rising window

Rising window is the term for a gap, in this case, an upward gap. (A downward gap is a *falling window*.) You can get more into gaps in Chapter 7.

In Figure 8-9, the gap separates two white candlesticks, which are themselves bullish. The next bar doesn't "fill the gap" (called "closing the window.") The gap between the two price bars is confirmation of the existing trend, and the market's refusal the following day to go back and fill the gap is further confirmation that the trend is okay.

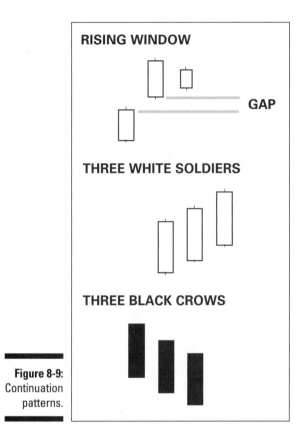

Figure 8-9:
Continuation
patterns.

Three white soldiers

The second exhibit in Figure 8-9 is of *three white soldiers*. In this pattern, what you need to note are the three large white candlesticks in a row. Seeing the close consistently over the open for three days confirms that the price series is in an uptrend, and the size of the bars indicates its robustness.

Three black crows

Three black crows is the upside-down mirror image of three white soldiers, only with black real bodies. In this pattern (refer to Figure 8-9), you have three periods of the close under the open and lower each time, with the bars fairly sizeable. The price series is now in a downtrend.

Combining Candlesticks with Other Indicators

You can combine candlesticks with other indicators to get a more-powerful description of what is going on in the hearts and minds of the people who trade the security.

Many traders who don't act directly on the information contained in the candlestick patterns still use the notation on every chart because of its visual appeal and because a candlestick bar or pattern often confirms some other indicator to which they give priority.

Figure 8-10 shows a set of parallel support and resistance lines called a *channel* (which I cover in Chapter 11). You use a channel to outline the probable limit of future prices moves, either up or down. Note that I describe each of the candlesticks on this chart in preceding sections in this chapter. The harami is followed by a rising window (upward gap) and a tall, white candle. These three candlesticks together are bullish and alert you to go back and start the channel at the lowest low, the bar before the harami.

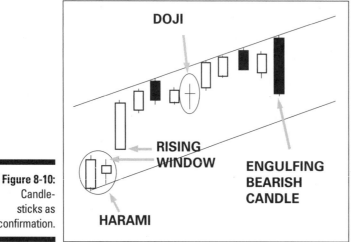

The real bodies in Figure 8-10 proceed to push against the top of the channel resistance line, but the doji, which suggests that traders are having second thoughts, is followed by two higher white candles. The two white candles indicate that the reconsideration of the move on the doji day culminated in traders' decision to keep taking the price up. In this occasion, the doji wasn't a reversal indicator, at least not for the next day. After the two white candles comes a bearish engulfing candle, a reversal warning that this up move may be ending. The engulfing candle alerts you to watch the next day's activity, especially the open, with an eagle eye.

You can also use candlesticks to confirm relative strength, momentum, and many other indicators. Check out Chapter 13 for details on relative strength and momentum. Note that in Japan, a favorite indicator to use with candlesticks is the moving average, which I cover in Chapter 12.

Some traders use specific candlesticks to identify *set-ups,* or a pattern configuration that is believed to have a high probability of delivering a specific outcome. Say that after a long series of falling bars, you see a doji bar (indicating indecisiveness) or a harami that closes near the upper end of the previous candle — and then a bullish engulfing candlestick. At the same time, another indicator like the stochastic oscillator or relative strength index shows the security to be deeply oversold. This scenario is a high-probability trade set-up, which means to get out the big guns because you want to buy! You can find many resources out there, including in print and online, for great ways to combine candlesticks with other indicators. I recommend books and Web work by John Person (pivot points and candlesticks) and Stephen Bigalow.

Trading on Candlesticks Alone

Reading candlesticks is like reading standard bars — endlessly fascinating, even addictive. But be aware that all bar reading takes practice. Some specific bars and patterns of bars are well known — and thus likely to get the expected response from market participants. But to do a good job interpreting candlesticks, you need to understand the dynamic and complex relationships of many patterns all at once, like juggling six oranges rather than three.

As with standard bar interpretation, the predictive power of a particular bar or pattern of bars may be limited to the next day or next few days. If you're a swing trader, candlesticks are going to be of more interest to you than if you're a position trader with a very long holding period (weeks and months).

Like all technical indicators, candlesticks work only some of the time to deliver the expected outcome. Evaluating candlesticks alone, without confirmation from other indicators, is a daunting task. First, you have to define, carefully, what each candlestick looks like. As noted in the section "Harami" in this chapter, a harami (for example) can be bullish or bearish, depending on the other bars around it.

Tom Bulkowski took on the task of measuring the predictive value of candle-sticks in his book *Encyclopedia of Candlestick Charts* (published by Wiley). Carefully defining each candlestick and set of candlestick patterns for a total of 103, Bulkowski ran them through a gigantic database of 500 U.S. equities over ten years and found that 69 percent of the candles delivered the outcome expected, such as continuing higher closes following "three white soldiers." Bulkowski tested 412 combinations of the 103 candlestick patterns and found that only 100 candles or patterns got the expected outcome, or 24 percent.

Wait — it gets worse. In statistics, you need a bare minimum of 30 to 40 instances of a pattern occurring to see whether it delivers the expected out-come. But Bulkowski found that patterns meeting his definitions didn't occur all that often. In fact, only 10 percent were found a sufficient number of times to "qualify" for workability testing. In short, you find only 10 percent of the can-dles in sufficient number, and these candles work as expected only 60 percent of the time. Refining the criteria further to a 66 percent success rate, meaning that the candle works as advertised in two out of three trades, only 6 percent of candles (or 13 candles total) are what Bulkowski calls "investment grade." These candles include some that I describe in this chapter, including the bear-ish doji star, bearish engulfing candle, and rising and falling windows.

Bulkowski's findings don't mean that you cannot find a specific candlestick that works (say) most of the time in your security. A higher incidence of success in candle-reading may be due to other traders in the same security seeing the same candlestick pattern and believing it will work — and so it does. In foreign exchange trading, for example, the hammer, shooting star, and engulfing bull or engulfing bear candles work nearly all the time.

A qualification of the Bulkowski study is that it was applied to U.S. equities, not commodities or other securities, and over a specific ten-year period. Still, the study confirms what you already knew — no technical indicator works all the time. That doesn't mean specific candlesticks won't work for you, espe-cially if you add confirming indicators like the MACD. This only emphasizes once again that chart-reading is an art.

Part IV
Finding Patterns

The 5th Wave   By Rich Tennant

"Right now I'm working with a combination of charting techniques. Japanese Candlesticks, some Elliot Waves, and a dash of Magic 8-Ball."

In this part . . .

Securities prices move in regular ways that most
professional traders (who dominate the market)
expect — and therefore create. The key concepts are *support and resistance* and *breakout*. Even a rough application
of these two concepts can save you a bundle or help you
make profits, because they're among the top technical ruling concepts in the market, even among non-technical
traders.

Chapter 9

Seeing Chart Patterns Through a Technical Lens

....

In This Chapter

▶ Discovering patterns

▶ Figuring out continuation patterns

▶ Going over reversal patterns

▶ Measuring the measured move

....

A pattern is a type of indicator traditionally drawn on the chart by hand. Technical traders have been developing patterns from the earliest days of technical analysis. Until personal computers came along, *Technical Analysis of Stock Market Trends* by Edwards and McGee was a Bible for chart readers. Chart patterns are powerful indicators, and some rudimentary knowledge of patterns is a good idea for the most sophisticated indicator trader and the beginner alike.

I cover some classic patterns in other chapters, such as the inside day (Chapter 7) and support and resistance lines (Chapter 10). Other bar patterns are also covered in Chapter 7 (island reversal), and all the candlestick formations are considered patterns, too (Chapter 8). In this chapter, I describe a few more of the most common patterns.

Introducing Patterns

Chart patterns are indicators consisting of geometric shapes drawn on the chart, such as a triangle. As with most indicators, a price forecast is embedded in the pattern identification. Here's a quick pattern primer:

- Most patterns employ straight lines (such as triangles), although a few use semicircles or semiellipses (such as head-and-shoulders).

- Pattern lines generally follow either the highs or the lows.

- You usually want to organize pattern types according to whether they forecast a continuation or a reversal of the current price move, although you can apply many patterns (like triangles) either way.

The lingo of pattern analysis — double bottom and dead-cat bounce, for example — makes some people laugh. Some of the names do seem a little silly but they describe the price action efficiently.

As with most aspects of technical analysis, a pattern is a work in progress. You may think you see a pattern developing, only to have the price action change course and fail to complete the expected formation. You may have to erase your work and start over a number of times on any single set of bars.

In short, pattern identification can be frustrating and time consuming. Resign yourself to making a lot of mistakes, and then, even valid patterns fail some of the time, like all indicators. The reason to tolerate the pattern recognition process is that when you get it right, you have a powerful forecasting tool that can deliver high returns. In the sections that follow, I cite performance data from Tom Bulkowski's path-breaking *Encyclopedia of Chart Patterns* (Wiley).

Got imagination?

Not everyone can see patterns right away. Pattern identification takes practice — and a lot of drawing and redrawing of lines and shapes until you get the hang of it. For example, consider Figure 9-1. Do you see the pattern?

Figure 9-1:
Find the
pattern.

The pattern in Figure 9-1 is a symmetrical triangle, as you can see in Figure 9-2. The triangle is characterized by a series of lower highs along which you can draw one trendline, and a series of higher lows along which you can draw another trendline. The two lines eventually come together at an apex. Before that point is reached, the price must pierce one of the trendlines simply in the course of trading in its normal range. Which one? Because most of the bars are trending downward, you imagine the odds favor a break to the downside.

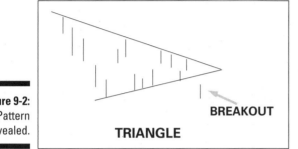

Figure 9-2:
Pattern
revealed.

TRIANGLE

BREAKOUT

And you're right. In the Bulkowski study of triangles, covering 500 stocks from 1991 to 1996, the symmetrical triangle pattern appeared 146 times. On 83 occasions, or 57 percent of the time, it was a downside breakout. The average decline was 19 percent, and the average decline lasted 74 days. In these cases, the triangle was a continuation pattern (see later section, "Cozying Up to Continuation Patterns," in this chapter).

But sometimes the breakout is to the upside. In the same study, the price delivered an upside breakout 63 times out of 146, or 43 percent of the cases. The average rise was 41 percent and lasted an average of 163 days. In this instance, the pattern forecast a reversal, not a continuation. Most patterns don't deliver a gift-wrapped buy/sell signal until near the end of the formation. As the symmetrical triangle pattern develops, the forecast is only that a breakout will occur, not the direction of the breakout.

You usually see a burst of higher volume when a pattern reaches completion. This observation makes sense — other chartists in the crowd are seeing the same pattern. For triangles, low volume often *precedes* the breakout, and serves as a bonus warning of an impending move.

Coloring inside the lines

Pattern identification doesn't require that each single price in a series line up perfectly. Not every price high hits an overhead resistance line, for example. It suffices that several hit the line. All triangles — symmetrical, ascending, and descending — incorporate support (top) and resistance (bottom) lines, as do flags and pennants, and other patterns. Opinion differs on whether the top and bottom lines must enclose every part of every price bar, or if it's okay for the bar to break the line by a tiny amount as a triangle pattern is developing.

Generally, when a pattern includes a form of support and resistance, "color within the lines," so to speak. Victor Sperandeo in *Trader Vic: Methods of a Wall Street Master* (another must-have book in every technical analyst's library), says that ignoring a break of the trendline is always wrong. Commodity price charts offer more usable patterns than equity price charts, according to Curtis Arnold, author of *Timing the Market* and *Curtis Arnold's PPS Trading System;* "PPS" standing for "Pattern Profitability Strategy." Arnold recommends using patterns (like triangles) together with confirming moving averages (see Chapter 12 for more on moving averages).

Cozying Up to Continuation Patterns

A *continuation pattern* tells you that buying or selling pressure is pausing. If a big-picture trend is well established, the pattern suggests it will accelerate after the pause. A continuation pattern, therefore, is a good place to add more to a position, because you expect an additional move in the same direction. Continuation patterns tend to be fairly short term, sometimes only a few days, and are often neglected as a consequence.

Continuation patterns serve as reassurance that you've identified the trend correctly. They also often point you to the ideal level at which to place a stop-loss order, such as the ascending line in the ascending triangle that I describe in the following section. (See Chapter 5 for a discussion of stops.)

Ascending and descending triangles

To draw ascending and descending triangles, you draw a line along the highs of a price series and another one along the lows (see Figure 9-3) — just like you do with symmetrical triangles.

In the ascending triangle, the price isn't making new highs, and the topmost (resistance) line is horizontal. You may worry that the failure to make new highs means that the up move is over. But the price isn't making new lows, either. You can often expect a breakout of the top line to the upside.

When you can draw a horizontal line along a series of highs, remember to look for a rising line along the lows at the same time. Not only does the ascending line of lows confirm the trend continuation, but it also provides you with a ready-made stop-loss level at this ascending support line. The ascending triangle pattern delivers the expected rise about two-thirds of the time, but according to Tom Bulkowski's study, it fails about 32 percent of the time. If you wait for prices to close above the top trendline, then the failure rate drops to a mere 2 percent. The *expected rise,* by the way, is equal to the height of the triangle pattern. See the section later in this chapter on "Evaluating the Measured Move."

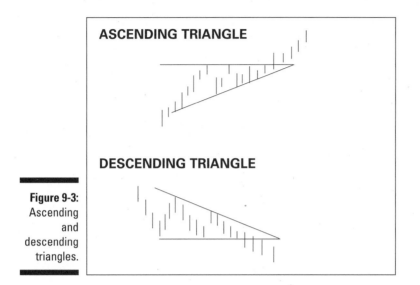

ASCENDING TRIANGLE

DESCENDING TRIANGLE

Figure 9-3:
Ascending
and
descending
triangles.

A descending triangle is the mirror image of the ascending triangle. The important point is that in this case, the price is failing to make new lows in the prevailing downtrend. You wonder if the trend is failing. But if you can still draw a line along the series of lower highs, it would be a mistake to buy at this point — the probability is high that the downtrend is going to continue.

Dead-cat bounce

A dead-cat bounce is a peculiar continuation pattern that looks like a reversal at the beginning, with a sizeable upward retracement of a down move, but then fades back to the same downward direction. Note that a dead-cat bounce occurs only in down moves and no equivalent named pattern exists for a parallel sequence of events in an up move.

The dead-cat pattern starts off with a negative fundamental event that triggers a massive down move. The average size of the down move is 25 percent — but the price can shoot down by 70 percent or more in only a few days. The *bounce* is an upward retracement that may make you think the drop is over. The pattern includes a breakaway downside gap about 80 percent of the time, and sometimes the bounce upward fills part of the gap. (See Chapter 7 for a discussion of gaps.) Many traders mistakenly think that if a gap is filled, even partly, the preceding move has ended. The dead-cat bounce is one of the patterns that disproves that idea — by the end of six months after the gap, only 54 percent of price moves had fully closed the gap in the Bulkowski study, which found 244 versions of the dead-cat bounce pattern in 500 stocks between 1991 and 1996. See Figure 9-4.

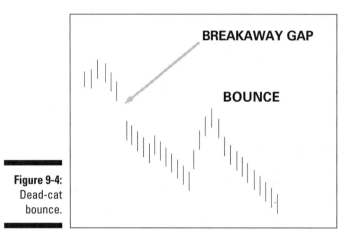

Bulkowski's statistics on the dead-cat bounce are extensive. A few of the points that stand out include the following:

- The bounce upward averages 19 percent from the lowest low.
- The average decline from the top of the retracement bounce is 15 percent and lasts an average of three months.
- The pattern fails to deliver an additional decline only 10 percent of the time, making the success rate 90 percent.

Recognizing Classic Reversal Patterns

Patterns come into their own when you use them to identify a trend reversal. No matter how a trend comes to an end, chances are good that a pattern exists to identify it. The reversal patterns I mention in the following sections are definitely ones you want to be able to recognize.

Double bottom

A double bottom looks like a W. The double bottom is essentially a retest of a low and predicts a price breakout to the upside, but only under certain conditions. See Figure 9-5.

The identification guide for a valid double bottom includes these factors:

✔ A minimum of ten days between the two lows and sometimes as long as two or three months.

✔ Variation between the two lows should not be more than 4 percent.

✔ A center up move of at least 10 percent from the lower of the two bottoms.

✔ The price must rise above the confirmation line to confirm that the pattern is indeed a double bottom and the forecast of a continued rise is correct. The *confirmation line* is a horizontal line drawn from the highest high in the middle of the W. The point where the price rises above the line is called the *confirmation point.*

Reaching the confirmation line drawn horizontally from the confirmation point, shown on Figure 9-5, is the most important identification key of the double bottom. This is where you buy.

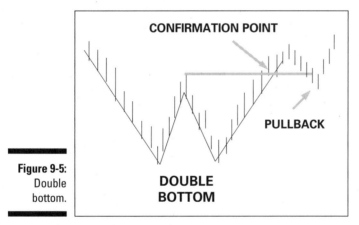

CONFIRMATION POINT

PULLBACK

DOUBLE BOTTOM

Figure 9-5:
Double
bottom.

Notice that some of the price bars break the lines you draw to form the double bottom pattern. Breaking some of the bars is allowed in a formation where the line is not a support or resistance line. Note the pullback, too. A *pullback* is a retracement to the downside right after the price breaks the confirmation line. A pullback occurs 68 percent of the time in confirmed double bottoms, making it hard to trust your pattern identification.

Bulkowski prefers the term *throwback* for the retracement after an upside breakout, as in the double bottom, and *pullback* for the retracement after a downward breakout, as in a double top, but these words aren't engraved in stone. You can use the words *retracement, correction, throwback,* and *pullback* (more or less) interchangeably.

Not every twin bottom is a true double bottom. Only about one-third of all the patterns that look like a double bottom end up meeting the confirmation criterion. In short, the pattern fails about two-thirds of the time.

These odds sound terrible, but wait — on the occasions when you do get confirmation, the double bottom is tremendously reliable. If you wait for the price to break above the confirmation line, the pattern delivers a profit an astonishing 97 percent of the time — and the average gain is 40 percent. The average number of days to the ultimate high is 204 or seven months, in the Bulkowski study.

The version of the double bottom that Figure 9-5 illustrates is clear and obvious, but not every pattern is so easy to detect. For example, one or both of the two lows of the double bottom could be rounded rather than pointed. When the first bottom is pointed and the second is rounded, Tom Bulkowski names it the *Adam and Eve* double bottom. You can imagine the other combinations, including two pointy bottoms (*Adam and Adam*) and the first one rounded with the second one pointed (*Eve and Adam*). This is, by the way, as racy as technical analysis ever gets.

Often the two lows of a double bottom are separated by several months or even a year, and you can easily miss the pattern altogether. Also, minor retracements and even other patterns within the W can obscure the pattern. Some analysts note that big patterns lasting months are easier to see on weekly charts that skim off the aberrations in daily data.

Double tops

A double top is the mirror image of the double bottom — it looks like the letter M. In a *double top,* the price makes a high, pulls back on profit-taking (as usual), and then bullish traders try but fail to surpass the first high. The failure to rally a second time through the first high means that the bulls were beaten and the bears are now in charge. A true double top is usually accompanied by falling volume as the second top is being formed.

As with the double bottom (see the section "Double bottom" in this chapter), you need to see the price surpass the confirmation level (the lowest point in the center bar of the M) for the pattern to be valid. When that condition is not met, twin tops fail to deliver a sustained down move 65 percent of the time. When the condition is met, however, the pattern delivers a down move 83 percent of the time, which is less reliable than the double bottom (97 percent), but still impressive. In the Bulkoswski study, the average drop after a confirmed double top is 20 percent and lasts two months to the eventual lowest low.

Again, as with double bottoms, the price pulls back after the confirmation 69 percent of the time, causing you to doubt the pattern. Fortunately, the pull-back period averages only ten days before the downtrend resumes.

Topping reversal patterns like the double top are usually more short term than bottoming reversal patterns like double bottoms. Tops take less time to form (57 days on average) than bottoms (70 days), because traders are more fearful of taking losses after a big gain than they are trusting of early signs of a bottom. Topping reversals are often more volatile, too, although they occur with equal frequency. According to Bulkowski, nearly all bottom chart patterns — of any type — perform better than tops. Bottoming patterns have average gains of 38 percent, but tops show losses of just 21 percent.

These statistics confirm market lore that bull markets are easier to trade than bear markets. Bull markets are more orderly and may suggest that greed is stronger than fear. Bull markets tend to have wider and deeper participation, too, because there are more traders who can go long than there are traders who can go both long and short, at least in equities. In equities (but not in securities like foreign exchange), buy-side gains are theoretically unlimited while gains on the short side are always limited — a stock cannot sell for less than zero.

The ultimate triple top: Head-and-shoulders

A triple top or bottom is somewhat rarer than the double version, but the meaning is the same — the price fails to surpass the previous low or high, signaling a trend reversal.

The *head-and-shoulders* pattern is a triple top that's easy to see: One bump forms the left shoulder, a higher bump forms a head, and a third bump forms the right shoulder. (See Figure 9-6 for two examples.) The head-and-shoulders pattern is the most widely recognized of all the patterns, and deserves its popularity because when the price surpasses the pattern's confirmation line, it delivers the expected down move a whopping 93 percent of the time.

The confirmation line connects the low point of each shoulder and is named the *neckline.* The price breaking the neckline predicts a price decline, whether the neckline is sloping upward or downward. Seldom do you see the neckline perfectly horizontal. A downward-sloping neckline tends to deliver the biggest price move.

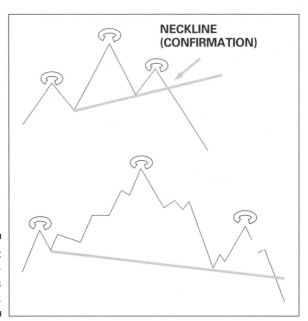

NECKLINE
(CONFIRMATION)

Figure 9-6:
Head-and-
shoulders
patterns.

If you stop and think about it, a head-and-shoulders pattern is a logical development of crowd behavior. A head-and-shoulders usually forms after a long
uptrend. The dip from the first shoulder represents the normal retracement
after a new high. The head then represents the triumph of bullish sentiment
and sets a new higher high. The dip after the higher-high head represents
more profit-taking, whereupon the bulls buy again. When the bulls are making
their third try at a rally, their price target is the last highest high, which is the
top of the head. The failure of the second shoulder to surpass the head is the
end of the rally. Buying demand diminishes and selling pressure takes hold,
forcing prices down, completing the pattern.

According to the Bulkowski study, which examined 500 stocks over the
period 1991 to 1996, the head-and-shoulders pattern appeared 431 times and
resulted in 406 reversals. A confirmed head-and-shoulders delivers an average decline of 23 percent from the neckline, and the most often-seen decline
is 15 percent. The average length of the pattern is 62 days.

As with double tops and bottoms, however, some traders refuse to accept
the pattern, and they cause a pullback to the confirmation line 45 percent of
the time. Pullbacks average only 11 days before the stock resumes its decline.
This is your last chance to jump off before the price hits the wall. Do not listen
to that little voice that says, "See, it's coming back." That little voice is wishful
thinking. The pullback is the only free lunch in technical analysis.

As with every trend that is losing steam, volume falls after the head, although about half the time the highest volume is at the left shoulder and about half the time at the head. Volume is low at the second shoulder. Volume on the breakout day and the next few days after the breakout day, however, tends to be very high. This is not surprising, because by now a great number of chart-oriented traders have identified the pattern and its neckline. Some traders may see only the break of support without having seen the head-and-shoulders pattern, adding to the number of traders who now want to sell.

The head-and-shoulders patterns shown in Figure 9-6 are easy enough to see, but many head-and-shoulders patterns are more complex and contain other patterns within them. The second head-and-shoulders pattern in Figure 9-6, for example, contains a little double top and a gap (see Chapter 7). You may also see what appears to be two heads or two shoulders, although one is always higher, which makes it the head.

Evaluating the Measured Move

The term *measured move* is used in a number of contexts in technical analysis, so it can become confusing. In essence, a *measured move* is a forecast of the upcoming price move after a chart event, including completion of a pattern. Unfortunately, these forecasts are seldom correct, or rather, they vary by too much from actual outcomes to serve as reliable trading guides. Below, I outline three types of measured moves. (Point-and-figure charting also features its own version of the measured move — see Chapter 15.)

Taking dictation from the pattern

One definition of *measured move* is the price change expected to result from a particular pattern. For example, in the ascending triangle pictured at the top of Figure 9-7, the gray lines denote the height of the pattern. Imagine that the distance between the high and low within the pattern is $5. After the price breaks out above the top of the triangle, you expect the subsequent rise to be the same amount, $5.

One useful (if general) observation is that the size of a move after a pattern is proportional to the size of the pattern. When a pattern takes a long time to form (three months or more) and when it is very deep (30 to 50 percent of the annual high-low range), the bigger the eventual reaction to the pattern.

As I mention in Chapter 11, you often get a sideways movement that results in a horizontal channel (a *Darvas box*), also called a rectangle. You project the height of the existing box into the future to gauge the extent of the break-out move. A measured move of this type has a certain amount of logic. The traders in a particular security may become accustomed to rises or falls of a certain amount before pausing or retracing.

Tom Bulkowski, in his books and articles, provides measurement guidelines for the range, average, and *mode* (most often seen) price change upon the completion of a pattern. Seldom are they exactly 100 percent of the height of a pattern. Every pattern is measured in its own way. The expected move after a head-and-shoulders pattern (described in the section "The ultimate triple top: Head-and-shoulders" earlier in this chapter), for example, is measured from the top of the head to the neckline. You then subtract that number from the neckline at the breakout point to derive the expected stopping point of the down move. This target is met only 63 percent of the time in Bulkowski's study, which falls short of a convincing forecasting technique.

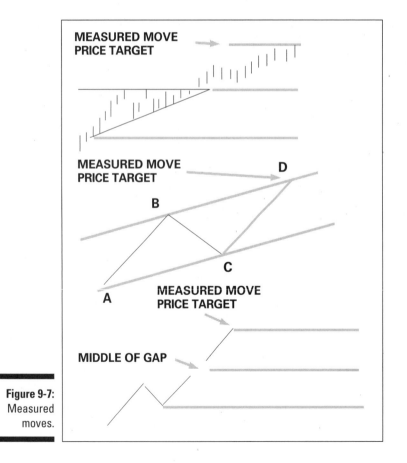

Figure 9-7:
Measured
moves.

Knowing that the down move on confirmation of a head-and-shoulders is equal to the expected move only 63 percent of the time doesn't mean that you shouldn't heed a head-and-shoulders pattern when you see it. This reversal pattern is still valid, and if you own the security, you should exit at the pattern confirmation neckline, because so many other traders are going to identify the pattern and do precisely that, causing a self-fulfilling prophecy.

Resuming the trend after retracement

Another type of *measured move* is when a price repeats the extent of a first move after a retracement. The retracement takes back 30 percent of the gain from the low to the high, or some other percentage. The point is that after the retracement, you often see the price resume the trend at the same slope and to the same extent as in the first move.

This type of measured move is illustrated in the second chart in Figure 9-7. Here you see an already established channel consisting of support and resistance lines. (See Chapter 10 for more information on support and resistance.) The price is oscillating between the two channel lines. After you see the price stop at Price C, you simply copy and paste the A-to-B move to C to arrive at price target D.

Bulkowski found that in a measured move up, the first A-B leg averages 43 percent over 87 days while the second leg, C-D, averages 37 percent in 65 days. You have to decide for yourself whether these numbers confirm or repudiate the idea of the measured move. In a measured move down, the first leg averages 25 percent and the second leg averages 27 percent, and that seems to affirm the idea of proportionality. Note that the retracement in measured moves up averages 14 percent over 45 days while in measured moves down, the corrective retracement averages 16 percent over 39 days.

Measuring from the gap

A third type of *measured move* is when you have a gap. (See Chapter 7 for a discussion of gaps.) A *gap* is a price bar whose high or low is separated from the preceding bar by open space, meaning that no trades took place at those intervening prices. A gap is important because it shows, graphically, that something happened to alter perception of the security. In Figure 9-7, you measure the distance from the lowest low in the up move to the middle of the gap, and then project that height from the middle of the gap to the upside (in an uptrend). You do the opposite in a downtrend.

Chapter 10

Drawing Trendlines

. . . .

. . . .

*O*ften you can see a trend with the naked eye, but to impose order on your visual impression, you can connect the dots, so to speak, by actually drawing a line along the price bars. A *trendline* is a straight line that starts at the beginning of the trend and stops at the end of the trend. You can do this the low-tech way by using a piece of paper, a ruler, and a Number 2 pencil, or go high tech with software like Excel or special charting software. Figuring out where trends start and stop can be complicated, but in this chapter, I explain how to spot them, plot them, and figure out what they're telling you.

Looking Closely at a Price Chart

Sometimes a trendline pops out when you look at a chart. The price is moving in a consistent fashion, either up or down. Usually your eye directs your hand to draw a trendline — but then you see another one that may be more representative. You may find yourself frustrated at this situation and be tempted to give up. Persevere for two reasons:

✔ You can feel a higher level of confidence that your trade is the right one when prices are following your trendline.

✔ A break of a trendline is a high-probability indication that the trend has ended and you need to take action.

You never know in advance when a trendline should start or stop. You know only after the fact. So a trendline is a work in progress that needs constant reevaluation. Yes, this means that you need to check the price after the close to see where it stands in relation to the trendline. You probably know people who check their prices every day. It's a mystery why they do that if they don't have an analytical framework on which to judge the day's outcome, even just a rough hand-drawn trendline. To help in the process, you may extend a trendline artificially out into the future in the hope and expectation that new prices will be near it, but remember that the extended line is only a hope and expectation, and not real.

The time frame of the chart you're looking at influences what you see. A trader with a long-term time frame may see one trend on a weekly chart, whereas a swing trader with a shorter time frame in mind sees multiple trends on the same chart. In order to see the single long-term trendline, you have to accept that charting is a dynamic process. Your work is never done. Every day (or hour or week) provides new data. You need to be ready, willing, and able to discard a trendline when it stops representing the trend — or to restore an old trendline with some minor modifications if your original drawing turns out to be right, after all. In this case, the move is a big-picture uptrend, but you don't know it for sure until late in the move.

You may not be able to see or place a trendline on certain charts. No security is in a trending mode all the time. On other occasions, you draw one trendline only to realize later that you can draw a better one. Some trends are orderly, making it easy to spot them, while other trends are disorderly and hard to see.

Following the Rules with Rule-Based Trendlines

You are welcome to draw any old line that your eye dictates, but rule-based lines have a long history of actually working to improve trading results, in part because everyone knows the rules and draws the same lines. This gives some practical meaning to the phrase "reading the mind of the market."

A rule-based trendline is one that starts and stops according to well-defined conditions, such as a line starting at the lowest low of the last three days and ending at the highest high of the last three days. A rule-based trendline is better than an impressionistic trendline for three reasons:

- ✔ It doesn't let you impose your personal view of what the trend should be.
- ✔ It improves your ability (and self confidence) to buy a security when its price is rising or sell it when the price is falling.
- ✔ It helps prevent loss by showing you the exit at the right time.

Drawing rule-based trendlines

Here's how you draw a rule-based trendline for an uptrend:

1. **Start at the lowest low and connect the line to the next low that precedes a new high.**

2. **As long as new highs are being made, redraw the line to connect to the lowest low before the last high.**

3. **When prices stop making new highs, stop drawing. Extend the line out into the future at the same slope.**

Here's how you draw a rule-based trendline for a downtrend:

1. **Start at the highest high and connect the line to the next high that precedes a new low.**

2. **As long as new lows are being made, redraw the line to connect to the highest high before the last low.**

3. **When prices stop making new lows, stop drawing. Extend the line out into the future at the same slope.**

Notice that this is a dynamic process. You often have to erase one line and draw another one as conditions change.

Using the support line to enter and exit

In Figure 10-1, the trendline illustrates the rule-based trendline named a *support line*. It's named *support* because you expect the line to support the price — traders won't let the price fall below it. You start at the lowest low and draw a line to the next low. This generates a line that can be extended at the same slope, but it becomes a trendline only when another daily price low touches the line and bounces off it. This touch-bounce is confirmation that the line is more than just a line and is a true trendline. When you use the support trendline as a trading guide, you initiate a new position on the confirmation, right after the third touch.

Some technical traders say that to require a third touch is to be overly cautious and to miss out on some perfectly good trends that fail to meet the third-touch qualification. This is true — many valid trends do have only two touches before they end. If you're waiting for the third touch, you may miss the entire move. You may even say that two touches is better than three or more because that means this security doesn't have a crew of wiseguys always testing support. But, experience shows that your trust is better placed in a trendline with three or more touches. You're taking more risk if you accept two touches.

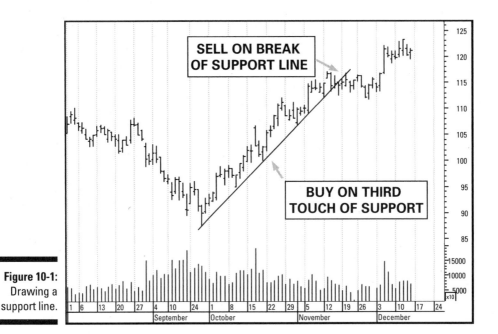

Figure 10-1:
Drawing a
support line.

The support line entry rule says: Buy on the third touch of the support line by the low of a price bar. On the flip side, the support line exit rule says: Sell when the low of the price bar falls below the support line. In some securities, including foreign exchange (FX), traders like to play games and push the price to break the support line but then buy it back so that the *close* remains over the support line. You need to watch your security to see whether it's the low breaking the line that matters, or if it must be the close.

You use the support line to identify an uptrend. The price is rising, and rising consistently. This provides comfort that the purchase of this security is returning a profit and may continue to return a profit. Notice that on many days in Figure 10-1, the low price touched the line but didn't cross it.

The more times that a low-of-the-day touches the support line without crossing it, the more confidence you should have that it is a valid description of the trend. This is called a *test of support* and encourages buyers of the security to buy more after the price passes the test. Fresh buying constitutes demand for the security and is called *accumulation*. Those who already own the security are reluctant to sell it after support has passed the test, and now require a higher price to put their inventory of the security on offer.

Here's a trader's trick: Sometimes traders engineer a test of support by selling the security down to the support line to see whether support will hold. If you put on a new long position above the support line, you're sweating bullets when traders test support. Will holders of the security rush in to buy more of the security to defend their positions? When the support line does hold, the traders who were selling become big buyers. They've just been given proof that the bulls put their money where their mouth is. If you had bought and survived a test of support, you are likely to get a fat gain after support was respected.

When any part of the price bar penetrates the line on the downside, support has been broken, and you may deduce that the trend is over. However, this trend end may or may not be true. In Figure 10-1, the move continues after the line was broken — but experience teaches that the trendline is no longer reliable. This analysis is logical because every market participant can draw the same support line. A break of support is literally just that — some holders of the stock were willing to break ranks with the other holders and to sell at progressively lower prices.

A *breakout* is any part of the price bar penetrating a line that you drew on the chart. Some traders require that to qualify as a breakout, the bar component that breaks the line has to be the close. The word *breakout* is used in a dozen contexts in technical analysis, but it always refers to a significant violation of the trend. Sometimes the offending breakout is quickly roped back into the herd, but usually a breakout means that the trend has changed its nature — and usually that is an impending change of direction. In some cases, though, a downside breakout of support that is *immediately* followed by a series of higher highs indicates that bulls got a second wind and are violently repudiating the breakout. A continuation move after a downside breakout tends to be uncommon, so don't count on it.

Sometimes the low extends beyond the support line for just one day, and then prices obediently fall back into line. Subsequent prices respect the support function of the line. A one-day break of the line is called a *false breakout*. The word *false* is misleading because the price really does break the line; what's false is the conclusion you draw from it.

To estimate whether a breakout might be false, master trader Larry Williams recommends that you consider the position of the close on the day before the breakout. In an uptrend, if the close is at or near the high, chances are good that it's a false breakout. The breakout was due to profit-taking that got carried away, it was triggered by a false rumor, or it was a random move. If the close on the day before is at or near the low, though, chances are the breakout is real.

Discard the support line as a trading tool after it has been broken. However, you may want to leave it on the chart for a while. Sometimes old support becomes new resistance and vice versa.

The other side of the coin: Using resistance to enter and exit

Resistance is the mirror image of support: A line drawn along a series of highs marks where buyers resist buying more — the price is too high for them. Traders expect sellers to emerge at the resistance line (taking profit). You may be wondering why you should care about resistance lines if all you ever do is buy securities. As a buyer, the only trendline you care about is the support line. But you should care about identifying a downtrend using the resistance line for two reasons:

- ✔ **When a downtrend ends, the next move may be an uptrend.** You want to get in on the action as early as possible, so you care when a downtrend is broken to the upside. The breakout is an important clue that an uptrend may be starting and you should start paying attention.

- ✔ **You may someday do the unimaginable — sell short.** If you have been trading exclusively in the U.S. stock market, chances are you're not familiar with *initiating a short position,* or selling a security first and buying it back later after its price has fallen. Commodity traders, on the other hand, are familiar with the practice. After all, we're striving to be emotionally neutral about whether prices are rising or falling. Why not profit symmetrically? To make a profit only when a price is rising is to lose 50 percent of the opportunity presented by trend-following.

Figure 10-2 shows two resistance lines drawn according to the rule. The uppermost line correctly advised shorting this security at the third touch of the line. The price falls off the cliff. But the price never returns to this first resistance line. Instead you get the opportunity to draw a new resistance line a few months later.

An experienced trader would probably see the new line as an opportunity to increase his short position. A long-only trader would be watching this second resistance line for the opportunity to buy the security — with a holding period that lasts only until the price nears the topmost resistance line, where it will face (you guessed it) resistance. Note that selling this security on the third touch of resistance and covering the short position when the price breaks the second resistance line would have given you a return of 20 percent.

The logic for trading using resistance lines is the same as for the support line (see the preceding section), but in reverse. The more times the high-of-the-day touches the resistance line and doesn't cross it, the more confidence you have that it is a valid description of the trend. This is called a *test of resistance* and encourages sellers of the security to sell more after the price passes the test. Fresh selling constitutes supply of the security and is called *distribution.* Those who own the security are reluctant to hold it after resistance was proved to resist an effort to break above it. They're willing to sell their inventory at increasingly lower prices.

Figure 10-2:
Drawing
resistance
lines.

To trade using support and resistance exemplifies the ruling principle of trend-following trading: You never enter at the absolute high and never exit at the absolute low. The goal is to capture a portion of the trend. Famous trader Bernard Baruch said he was willing to let others have the first third of a move and the last third of a move — he just wanted the middle third.

Fine tuning support and resistance

You need patience and persistence to work with trendlines, because you need to adjust the lines often, sometimes daily. You will hardly ever be lucky enough to get a clear uptrend along a support line and then a breakout of the support line that turns into a downtrend with a tidy resistance line. Instead the price will wander around and perhaps test the last high, which can be very annoying if you sold at the break of support.

See Figure 10-3. This chart is an adaptation of one shown by Victor Sperandeo in *Trader Vic: Methods of a Wall Street Master.* First is the break of the support line. But instead of an inverted V-shaped down move coming right afterward, the price tests both the highest high and a significant low along the up move. It is only when it crosses under this previous significant low that you are 100 percent certain that the move is over. Sperandeo calls it the *1-2-3 method* for identifying a change in trend. Not every break of support looks like this, of course, but it's an excellent model, not least because it reminds us that trends hardly ever end and reverse in one fell swoop.

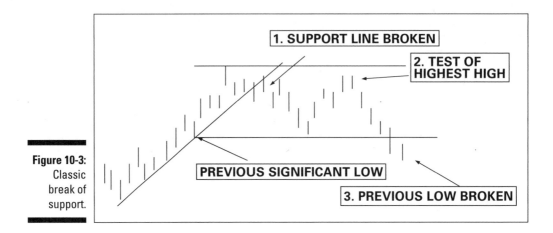

Figure 10-3:
Classic
break of
support.

If you grasp the 1-2-3 concept, congratulations! You have just met the most irksome, vexatious phenomenon in technical analysis — the pullback. It is also called a *retracement* or *correction*. This usage can get confusing because *retracement* and *correction* have specific meanings in other contexts, so you stick to the word *pullback* to be safe.

The pullback is usually characterized by a roughly sideways movement that occurs after a trendline breakout and very often, just before it, too. The pullback is a symptom of *congestion,* aptly describing the market participants milling around like people on a crowded sidewalk trying to dodge one another and impeding progress in both directions as a result. Another term for a sideways price movement is *consolidation*, referring to market participants consolidating their ideas about the security being traded. Consolidation often — but not always — precedes a breakout of the trendline.

Congestion and consolidation describe the same thing — trendless prices trading in a range. Often the range is defined by a previous high or low. Consolidations often precede *and* follow a breakout. If you see a period of sideways price movement and can't find the trend, widen your chart to include more data and switch to a longer time frame (such as weekly). Chances are you are about to get or have just gotten a breakout.

Playing games with support and resistance lines

The chief issue with support and resistance is that the line itself becomes the focus of attention, rather than the *trend.* People make decisions about buying and selling because of what happens to the line — without anything real actually happening within the underlying trend.

Support and resistance lines occur so often on charts, and nowadays so many people are aware of them, that to some extent they become self-fulfilling prophecies. A large number of people draw and respect the same lines. Some people want to defend the price because they own the security and want to see it survive a test of support so that more buyers are encouraged and it can rise some more.

Others want the price to fall so they can buy the security more cheaply, or to cover a short position. In some instances, the big players in a market know where the small players have placed their buy or sell orders, because as amateurs, they select the obvious support or resistance levels. The professionals can then pick off the amateurs for a quick buck. As I note above, the pros may push the price under a support line just to spook the amateurs into selling. You end up going through a tricky and complicated train of thought whereby you don't place your order at an obvious level because that's exactly where the big guys expect you to — and then you miss an entry or exit at the best level.

Drawing good and valid trendlines isn't enough. You also want to study how often the crowd that trades your specific security chickens out at a resistance level or breaks support by a hair only to take the price up afterward. It's not the line that counts — what counts is the crowd psychology that created the line.

Drawing Internal Trendlines

Wouldn't it be nice to know the "true" trendline? This line would reveal the hidden trendedness of the prices without at the same time alerting everybody and his brother to attack or defend specific levels.

Such a line does exist. It's a line that goes through the center of the price series rather than along its edges, like support and resistance (see the section "Following the Rules with Rule-Based Trendlines" earlier in this chapter). How do you draw a straight line through the center of each price bar? Technically, you can't, as least not on any chart where the prices jump around at all.

But scientists have a solution to jumpiness: To "fit" a line that minimizes the distance from itself to each price close along the line. The best-fit line is named the *linear regression line, linear* referring to *line* and *regression* referring to the mathematical calculation. You don't need to know how the line is calculated to be able to use it. You probably can't explain an auto transmission, either, but you can still drive your car.

You can't draw an accurate linear regression without first performing a complex statistical calculation. Spreadsheet software and all charting packages come with the linear regression already built in. Don't shoot yourself in the foot trying to do the calculations yourself when you could just as easily be sipping a latté while a program does it for you.

Rules for drawing a linear regression

This section is a short one — you have no rules. Figuring out where to start and where to end a linear regression line is the first big obstacle in using the line in a practical way to help you make trading decisions. The simple answer is to start it at an obvious high or low, meaning that you need to look backward at the historical data on the chart to see where the current move began.

This history check can be trickier than it sounds. You can get very different slopes, depending on how tightly you want the data to fit to the line. Seeing a welter of slopes covering up your chart can get very frustrating. Stick with it — pare back the surplus lines until you get one that looks the best to your eye.

Where do you end a linear regression? This takes some practice with other indicators, such as a gap, a giant outside day, a moving average crossover, a change in momentum, or even a nontechnical development.

You may see charts by self-appointed gurus that show a linear regression and advice that prices are "mean reverting" and exhibit a "central tendency," meaning that a big variation away from the linear regression line will automatically correct back to the linear regression. This is nonsense. I am not aware of any reputable trading system that features the linear regression as a trading tool.

Identifying trendedness

In Figure 10-4, the linear regression line doesn't actually go through the center of each price bar. In fact, some price bars are quite far away from the line. But if you look more closely, you can see that no other line gets you as close to Point A *and* to Point B at the same time. Only one linear regression exists for any set of prices on the chart. Despite its somewhat intimidating name, the linear regression should have you breathing a sigh of relief right now because nothing is subjective or judgmental about it. It's "science." Everybody gets the identical line if they are given the same chart and the same starting and ending points.

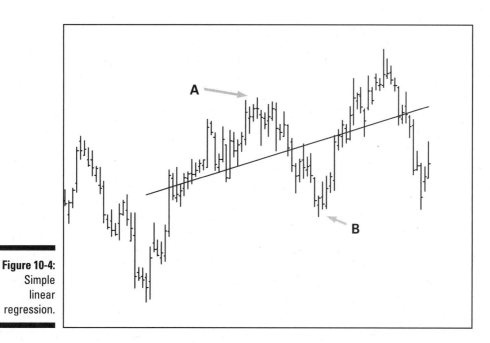

Figure 10-4:
Simple
linear
regression.

A linear regression is the true, pure trendline. This is wonderful news. If you accept the core concept of technical analysis, that a trend will continue in the same direction, at least for a while, then you can extend the true trendline and obtain a *forecast*. In some software packages, a linear regression extension is called exactly that — *a time-series forecast*. This tool is tremendously useful. You have created a high-probability forecast for the upcoming period that gives you perspective on what to expect.

If someone says, for example, that the price of Blue Widget stock is going from $5 to $10 in one month, you can take the current linear regression line and extend it out one month to evaluate whether that forecast has any relationship to reality, or is silly hype. That's the good news.

The bad news is that the linear regression line can slope this way or that way or no way (horizontal), depending on where you start and stop drawing. If you take a V-shaped price series like the one in Figure 10-5 and draw a single linear regression line, you get . . . garbage. Unless you have a very long holding period in mind, this chart shows two trends, and you need two linear regressions to reflect that. This conundrum leads to the common-sense observation that the less daylight between the line and the price points on the chart, the better the fit and the more likely it is that extending the line is a valid technique.

You can draw linear regression lines that are totally useless. They'll still be scientifically accurate in that they depict the best fit possible to the data, and everyone else will get the same result. However, they won't advance the cause of making a profit in the market or preventing a loss.

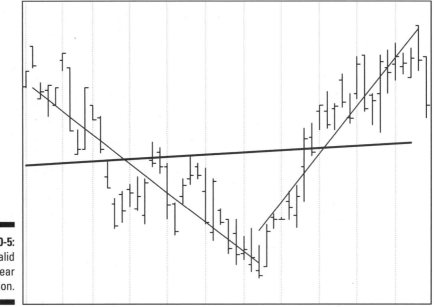

Figure 10-5:
Invalid
linear
regression.

How to use the linear regression

The linear regression does not take the place of support and resistance lines. It should be viewed as a supplement and confirming indicator to identify the trend. If you select a good starting point, the linear regression delivers pure trend. Unlike support and resistance lines (see the section "Following the Rules with Rule-Based Trendlines" in this chapter), the linear regression line doesn't have any trading rules associated directly with it, but visually, the linear regression line is the most informative.

If you draw a support or resistance line whose slope varies dramatically from your linear regression line, one of them is wrong. In a similar vein, if the line has a very steep slope and no other linear regression line on charts of the same security has such a steep slope, you can deduce that the price movement is statistically abnormal. It is unsustainably fast and likely to come to a sad end when traders start taking profit.

This crash and burn is exactly what happened in the NASDAQ in March 2000, the "tech wreck." Look at Figure 10-6.

TRUE LINEAR REGRESSION TREND-
LINE ENDED AT START OF BUBBLE

TRUE LINEAR REGRESSION TREND-
LINE EXTENDED BY HAND INTO THE
FUTURE

Figure 10-6:
Anatomy of
a bubble.

The linear regression line from the low in October 1998 to the peak in March 2000 is so steep (and unprecedented) that anyone with an ounce of technical savvy could tell it was going to blow out and come crashing down — exactly as gurus were predicting. That doesn't mean people shouldn't take advantage of rising prices. It does mean that they shouldn't have expected high and rising prices forever and should've placed trailing stops every day to lock in the extraordinary gains. See Chapter 5 for a discussion of stops.

Here's an interesting way to draw a linear regression:

1. **When you suspect that the price is accelerating (in either direction) at an abnormally high speed, first you draw a true linear regression. from the beginning of the data series but *stop* it at the point where the abnormality — the bubble — begins.** You can see this only in hindsight, but it doesn't take a lot of hindsight.

2. **Extend the line by hand, cutting off the bubble.** The extension of the trendline becomes a more realistic forecast, because we know that bubbles always burst.

Anyone drawing this linear regression trendline extension before March 2000 (the market high) had a pretty good idea of where the market would land after the bubble burst. Yes, this is a highly subjective process, and it doesn't always work. But it gets you thinking about the overall trend of the security or the market index.

You can do some really dumb things when using the linear regression line. For example, a linear regression line that is very far away from some of the prices on the chart is probably not valid. Also, if you extend a line out into the indefinite future, you get a fantasy, not a forecast. The market is a collection of human beings, not a science project. Prices simply don't move in a straight line indefinitely.

The linear regression could save your bacon someday, like it saved many technical traders in the Nasdaq crash of 2000 and the S&P crash in 2007. See Figure 10-6, showing the linear regression line from the lowest low in 2002 to the highest high of 2007. I also put the 200-day moving average on this chart (see Chapter 12). Anyone who didn't buy in 2003 when the price diverged from the downsloping linear regression, and then sell everything at the beginning of 2008, was not paying attention.

Chapter 11

Transforming Channels into Forecasts

*D*rawing a straight-line trendline and extending it out into the future suggests what the price may be in days to come. Actually, a trendline suggests only the general neighborhood of future prices. If the trendline is a support line, you expect the price not to fall below it, but that doesn't tell you anything about how high it may go. With a linear regression line, you expect future prices to cluster around the line, but some outliers are always possible. In short, common sense tells you that you can't forecast future prices to the penny.

While nobody can create a pinpoint forecast, we can forecast the range of probable future prices. *Range* refers to the same high-low range of the price bar described in Chapters 6 through 8, only encompassing a larger number of price bars in a series — weeks and months rather than only a few days.

In this chapter, I describe the straight-line channel and its forecasting capabilities. I show you two ways to build a straight-line channel forecast and outline how to interpret the information you see on the chart. I also talk about using pivot point analysis to draw horizontal support and resistance, for use either in nondirectional situations or with trend channels.

Diving into Channel-Drawing Basics

A *channel* is a pair of straight-line trendlines (see Chapter 10) encasing a price series. It consists of one line drawn along the top of a price series and another line, parallel to the first, along the bottom of the price series.

The purpose of the channel is to train your eye to accept prices within its borders as *on the trend* and to detect prices outside its borders as *off the trend* (and perhaps ending the trend). In other words, the channel is a wider measure of trending behavior than a single line. As long as prices remain within the channel, you deduce that the trend is still in place.

Depending on the raw material of your price bars, you can either

- ✔ Start with a top line connecting at least two highs, and draw the bottom line parallel to it.

- ✔ Start with the bottom line connecting at least two lows, and draw the top line parallel to that.

- ✔ Draw a linear regression line, and draw the top and bottom of the channel at equal distances on either side of it.

How do you know when a high or low is obvious and the right place to start a trendline? An obvious high or low is named a *swing point,* because it's the last highest high or lowest low in a series of higher highs or lower lows. The trend may seem to continue for a few more bars after the highest high or lowest low. You don't always get a sharp, clear-cut reversal exactly at the swing bar. But a few days after a swing bar, the reversal or swing point becomes visually obvious. Can you mistakenly identify a swing point? You bet. When drawing trendlines, you have to resign yourself to erasing a lot.

You can draw channels to enclose every part of every price bar in the series, or you can draw the channels to allow some minor breaking of the lines. (In the section "Neatness counts" later in the chapter, I describe the pros and cons of allowing minor breakage.) Whatever your starting point (top, bottom, or linear regression) and whether you encase some or all the price series, consider the top line of the channel to be resistance and the bottom line of the channel to be support (see Chapter 10 for definitions of these terms).

Constructing a channel by drawing parallel support and resistance lines organizes your vision. You expect future price highs not to exceed the top of the channel (resistance) and upcoming price lows not to exceed the bottom of the channel (support). The parallel lines tell you the maximum probable future price range. Note that word *probable.* Channels are visually compelling and can seduce you into thinking that the forecast range *must* occur. It's all too easy to start drawing channels and forget that they're only a forecast. A zillion factors can come out of the blue and knock your trend off the rails.

Channels, whether hand drawn or software drawn, aren't always as neat and tidy as the examples I use in the following sections. Some securities never offer the opportunity to draw a tidy channel, and some securities offer a tidy channel only some of the time. But the longer a tidy channel lasts, the more confident you can feel that you have correctly identified a trend.

Drawing channels by hand

Figure 11-1 is a model-perfect channel, but you may be astonished at how often you can draw a channel like this on a real security. Here's how you do it:

1. **Start by connecting the two lows at the lower left. This is the support line.**

   Notice that they're the two relative lows because a bar with a higher low comes in between.

2. **With your ruler or through the magic of software, extend that line into the future.**

3. **To form the top of the channel, you have to wait for the next relative high.**

   A relative high can be seen only after you get an intervening lower high (got that?). On the chart, the highest high is the last of three higher highs. You go back to the highest high and start a line parallel to the support line from it. This is the resistance line.

4. **Extend the resistance line into the future.**

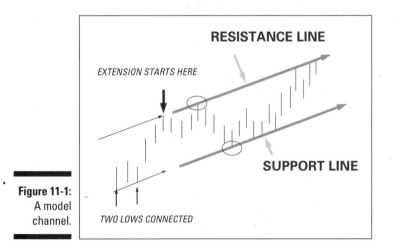

Figure 11-1:
A model
channel.

RESISTANCE LINE

EXTENSION STARTS HERE

SUPPORT LINE

TWO LOWS CONNECTED

Why are the lines parallel?

When you draw a support line connecting a series of lows, you often see a parallel resistance line that mysteriously connects the highest highs. This is so common that most charting software programs have a standard command — "create parallel line." No one knows why support and resistance lines are so often parallel. Here are a few explanations:

✔ This kind of orderliness appears when the high-low trading range is stable. Volume is steady, too. An orderly crowd promotes an orderly channel. Market participants know where the price is relatively high — at the top of the channel. They expect no more gains at this point and are prepared to sell at the top to put their money to better use in some other security. Die-hard buyers, in turn, see when the price is relatively cheap — down around the support line. They add to their position, propelling the price upward.

✔ Many technical analysts perceive a cyclical quality to the ebb and flow of prices within a channel. They rely on the security alternating between support and resistance, and the perceived cycle is the basis of their trading plan. This often works, at least for short periods, as long as you don't project the price bouncing off the support or resistance line several cycles into the future. In other words, don't get cocky. You never know when fresh news is going to come along and cause prices to break the channel.

✔ Humans have an innate need to impose order on a chaotic universe — or market. Parallel lines don't always appear, of course, but they appear often enough that observers speak of trading ranges with a certain air of authority. When you hear of a trading range, this kind of parallel support and resistance channel is usually what the commentator has in mind.

Note that sometimes you later get a higher high and have to shift the entire resistance line up, keeping it parallel. Oddly, a high proportion of new highs stop at the old resistance line, even though some stop at the new resistance line, too. It's like having two equally valid resistance lines. To be on the safe side, consider the farther-away channel line as the more-important one. The same thing is true of a second, farther-away support line.

On the chart in Figure 11-1, the extension lines are gray. At the time they're first drawn, the extended lines are hypothetical support and hypothetical resistance. *Hypothetical* means not proven.

The lines stop being hypothetical and become actual support and resistance when the next high or low touches the extended line but doesn't break it, validating the extension process. The circles in Figure 11-1 mark where the next high and low occur in this price series — and they occur at the hypothetical support and resistance lines. You know that you've drawn your channel line correctly when a third relative high or low makes a touch of the line but doesn't cross it, making that touch a confirmation point.

Letting software do the drawing

Another way to capture the collective habit of market participants is to draw the linear regression line, as I describe in Chapter 10, and then to build a channel on either side of it. Instead of drawing the support and resistance lines by hand and extending them out, you let the software do the drawing. See the later section "Riding the regression range," for information on how the channel is calculated mathematically.

Whichever way you draw the channel, apply the same expectations about the collective behavior of the market participants, and assume that future relative highs and relative lows are going to fall within the same range. The principle of extending support and resistance lines is the same whether you draw them by hand or use the linear regression as an anchor.

Considering the benefits of straight-line channels

When you use straight lines to represent a range, you get a chart that's easy to read. Your eye fills in the blanks. The benefits include the following:

- ✔ Straight-line channels imply absolute limits that give you comfort and the sense that you know where you stand.

- ✔ When a new price touches the channel top or bottom, but then retreats, you believe that the channel limits are correctly drawn and valid — and will likely work next time, too. As I explain in Chapter 10, the more often a price touches a support or resistance line but doesn't cross it, the more reliable you can consider the line to be.

- ✔ If a channel line is broken, you feel certain that something significant has happened to the perception of the security by its market participants. Violation of the channel alerts you to changing conditions and the need to consider making a trading decision.

A sense of certainty can be illusory and therefore dangerous. Like all technical indicators, channels only indicate; they don't dictate.

Delving into the drawbacks of straight-line channels

If your price series is orderly and doesn't vary much day to day from the average, the straight-line channel is fairly narrow. But if your chart contains a disorderly price move where prices jump around all over the place, your channel lines have to be so far apart that you can't judge what is usual or normal.

To some extent, a channel is valid because many others can see the same thing. One of the reasons that a technical analysis method works is because it creates a self-fulfilling prophecy. When everyone can see the same lines, a consensus builds as to what constitutes breaking the lines. When you draw a channel so wide or so narrow that only you can see it, you can't expect other traders to respond to it. To forecast a price range is really to forecast the probable collective behavior of the people who trade the security.

Using channels to make profit and avoid loss

When you have confidence that the channel broadly describes the trend, you can

- ✔ Buy near the channel bottom and sell near the channel top — over and over again, as long as the channel lasts.

- ✔ Estimate your future gain. If the width of the channel is $5 and you bought near a support line, your maximum probable gain over the next few days is about $5 — as long as the channel remains in place and you're able to sell near the resistance line. This is more useful than you may think at first, because

  - • It's a sanity check. You can't reasonably expect a gain that would call for a price far outside the channel.

  - • It's a reality check. You can use the channel to evaluate a forecast made by someone else. If the forecaster is calling for a price far outside the channel, you have grounds to question the forecast.

- ✔ Calculate your maximum loss. Regardless of where you bought the security, you know that when a price bar breaks the bottom support line of the channel, the channel is no longer valid. The trend is likely over. This is the point at which you want to sell. And you don't have to wait for the actual breakout. You can place a stop-loss order with your broker at the breakout level (see Chapter 5).

Dealing with Breakouts

The *breakout* is one of the most important concepts in technical analysis. It's a direct, graphic representation that something happened to change the market's sentiment toward the security. In the simplest terms, a breakout implies that a trend is over, at least in its present form. After a breakout, the price can go up, down, or sideways, but it seldom resumes at exactly the same level and rate of change you had before the breakout.

A breakout must always be respected, but you want to be sure it's authentic, which is what the following sections are all about. As I mention in Chapter 10 and elsewhere, because so many traders draw support and resistance lines, there's always some wiseguy in the market who tries to push the price through the lines. In an uptrend that's retracing downward, he tries to break the support line and panic holders into selling. He may believe in the uptrend; he's just trying to get a lower price for himself. In a downtrend, he's the joker who buys so much that the price puts in a new high and a close higher than on previous days, which scares the pants off sellers, who then cover their shorts and propel the price higher. In addition, a breakout can be just a random aberration.

Distinguishing between false breakouts and the real thing

You often see a tiny breakout and don't know how to evaluate it. Say your support line is at precisely $10 and the low of the price bar is $9.75. Is that a legitimate breakout or just an accident? As I note in many places in this book, sometimes you have to accept imperfection and live with ambiguity. The channel lines are an estimate, not a certainty.

Or sometimes you get a minor break of a channel line that lasts one or two days but then the price returns back inside its channel and performs just as before. The breakout was a *false breakout,* which is a breach of a trendline that then fails to deliver the expected additional moves in the same direction (see Figure 11-2). As I note in Chapter 10, to call it false is misleading, because the price bar unmistakably breaks the trendline. What's false is the conclusion you draw from it — that the trend is over.

In Figure 11-2, the channel does define the high-low trading range, after all. Sometimes you have to accept one or two violations of your lines. The challenge, of course, is that you don't know right away whether a breakout is meaningful or just a random outcome. I provide some answers to this question in the following sections.

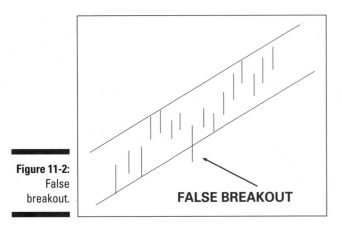

Figure 11-2:
False
breakout.

FALSE BREAKOUT

The first line of defense

Your first line of defense is the configuration of the breakout bar. A simple judgment is to see whether the breakout is a violation of the channel line by the *close,* and not just the high or low. As I explain in Chapter 6, the close is the bar component that best summarizes sentiment. A high or a low can be a random aberration. The close is less likely to be random.

A special version of the close rule is to evaluate whether the bar that breaks the line is a *key reversal bar,* which is a form of outside day (see Chapter 7 for the outside day). When you're in an uptrend, the key reversal bar has a promising open — above yesterday's close. The price even makes a new high over yesterday's high, but then the price crashes and delivers a close at or near the low and below yesterday's low. The market psychology isn't hard to read — the day started out well but then something happened to make negative sentiment rule the day, right into the close.

In a downtrend, the key reversal bar initially confirms the trend — the open is below yesterday's close and the price even makes a lower low. But then the price reverses direction and rallies strongly into the close, so that the close is above yesterday's high. Good news must have come out.

Opinion differs on whether the key reversal bar is definitive. Some traders swear by it, while others say that you wouldn't want to make trading decisions on the key reversal bar alone — you should have additional confirming factors or at least be able to verify the "news" that caused the abrupt change of sentiment during the day.

Does volume verify?

Breakouts are often accompanied by a change in volume, usually an easily noticed higher level. Consulting volume for confirmation is in keeping with interpreting events on the chart in terms of supply and demand, as described in Chapter 6. You can verify that the breakout isn't random by seeing an equivalent change in volume:

- ✔ **Increase in volume:** Extraordinarily high volume on one or two days is named a *volume spike* and often accompanies the end of a strong trend, either a rally or a crash. Buying and selling interest is frenzied.

- ✔ **Decrease in volume:** If volume declines steeply after holding steady at about the same level over the life of your trend, demand is falling off but so is selling interest. You don't necessarily know what falling volume means, but it may foreshadow a breakout. All the people who wanted to sell have done so, and the people still holding an inventory aren't willing to sell at the current price. It's like a logjam. It will be broken up when either the bull camp or the bear camp takes the initiative and causes a new high or new low, with accompanying higher volume.

Clues from other indicators

While the breakout is a powerful technical indicator, you still want as much confirmation as you can get. As I note in Chapter 8 on candlestick patterns, momentum and relative strength are useful to confirm or deny that a breakout is real. A loss of momentum and/or relative strength in an uptrend almost always precedes a downside channel breakout.

Size matters — and so does duration

You can use a filter to estimate whether a breakout is meaningful or can be ignored. A *filter* is a formula or a procedure used to modify an indicator. In this instance, the indicator is the break of the channel line. A filter can modify the amount or duration of the breakout. Here's how you do it:

- ✔ To modify the size of the indicator, you add some percentage of the total range to the channel line. You stipulate that to constitute a real break of the channel line, the new high or low must surpass this extra amount.

    If the channel is $5 wide, you can specify that a price has to violate the line by more than 5 percent (or 25 cents). Anything less wouldn't be a real breakout. Where does 5 percent come from? Why not 10 percent or 20 percent? Either one may be effective, or neither. You need to experiment with each security to see whether it has a habit of breaking its lines by this amount or that amount. You can also specify that the *close* has to break the line by x percent to qualify as a real breakout. In either case, the result is a new channel line that is a little farther out, effectively widening the channel.

- ✔ To modify the duration, you can specify that you're willing to accept one price bar violating the channel line, but not two. Or perhaps two days of violation, but not three. Again, you have to experiment with each security to see what its habits are. Also, you can combine the duration rule with the close rule and specify that the close beyond the line for x number of days is the sign of a true breakout.

Experienced technical analysts warn against making size and duration filters too complex and fancy, for a number of reasons:

- ✔ **Rules count.** The breakout principle is a powerful and well-known concept. A lot of other traders in your security are likely to heed a breakout in a black-and-white way. They *always* exit on a downside breakout of a support line by the low, for example. They feel that a breakout is a breakout, and traders shouldn't try to second-guess it.

- ✔ **One size doesn't fit all.** You can only know that 10 percent is the right amount to put into your filter if 10 percent was the amount that worked in the past on this security. Each security has its own habits; or rather, the people who trade it have their collective habits. In one security, the best filter may consistently be 10 percent and in another, it may consistently be 40 percent. (In the 1930s and 1940s, a filter of 3 percent was standard.) No single correct filter exists for every security under all circumstances. You only know whether a filter is usable by testing different filters on the price history of each security, one by one.

- ✔ **Blending works only with coffee.** The orderliness of your security can change without warning. During some periods, a 5 percent filter may be the most effective, but later, volatility can increase and you would need a 10 percent filter to capture all the price highs and lows that really do belong inside the same channel. Looking back over historical data to find the best filter has an enormous flaw: Chances are that you'll come up with a blended percentage filter that's too small for an orderly move and too big for a volatile one. And if today is the breakout day, you don't know how volatile the upcoming move is going to be.

Putting breakouts into context

A genuine breakout means that your trend channel is now defunct. You need to discard it. To verify that the breakout truly ended the trend, you need to evaluate it in the *context* of the general volatility characteristics of the security itself. By examining conditions at the time of the breakout, you may gather clues as to what the price is likely to do next.

Neatness counts

As a general rule, a breakout that occurs in the course of an *orderly* (low volatility) trend is more meaningful than a breakout that occurs in a *disorderly* (high volatility) trend. See Chapter 14 on volatility.

Figure 11-3 illustrates this point. In the first chart, the security is orderly — prices line up neatly within the channel. The breakout is obvious. In the second channel, the security isn't so tidy — prices jump around a lot. The breakout bar is exactly the same size as the orderly channel breakout bar, but in the disorderly price series, you can't be sure that it's authentic. The people who trade this security are accustomed to big bars and big jumps.

You can see that it broke the support line, but perhaps others won't find it meaningful.

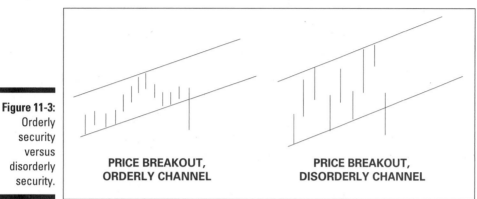

Figure 11-3:
Orderly
security
versus
disorderly
security.

**PRICE BREAKOUT,
ORDERLY CHANNEL**

**PRICE BREAKOUT,
DISORDERLY CHANNEL**

Orderliness isn't a word you find in the technical analysis literature. Instead, you find volatility. *Volatility* refers to the extent of variation away from a central reference point (like an average). You should consider that low volatility constitutes orderliness and high volatility implies disorder.

The more orderly your price bars, the more reliable your channels are. A breakout of an orderly channel is more likely to be the real thing than a breakout of a high-volatility (disorderly) channel. If you chose to trade a disorderly security, you must be able to tolerate a high number of false breakouts — and modify your filters accordingly.

If your security generates a lot of false breakouts and they make you nervous, find another security. A number of vendors offer software you can use to scan a collection of securities for those which are low volatility and therefore less likely to generate a lot of false breakouts.

Transition from orderly to disorderly (and back)

When a price series morphs from an orderly to a disorderly mode, the transformation is almost always accompanied by a breakout and a change in volume. Weirdly, a shift the other way also foreshadows a breakout. When prices shift from disorderly to orderly, the sharp decrease in volatility warns you that a breakout is impending; buyers and sellers alike don't know what to do, so they do nothing. On the day of the breakout and in the day or two following, you see a big increase in volume.

Driving faster is always risky

You also want to know the context of the breakout in terms of where the prices were located within the channel just before the breakout. The usual breakout is in the opposite direction of the prevailing trend.

But sometimes you see prices pressing against the top or bottom of the channel line, and this can lead to a breakout in the same direction as the trend. In other words, higher volatility can mean an acceleration of an existing trend. A breakout can be to the upside in an uptrend as well as to the downside in a downtrend.

Figure 11-4 illustrates an upside breakout in an uptrend. It's still a breakout, and you should expect that it still marks a change in the trend even though it is in the same direction. The acceleration of an existing trend should make you sit up and take notice. While it may simply signal a steepening of the trend as the crowd develops enthusiasm for the security, it can also occur near the end of a trend. It is sometimes called a *blowout* (or *blowoff*) *top* or a blowout bottom. In other words, an upside breakout in an uptrend is often a warning of an impending *downside* breakout, counterintuitive as that seems at first.

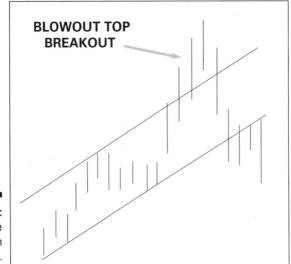

Figure 11-4:
Upside
breakout in
an uptrend.

How can such a pattern come about? Easy. The crowd becomes overheated with greed to buy a security that is rising with tremendous force, or overwhelmed by fear to dump a security that is declining with great momentum. At some point, everyone who was going to buy has bought. Because these are traders who bought only to get a fast profit, when the rise slows down and a lower high or a lower low appears, these buyers exit in a horde. (For a discussion of a lower high together with a lower low in an uptrend, see Chapter 6.) By selling a lot of the security in a very short period of time, the market has an oversupply, and just like the price of tomatoes falling to ten cents in late August, buyers can command a low price.

The same thing happens when a down move exhausts itself. Everybody who was going to sell has sold. Supply is now limited. Anyone who wants to buy has to start bidding the price up until he induces a longer-term holder of the security to part with it.

Riding the Regression Range

You can construct a more "scientific" set of parallel lines by drawing channel lines around the linear regression line. As I describe in Chapter 10, the *linear regression* is the line that minimizes the distance from itself and every point of the chart. It is the true, pure trendline, and thus the channel built on it, named the *standard error channel* (also called the *linear regression channel*) should be the true trend channel. You can calculate the standard error by hand, but it's laborious. Software is less error prone and a lot faster.

You use a channel based on the linear regression line the same way that you use a hand-drawn support and resistance channel, as you can see in the following sections. By projecting the lines out into the future, you get a forecast of the future price range, and you deem a significant breakout of a channel line as ending the trend.

With hand-drawn support and resistance channels, the channel is defined by the outer limits (the series of higher highs with higher low, or lower lows with lower highs). No centerline exists. In the linear regression channel, you build the channel from the inside out, so to speak. You start with a center linear line and draw the outer lines from that.

Introducing the standard error

Computer software places the standard error channel on either side of the linear regression line, according to the statistical measure named the standard error. Like the standard deviation you discover in Chapter 2, you don't need to know how to calculate this number or even precisely what it means in order to use it effectively.

The *standard error* measures how closely the prices cluster around your linear regression line. Most chartists use two standard errors, which results in a channel top and channel bottom that enclose a high percentage (95 percent) of the highs and lows. An extreme high or low constitutes a bigger error away from the trendline than 95 percent of the other highs and lows.

The closer prices are to the linear regression line, the stronger the trend. Here are a couple points to keep in mind:

✔ If you have an orderly trend, the prices don't stray very far from one another or from the linear regression, and therefore the channel is a narrow one on either side of the linear regression. A price that doesn't vary at all from the linear regression is literally "on the trend" and has a zero standard error.

✔ If you draw a channel and see that it's very wide, your price series has a lot of variation away from the linear regression. Prices far from the norm, the linear regression, are called *outliers* and when you have a lot of them, they are collectively called *noise.* The more noise, the less reliable your channel.

Drawing a linear regression channel

How "true" the linear regression and its channel turn out to be depends on where you start drawing. See Chapter 10 for a discussion of starting the linear regression in a reasonable place.

You start a linear regression channel at an obvious low or high, draw a channel line from there to a second relative low or high, and then extend it out. The parallel line comes along for the ride, which often helps you adjust the slope of the line by discovering relative highs or lows that you didn't see at first.

As with the hand-drawn support and resistance channel lines (see earlier sections in this chapter), you know that you have drawn your channel line correctly when a third relative high or low makes a touch of the line but doesn't cross it. Sometimes the "obvious" swing high or low occurs within a previous channel that has been broken and discarded: Go back to the swing bar and use it as the starting point for the new channel.

Figure 11-5 shows a nicely uptrending security with two channels. Look at the shorter one first. I start it at the lowest low, and let the software do the drawing to the bar after the next relative low. Then I stop drawing and extend the lines by hand, using dotted lines to mark them as hypothetical.

It isn't until three months later that prices break out of the channel — to the upside. Oh, oh. A breakout always means something. When it's a breakout in the same direction as the trend, you start worrying that it may be a blowout breakout, as I describe earlier in the chapter in the section "Driving faster is always risky." Whatever it turns out to be, you still need to discard the old channel. It has been broken. In this case, I left it on the chart.

Now I draw a new linear regression and its channel (the darker lines on the chart) from the same lowest-low starting point, and keep drawing until just after a new relative high appears. I know it's a relative high because it's breaking the top of the channel and followed by a lower high. I stop drawing at that relative high and extend the channel lines out, as before. Notice that the price does it again! It breaks out of the top of the channel a second time.

Figure 11-5:
Two
standard
error
channels.

As a practical matter, every time a price breaks a channel line, you face a higher risk. The channel defines what is normal, and any foray outside the channel is not normal. What does this breakout in Figure 11-5 mean?

✔ The latest high prices can mark a third shift to a new, more steeply sloping channel yet to be drawn.

✔ A blowout breakout may be forming.

✔ The price series may subside back into the channel.

You have no way to know which of these three outcomes is the most likely from the information on the chart. You may choose to exit on every channel line breakout, or you can add another indicator to guide your decision.

Confirming hand-drawn channels

You can validate a hand-drawn support and resistance channel by superimposing a standard error channel on top of it. Starting at the same low (or high) point that you used to draw by hand, draw the standard error channel and see how closely it tracks your hand-drawn lines. Sometimes the standard error channel falls exactly on top of your hand-drawn lines, which is "scientific" validation that you drew them right and they accurately represent the trend. More often, the standard error channel has a slightly different slope.

Trading a security that moves neatly within its channel, especially a validated double channel (hand-drawn *and* standard error), reduces the stress of trading.

Sizing up the special features of the linear regression channel

You use the linear regression channel the same way you use a hand-drawn channel — to estimate the future range and to determine when a trend has ended by observing a breakout of one of the channel lines.

The linear regression has a few special characteristics, though. For instance, when it comes to the linear regression channel, you want to know the following:

- The linear regression doesn't encompass every price extreme in a series. It encompasses a very high percentage of them. Therefore, some price bars will always break the channel lines without invalidating the channel, unlike the situation in a hand-drawn channel.

- To make it more unlikely that you'll mistake a normal breaking of the channel line with a breakout, you can widen the channel lines to encompass the first two or three highest highs and lowest lows, and then extend it out. This modification is named a *Raff regression channel* after Gilbert Raff, the man who devised it.

- You can adjust the width of the channel lines by instructing your software to use three errors rather than the usual two. A three-error channel encloses 99 percent of the prices. This is handy for a just-emerging channel where you don't have many prices yet.

- The linear regression is self-adjusting. Every time you update the channel, your software includes the new day's data and modifies both the linear regression line and the slope and width of the channel accordingly. It's therefore a bit of an odd duck — a set of straight lines that isn't fixed, at least until you fix it by halting the updating process.

- In order to see a breakout to confirm a trend change, you have to stop drawing at some point. Otherwise, the channel simply adjusts to the new data and you never get a breakout. Don't forget, it automatically incorporates all the price data you put into it. Garbage in, garbage out.

You can draw new channels on top of your existing forecast channel. You begin at the same starting point but continue the true channel to the current day. If the width and the slope of the fresh true channel are about the same as your forecast channel, you deem the forecast channel to be stable. A *stable* channel implies that the forecast embedded in the farther-out lines is probably pretty good. If you notice that the new, true channel that incorporates the latest prices is starting to widen, narrow, or change slope, examine the price bars themselves to see if they indicate a trend change. See Chapter 6 and 7 for information on the price bars.

Discovering the drawbacks of linear regression channels

Linear regression channels are more difficult to work with than hand-drawn support and resistance — you have to exercise more judgment, and it is more of an art. Some of the complications are

- ✔ **Not a majority process:** A large number of people draw support and resistance lines and channels, but not everyone draws linear regression channels. A big part of why technical analysis works is that many people are observing the same thing and acting on it, like breakouts. The same can't be said of linear regression channels.

- ✔ **May not stand alone:** You can draw a very large number of channels on the same chart, and each of them is "right." Often you draw one channel from an obvious starting point but after fixing it and extending it out into the future, you find that you can draw another channel from a nearby starting point that points to a different outcome. I call this dueling channels, and it always occurs at trend turning points.

- ✔ **Not really "scientific":** The linear regression channel is scientific in the sense that the software calculates it to enclose a preponderance of prices, but that doesn't mean that you started it or stopped it at the ideal spot, or that the channel extension is correct. The mathematical principle isn't subjective, but your application is always subjective. Consider that your car works on scientific principles of internal combustion and the like, but that doesn't necessarily make you a good driver.

Pivot Point Support and Resistance Channel

What do you do when you stop getting higher highs (in an uptrend) or lower lows (in a downtrend)? In other words, the price is still within its channel but now it is moving sideways.

The pause in movement may be temporary, but the sideways action can also be a warning that forward momentum is gone. From this you may deduce that if you're going to take profit, now is the time. The sideways action may also imply that a breakout in the opposite direction is impending.

One technique for dealing with sideways moves within a channel is to draw horizontal support and resistance lines off pivot points. Technical traders use the term *pivot point* in many different ways. One standard definition is that the pivot point is the center bar of three bars (or more) where the center bar is the highest high or lowest low. Another definition of pivot is the median price (the numerical average of the high, low, and close). Other traders cook up yet more definitions. Today, the median price version is probably the most accepted. Keep reading for more handy tips on pivot points.

Calculating the first zone of support and resistance

The logic of the pivot point is that after a trend pauses, you need a breakout that's a significant distance from the median price to decide whether the old trend will resume or a reversal is really at hand. So you start with the median price and to that you add a factor to get upside resistance, and you subtract a factor to get downside support.

To calculate the first (inner) line of resistance, multiply the pivot point value by two and, from that number, subtract the low of the pivot day. This is named R1. To calculate the first (inner) line of support, or S1, multiply the pivot value by two and, from that number, subtract the high of the pivot day. This procedure sounds like a lot of arithmetic, but don't sweat it. It's easy enough to do in a spreadsheet or by hand, and many trading platforms offer it as a standard option. Plus, the procedure itself is quite sensible — you use a multiple of the median price to estimate a range going forward that subtracts the high and the low to yield a norm. Any price higher or lower would be an extreme. If the upcoming price breaks the horizontal support and resistance lines calculated this way, the direction of the breakout is your clue that the trend is truly over.

You can create a series of pivot support and resistance lines according to these formulas or some variation of them:

Pivot Point = (High + Close + Low)/3Support 1 = 2 × Pivot − High
Support 2 = Pivot − (R1 − S1)
Support 3 = Low − 2 × (High − Pivot)

Resistance 1 = 2 × Pivot − Low
Resistance 2 = Pivot + (R1 − S1)
Resistance 3 = High + 2 × (Pivot − Low)

In Figure 11-6, R3 is very close to the highest high and S3, while higher than the recent lowest low, meets the hand-drawn support line connecting two lows. Pivot point analysis has become very popular in recent years. Advocates say that by projecting out a reasonable range to the next few days, you can easily see a breakout, and pivot points are therefore predictive instead of lagging, like every other indicator. This is not, strictly speaking, accurate. Any band or channel has predictive value in the sense that upcoming prices, if they are normal, will remain within the band or channel and a violation of the channel top or bottom constitutes a breakout. What is valuable about pivot points is that when many market participants are looking at the same lines, you can expect price movement at exactly those lines.

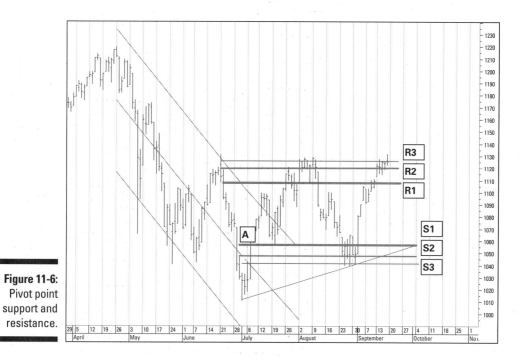

Figure 11-6:
Pivot point
support and
resistance.

Using pivot support and resistance

You can use pivot support and resistance all by itself, and many day traders do. You can also add other indicators like the two moving average crossover (see Chapter 12). In the case I present in Figure 11-7, if you had bought at Point A, you would set your target at R1 if you are risk averse, R2 if you are an optimist, and R3 if you are swinging at the bases. Note that a test of a previous high is commonplace in a bounce off a low. If you're able to go short, you may sell at R3 and target a gain to S3, which conveniently meets the hand-drawn support line.

What's important about the pivot-based support and resistance lines is that they effectively outline a period of activity where traders don't know the trend. Bulls try to make a new high and get only a few pennies worth. Bears try to make a new low but fail to get a significant lower low.

Pivot analysis is most useful in periods of congestion or sideways action after an old trend has ended and a new one has not yet emerged.

Figure 11-7:
Pivot point
levels
overlaid
with a
standard
error
channel.

In Figure 11-7, you can see two standard error channels overlaid on the same pivot point chart as in Figure 11-6. The first channel is drawn from the intermediate high in the topmost oval, and the second channel is drawn from the lowest low in the bottommost oval. Both channels slope upward, suggesting it is a credible identification of the direction, and both are near the hand-drawn support line. This evidence certainly suggests that an uptrend has formed, and yet the moves are choppy and failing to make new highs or new lows. It's a range-trading market and the up-sloping standard error channel could be just wishful thinking. In contrast, the pivot-based support and resistance "channel" offers hands-on, specific places to buy and sell whether the trend uptrend is the real deal or not.

Part V
Flying with Dynamic Analysis

The 5th Wave   By Rich Tennant

"I'm in technical analysis, Doug. This keeps me sharp."

In this part . . .

Math-based indicators are commonplace today, even among non-technicians. The purpose of these indicators is to refine and better quantify the same questions asked in all technical methods: Is the security trending? How strong is the trend? Is the trend ending?

Every indicator uses basic arithmetic to fiddle with the various components of a series of bars. If you have a grasp of the bar components, you don't need to bother with the exact formulas unless you like formulas. In this part, I walk you through the most commonly used indicators and show how they capture various aspects of crowd behavior.

Chapter 12

Using Dynamic Lines

Moving averages are the workhorses of technical analysis. Most traders start out in technical analysis with moving averages, and some traders never see a need to look into any other technique — that's how successful moving averages can make your trading.

A *moving average* is an arithmetic method of smoothing price numbers so that you can see and measure a trend. A straight line (see Chapter 10) is a good visual organizing device, but a dynamic line — the moving average — more accurately describes what's really going on. In addition, you don't need to choose starting and ending points, removing that aspect of subjectivity, although choosing how many periods to put in your moving averages is subjective. In this chapter, I discuss several different ways you can calculate and use moving averages to get buy/sell trading signals.

Be careful not to attribute a forecasting capability to the moving average. Moving averages are *trend-following*. The moving average is a lagging indicator — it can still be rising after your price hits a brick wall and crashes.

Introducing the Simple Moving Average

You know what an average is — you measure ten of something, add up the measurements, and divide by ten. Here's how you get the average "moving": Start by finding the average of a number of prices — say ten. The next day you add the newest price to the total and subtract the oldest price, keeping the total number of prices constant at ten. The standard simple moving average uses the close, because the close is the summary of the period's action and sentiment (see Chapter 6).

Yes, using the moving average means recalculating the whole thing every time you have a new price. Before PCs, it was a laborious process. In fact, a preference for the 10-day average started in the 1930s, because it's easy to calculate by hand (plus it measures two weeks), and it remains popular today. (For a discussion on choosing the number of days to use with a moving average, see the "Fixing lag" section later in the chapter.) Figure 12-1 displays a 10-day simple moving average.

Right off the bat, you can see that the moving average clings to the prices and represents their movements better than a straight line and, at the same time, smoothes away the occasional erratic price. You almost stop seeing price variations after you draw the moving average on a chart.

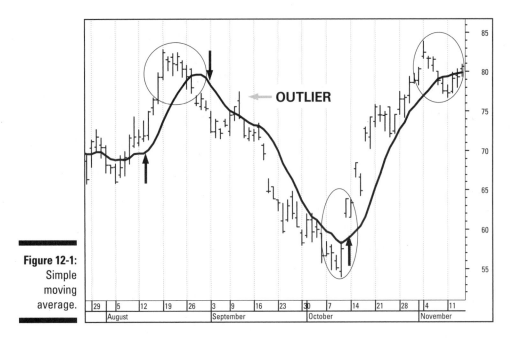

Figure 12-1: Simple moving average.

Starting with the crossover rule

When the price is moving upward or downward, so is the moving average line, albeit with a lag. After a price turning point, the price crosses the moving average line. At the V-shaped bottom on Figure 12-1, for example, prices are below the line until the gap (ellipse), and then prices cross above the line. (See Chapter 7 for information on gaps.)

The crossover rule states that you buy at the point where the price crosses above the moving average line and sell at the point where it falls below the moving average line. In practice, you execute the trades the next day at the open if you're working with daily data.

You can easily see that the moving average on Figure 12-1 captured the trends. The crossovers captured the trend reversals, too. The result is buying at lows and selling at highs. The moving average crossover rule generates a profit. What could be better? Right about now, you may be tempted to shout "Eureka! I have discovered a systematic, objective trading system."

Not so fast. For one thing, the price doesn't always obediently stay above the moving average after an upside crossover (or below the moving average after a downside crossover). See the price bars on Figure 12-1 marked "Outlier." First you get a close above the moving average and then the next bar is almost entirely above the moving average. An *outlier* is just what it sounds like — a data point that lies far off the trendline. This particular chart is tidy — it has only a pair of outliers. Usually you see a lot more.

If you use the crossover rule to buy and sell a security every time the close crosses the moving average, you get a lot of buy/sell signals that reverse in fairly short order, as this one does. In Figure 12-1, you don't know at the time it's happening that the outliers are abnormal. For all you know, the crossover above the moving average is a genuine indication of a reversal. You know only after the price resumes the down move that they were outliers.

Table 12-1 shows the gains and losses following the moving average crossover trading rule. Notice that I include the short side, which is selling something you don't own in the expectation that you'll be able to buy it later at a cheaper price. To sell short is only to reverse the normal order of the buy/sell equation. Usually you buy before you sell, but if you see a price clearly trending downward, in many cases you can sell it today and buy it back later for a profit. Even if you never sell short, calculating total profitability accurately is important when you evaluate a trading rule like the moving average crossover rule. For one thing, a rule that applies equally well to down moves as to up moves is more likely to be correct in all cases. For another, the end of a short sale may be the start of a purchase trade.

To evaluate a trading technique, including moving averages, you judge its effectiveness on the basis of its profitability from identifying trends going in both directions.

Table 12-1	Hypothetical Profit from the Simple Moving Average Crossover Rule			
No. of Days	*Action*	*Price*	*Crossover Profit*	*Buy-and-Hold*
19 days	Buy	$70.61		$70.61
	Sell	$76.00	$5.39	

(continued)

Table 12-1 *(continued)*

No. of Days	Action	Price	Crossover Profit	Buy-and-Hold
14 days	Sell	$76.00		
	Buy	$76.40	($.40)	
2 days	Buy	$76.40		
	Sell	$71.50	($4.90)	
28 days	Sell	$71.50		
	Buy	$62.00	$9.50	
38 days	Buy	$62.00		
	Sell	$78.50	$16.50	$78.50
Total			$26.09 (37%)	$7.89 (11%)

If you traded every crossover signal as shown in Table 12-1, the return is $26.09 on starting capital of $70.61, or 37 percent in less than one year. This gain is more than three times higher than simply buying at the beginning of the period and holding to the end. But in the process of trading the cross-overs, you take two losses caused by the outliers.

In measuring the profitability of the crossover rule, I assume a policy of *stop-and-reverse,* which means you close out one trade and put on another in the opposite direction at the same time and at the same price. This method is the conventional way to calculate the profitability of a trading rule, at least the first time around. Later you may adjust your entry and exit rules, as I discuss in the section "Filtering out whipsaws" section later in this chapter.

Dealing with the dreaded whipsaw

A buy/sell signal that's wrong (in hindsight) is called a *false signal.* In moving average work, the false signal is a crossover that reverses within a few days, like the outliers in Figure 12-1. False signals usually reverse fairly quickly, putting you back in the trade in the right direction, but in the meanwhile, you take a small loss, called a *whipsaw loss. Whipsaw* refers to the whipping action of the price quickly moving through the moving average in both directions, resulting in a series of back-and-forth trades. Whipsaws occur in even the best-behaved trend and are common in a sideways market where traders are indecisive about trend direction.

Whipsaws have a pernicious effect on your profit and loss statement in two ways:

✔ When trading a trend-following technique like the moving average cross-over, you make most of your gains by riding big trends, and you accept that gains are going to be reduced by the occasional whipsaw at reversal points, sideways periods, and any spiky outlier. But if your big trends also contain whipsaws, you end up *overtrading,* which is to make a lot of trades for only a small net gain or loss.

✔ Overtrading almost always results in net losses because on every trade you have to pay brokerage commissions and fees. In all the cases in this chapter, I am conveniently not subtracting commissions and fees, but remember that they reduce profits and raise losses in real life.

Filtering out whipsaws

Instead of using the raw crossover of price and moving average to generate a buy/sell signal, you can set up additional tests, called *filters*. If the crossover passes the filter tests, chances are it's a valid buy/sell signal and not a flash in the pan. Filters come in several varieties, and you can apply any or all of them to reduce the number of trades. Note that filters may delay entry and exit, and therefore may reduce total gains while reducing whipsaw losses.

Consider the following filters:

✔ **Time:** The close has to remain above (or below) the moving average for an additional x number of periods after the crossover date.

✔ **Extent:** The price has to surpass the moving average numerical value by x percent of the price or x percent of some other measure, such as the trading range of the past y days (see Chapter 7 for information on the trading range).

✔ **Volume:** The crossover has to be accompanied by a significant rise in volume.

✔ **Extreme sentiment:** In an uptrend crossover, the low has to surpass the moving average and not just the close; in a downtrend, the high has to be under the moving average, and not just the close. See Chapter 6 for a discussion of the high, low, and close.

Using the moving average level rule

Instead of looking at the crossover, you can call the end of an uptrend when the moving average today is less than the moving average yesterday, and you call the end of a downtrend when the moving average today is higher than yesterday's. The moving average level rule usually calls the end of trend earlier than the crossover, although not always.

A moving average always lags the price action. In Figure 12-1, look at the prices and moving average in the left-hand ellipse. From the peak close, it takes the price six days to cross below the moving average — and *ten* days for the value of the moving average to be lower than the day before. By the time the moving average puts in a lower value than the day before, it's Day 10 and the price has fallen from $82.49 to $75.38, or by 8.6 percent.

But despite giving up 8.6 percent from the highest close while you wait for the moving average to catch up with prices, to trade *this* stock by using *this* indicator during *this* period would have been profitable. (See the "Fixing lag" section in this chapter for more information.)

The black arrows on the chart in Figure 12-1 mark the buy/sell entry and exit points, using the moving average level rule. You buy and sell at the open the day after the moving average meets the rule. Table 12-2 shows the profit you make by applying the rule. Your gain is $43.07 on an initial capital stake of $71.05, or 61 percent, compared to 14 percent if you buy on the first date and account for the gain on the last date.

Accounting for the gain is what *mark-to-market* means in Table 12-2. Cash in the bank from closed positions, named *realized gain,* is the main way to keep score in trading, but mark-to-market is the way to keep score on positions that are still open. It means to apply today's closing price to your position to see how much it's worth in cash terms, even though you didn't actually exit the position today. Mark-to-market gains are named *unrealized,* and it's a good phrase, meaning that the gain is only an accounting convention — and not real, although in futures trading you may use unrealized gains to add to positions. Needless to say, a mark-to-market valuation is valid only until the next market price becomes available.

Be on the lookout for trading system vendor performance track records that rely on mark-to-market gains for wonderful end-of-period gains. Mark-to-market gains are only paper gains and can vanish in a puff of smoke. To evaluate a technique, look at its performance on closed trades.

Table 12-2		Hypothetical Profit from the Moving Average Level Rule		
N. of Days	**Action**	**Price**	**Level Rule Profit**	**Buy-and-Hold**
22 days	Buy	$71.05		$71.05
	Sell	$78.24	$7.19	
42 days	Sell	$78.24		
	Buy	$61.54	$16.70	
29 days	Buy	$61.54		
	Mark-to-market	$80.72	$19.18	$80.72
Total			$43.07 (61%)	$9.67 (14%)

Dealing with limitations

You may have seen Table 12-2 and are starting to get excited by the 60 percent plus return in four months. But before you go off the deep end, consider that I rigged the case by finding an ideal chart like Figure 12-1. It wasn't hard to find, but for every ideal situation like this, thousands more can be found where applying a 10-day simple moving average crossover or the moving average level rule results in heartache and losses.

The security in Figure 12-1 is trending, and in a tidy fashion. Aside from one outlier, prices don't vary much away from the moving average. But this same security goes through periods when it is neither trending nor tidy. Moving averages lose their power to help you make money when either of these two conditions arises:

- **Not trending:** Prices can move sideways for long periods of time while the market makes up its mind what to do next (congestion). In that instance, the moving·average is a horizontal line. You get no buy/sell guidance from moving average techniques in a sideways move like the one shown in Figure 12-2. This particular one is tidy, too — no outliers. But a sideways movement defeats trend-following by definition.

- **Noisy:** A price series with many prices varying far from the moving average is said to have a lot of *noise,* likening outliers to the static you get on a car radio as you move out of signal range. The second chart in Figure 12-2 shows a tidy trend, with few outliers. The third chart is the same moving average, but it arises from a price move with many outliers.

The trader using moving averages faces a perpetual task of reducing noise while also reducing lag, and these two goals are hard to achieve simultaneously. Fixing noise entails using a higher number of periods in the moving average, while fixing lag entails using a shorter number — as you can see in the following sections.

Fixing noise

You can't do anything about a sideways move (except perhaps trade the security on a shorter time frame that may contain minitrends). But you can do something about noise — apply a moving average with more days in it. You want to minimize losses, and a noisy price series makes you vulnerable to false buy/sell signals. When you use a higher number of days in the moving average, say 50 days, noisy outliers get put in their place, arithmetically speaking. An abnormally high or low price relative to the existing average is less important in a 50-day moving average than in a 10-day moving average, because it literally carries less weight in the calculation.

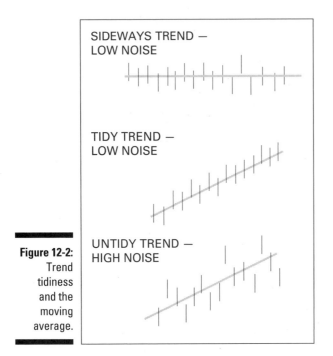

Figure 12-2:
Trend
tidiness
and the
moving
average.

But if you're using a 50-day moving average, your buy/sell signals are even later than the 10 days that cost 8.6 percent in the case above. Besides, in some periods, the security is tidy, and in other periods, it's noisy, and you don't know in advance which it is going to be. Fixing noise by altering the number of periods in the moving average is an endless challenge that has launched a gazillion hours of research. Because new data comes along all the time, a lot of this noise-targeting research is wasted.

Fixing lag

Often you can see a dramatic price move, but you know it's going to take days for the moving average to catch up. You're disciplined and committed to following the crossover rule, but potential profits are going up the chimney while you impatiently wait. Why not simply reduce the number of days in the moving average? A short moving average is more sensitive to recent prices.

As a general rule, you want to use as few days in the moving average as possible without running into a high level of wrong signals. When you use a very short moving average, like three days, you not only lose the descriptive visual power of the line on the chart, but you also get a lot of whipsaws. In fact, using a 3-day moving average on the same data in Figure 12-1 cuts the profitability to under 5 percent — worse than if you used the buy-and-hold approach.

No single number of days is best for a moving average. The best number is the one that fits how noisy the prices are. If your prices are so noisy that you would have to use a high number of days in the moving average, resign yourself to getting late exits long after the price peak. Or you can find a different, more orderly security to trade.

Magic moving average numbers

Some technical traders think that securities prices move in cycles that are relatively fixed, such as three-to-four weeks, three-to-four months (and its double, six-to-eight months), and three-to-four years. Therefore, they imagine that you should gear the number of days in your moving average to these cycles. But while cycles do exist, too many of them exist. They overlap, and nobody can agree on a single one that rules securities prices all the time, or which one is ruling the market at any one time. You won't find statistical proof of cycle theories consistently working in securities markets, and you will certainly see thousands of situations that don't conform to them.

As I note in Chapter 2, whether or not fixed-length cycles are true doesn't matter. If a sufficient number of traders believe they're true, sometimes traders cause the predicted cycle to occur. Popular moving averages are 28 days and half of 28 days (14 days), and the combination 5-10-20 days, or a variation, 4-18-40. The 28-day number was devised as a monthly number in apparent disregard of the trading month having 20 to 22 days compared to the lunar or calendar month. Systems designers joke that the 4-day moving average was devised to ace out the people using the 5-day, and the 9-day to get in front of the traders using the 10-day moving average.

The bottom line: Be skeptical of buying into a magic number. The spirit of technical analysis is empirical: What does the data say?

One moving average really does stand out — the 20-day. When a security is trending, the 20-day moving average often works the same way a support line works — sellers stop selling when it's reached. Less often, the 20-day moving average constitutes resistance. (I describe support and resistance in Chapter 10.) The virtue of a moving average that works as support or resistance is that you don't have to choose a starting and ending point — the moving average is nonjudgmental and everyone gets the same line. Many traders plot the 20-day moving average on every chart to get a feel for what other traders in the market may see as a benchmark level.

You may also see the 20-day moving average tracking the linear regression. When you see this confluence, you get a sense that maybe the market has some underlying order after all. Beware of superstition! The sense of orderliness may not be an illusion in any particular case, but remember that no trend lasts forever. At the turning point, the 20-day moving average is dead wrong, so enjoy it while you have it.

Folklore versus trading tools

You see reports that Blue Widget stock just surpassed its 50-day moving average, or its 200-day moving average, or that its 50-day moving average crossed its 200-day moving average, a so-called "golden cross." This type of information may or may not be interesting and useful. Maybe the price had been within a few pennies of the 200-day moving average for months on end, and just managed to inch over it. Why is this news?

Without a context, a price crossing a moving average of a fixed number of days is just another statistic. Because of research by technical trader Richard Donchian, the 5-day and 20-day moving averages became popular, and that makes sense — 5 days is a week and 20 days is (roughly) a month. But 50 days and 200 days are just round numbers unrelated to the calendar (the number of business days in a year is about 240). And as I note in this chapter, the best number of days to put in a moving average is the *smallest* number that still generates as few whipsaws as possible. By choosing a number as high as 50 or 200 days, you're condemning yourself to an inefficient parameter practically by definition.

But that would be to mistake a barometer of the environment for a trading tool. If you're looking for an indicator to describe the general tone of a security or market index, the 200-day moving average is pretty good — mostly because it *is* in vogue. To use a fixed number like 50 or 200 makes sense only if everyone else is looking at the same number, and increasingly, they are. Even people who profess to dislike and distrust technical analysis give credence to the 200-day moving average.

But what *exactly* does it mean? Well, the 200-day moving average doesn't have a proven meaning. A security whose price falls below the 200-day moving average has fallen out of favor with traders, and one whose price is in the process of crossing above the 200-day moving average is back in favor. The financial press sometimes reports a "death cross," or the 50-day moving average crossing below the 200-day. *Death cross* is a semantically loaded term that has no statistical basis for reliably predicting outcomes. This technical jargon example is an instance where language influences the outcome far more than the event the language is purportedly describing.

Adjusting the Moving Average

You can adjust the moving average to make it track current prices more closely without sacrificing all the benefits of the averaging process. Keep reading this section to find out how.

Getting acquainted with moving average types

Moving averages are often abbreviated. You may see SMA and wonder what *that* is. SMA stands for the *simple moving average* (and you feel like an idiot after you figure it out). Likewise, the moving averages I cover in the following sections are also often abbreviated: WMA refers to *weighted moving average,* EMA refers to *exponential moving average,* and AMA refers to *adaptive moving average.*

Weighted and exponential moving averages

Instead of reducing the number of days in the moving average, a different way to make the moving average more responsive to the latest prices is to weight the latest prices more heavily. You get the *weighted moving average* by multiplying each price in your series according to how fresh it is. In a 5-day moving average, for example, Day 5 (today) would be multiplied by 5, Day 4 by 4, Day 3 by 3, and so on. Remember to divide the total by the sum of the weights, not the sum of the days (5 + 4 + 3 + 2 + 1 = 15).

More popular than the weighted moving average is the *exponential moving average.* This moving average is hard to calculate, and fortunately, all the charting software packages can do it for you. The principle is to subtract today's closing price from yesterday's exponential moving average.

When you begin, start with a simple moving average. Multiply the difference between today's price and the moving average by a constant smoothing factor (the *exponent*). The factor is determined by the number of days you're using in the moving average, say 10 days. The exponent is calculated by dividing 2 by 10, yielding 0.2 as the factor. If you're using 20 days, you divide 2 by 20 and get 0.1 as the factor. Here's why:

- ✔ The factor minimizes the change between the existing moving average and the latest price, creating a smaller bridge than in a simple moving average, which has to bridge the entire distance between today's price and yesterday's. This factor gives the moving average a numerical value closer to the last price and thus makes it more representative of recent prices.

- ✔ The fewer the number of days in the moving average, the bigger the factor. This principle closes the gap between the moving average and the latest price even more.

Adaptive moving averages

The adaptive moving average works like a long-term moving average in that it diminishes the effect of outliers, but without sacrificing sensitivity to trended prices. You always want a moving average to be as short as possible to identify the beginning of a trend quickly, but as long as necessary to avoid whipsaw losses.

In other words, sometimes you want the moving average to contain a small number of days, and other times you want it to contain a higher number of days. You don't want to be forced to select the number yourself, because you have no way of knowing in advance which is right. You want some automatic mechanical adjustment to kick in when variability changes, to adapt the moving average to the new condition. You can't change the number of days according to conditions, but you can get the same effect by making the moving average adaptive.

A trading systems designer named Perry Kaufman devised an ingenious way to achieve this adaptiveness for trading purposes and called it the *adaptive moving average.* It is abbreviated KAMA, for *Kaufman's adaptive moving average,* while other versions of the adaptive moving average are usually named just AMA or have the inventor's initial, like Richard Jurik's JAMA. The Kaufman process of performing the adaptive calculation begins with a concept called an *efficiency ratio,* which measures how straight the line prices follow as they move from one point to the next.

Efficient prices follow a straight line. They receive an efficiency rating of 1. Prices that are inefficient resemble the meandering path of a drunken sailor. They get an efficiency rating of zero. Most prices are somewhere in between. The rating is then converted to a *smoothing constant* (which is confusing because in this application, it's not constant, but changes depending on the numbers; *constant* is a term used by mathematicians for a term in a formula because it's constantly there, whatever its numerical value). As the smoothing constant gets closer to 1, the moving average tracks the prices more closely. When the smoothing constant is zero, the moving average value doesn't change and is carried over unchanged from yesterday — in other words, a spiky outlier is simply ignored.

Choosing a moving average type

Traders debate which type of moving average is the best. Figure 12-3 shows examples of all four of the moving averages I discuss in this chapter, and that doesn't come close to exhausting all the possible modifications.

Each version of moving averages has strengths and weaknesses. The weighted moving average is the most sensitive to the latest price moves, followed by the exponential moving average. Notice that the KAMA is the best at chopping off the spiky outlier prices that make the price series noisy. That means it works best at reducing whipsaw losses, too. But it gives a value of zero to the breakaway gap like the last bar on this chart. (See Chapter 7 for a discussion of gaps). In a trend reversal like the one depicted on this chart, that's a drawback. You enter the new trend later than if you used a nonadaptive technique, but as an offset, you don't get very many false signals.

Don't invest the moving average with supernatural powers. It's only arithmetic. A moving average can't capture every important move and in fact, rides roughshod over some important chart events, like breakaway gaps. The moving average is a repackaging of the price series, not the price series itself.

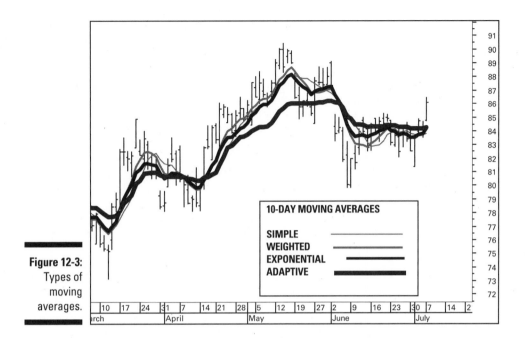

Figure 12-3:
Types of
moving
averages.

Using Multiple Moving Averages

You like a short moving average because it responds quickly to new conditions, and you like a long moving average because it reduces errors. So why not use both of them? Or three — a short-, medium-, and long-term moving average? You can. Read on!

Putting two moving averages into play

Here's where the crossover concept (which I introduce earlier in this chapter) comes back into the picture, and it shines. Instead of looking for the price to cross a single moving average, you look for a shorter moving average (say 5 days) to cross a longer moving average (say 20 days). When you use 5 and 20 days, you chart a one-week moving average against a one-month moving average.

When the shorter moving average crosses the longer moving average on the upside, you buy. When the shorter moving average crosses the longer moving average on the downside, you sell.

You are free to use any parameter set in the two moving average crossover model. Before getting into how to customize the two moving average model, look at Figure 12-4, which shows the same security and time frame as in

Figure 12-1, only this time with two moving averages, the short one at 5 days and the longer one at 20 days. You buy when the short-term moving averages crosses above the long-term moving average, and sell when it crosses below. Again, the arrows mark the buy/sell crossovers.

You may notice the similarity of the buy/sell arrow placement on Figure 12-4 to those in Figure 12-1. But you can also see that the problems present on the first chart are absent from this chart. The outlier is still there, but the short-term moving average is clearly below the long-term moving average, so you don't care. You hardly see it. On the right-hand side of the chart, some prices close below the short-term moving average, and again, you don't care. The short-term moving average remains nicely above the long-term one, and in fact, you can see a fair amount of daylight between the two moving average lines.

Figure 12-4:
Two
moving
average
crossover
model.

The more open space — daylight — you see between two moving averages, the more confident you can be that the signal is correct and will continue. When the two moving averages converge (as they do near the outlier, for example), you have less confidence that the signal is going to last.

If you trade the two moving average model, your gain is $25.31 on an initial capital stake of $70.61, or 36 percent, as shown in Table 12-3. This gain is considerably less than the 61 percent you can make by using the moving average level rule, shown in Table 12-2, but consider the advantages of the two moving average crossover:

✔ You can *see* the crossover and don't have to calculate the numerical value of the moving average every day, which is a nuisance. You still may want to add a filter, such as waiting a day or two after the crossover to put on the trade or qualifying the crossover by a percentage amount.

✔ The two moving average crossover is more reliable than the single moving average in that it is less sensitive. It lags more (see the section "Fixing lag" earlier in this chapter), but is wrong less often. You're swapping risk for return, as usual.

✔ You have fewer trades and therefore lower brokerage expense. In the crossover of the moving average and price, you have ten trades (five in and five out), whereas in the level rule and two moving average crossover, you have six.

Table 12-3	Hypothetical Profit from the Two Moving Average Crossover Rule			
No. of Days	*Action*	*Price*	*Profit*	*Buy-and-Hold*
25 days	Buy	$70.61		$70.61
	Sell	$74.20	$3.59	
43 days	Sell	$74.20		
	Buy	$66.60	$7.60	
29 days	Buy	$66.60		
	Mark-to-market	$80.72	$14.12	$80.72
Total			$25.31 (36%)	$10.11 (14%)

Trying the three-way approach

If two moving averages are good, three must be better. For example, you could plot the 5-day, 10-day, and 20-day moving averages on a chart, and you would consider a buy/sell signal to be confirmed only when both the 5-day *and* the 10-day cross the 20-day moving average. If you're always a buyer and never a short-seller, you can add a qualification that a sell signal occurs when the 5-day moving average crosses *either* of the other two moving averages.

This approach is the belt-and-suspenders school of trading, where you're willing to accept a lot of delay in entering a new trade in exchange for hardly any wrong signals. The three moving average model has one very useful feature — it keeps you out of a trade if the price movement stops trending and starts going sideways, or if it becomes very choppy and volatile, so that you would need an exceptionally long moving average just to see the trend.

In the conventional two moving average model, you're always in the market. When you sell, you not only get rid of the security that you bought, but you also go short. But when the security enters a sideways or choppy period, you're going to get chopped up on whipsaw losses. The three moving average model overcomes that problem by refusing to give you a confirmed signal. You stay out of the security and out of trouble.

See Figure 12-5. The first arrow on the left marks where the short-term moving average rises above the medium- and long-term moving averages. The arrow in the center marks where the short-term moving average crosses below the medium-term moving average — and you're out. You don't enter short at the same time, as in the two moving average case. If you had entered short, you would have been whipsawed several times over the next few weeks. Look at how choppy the prices became, up and down by large amounts over a short period of time. Finally, near the end of the chart, the short-term moving average crosses above both of the other moving averages, and you get a buy signal.

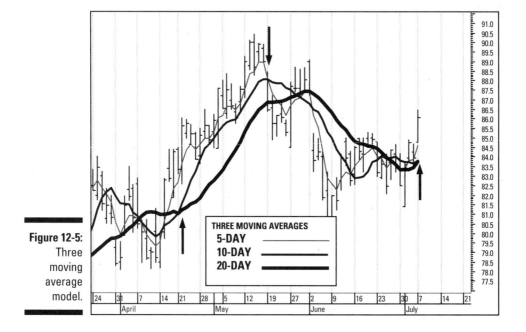

Figure 12-5: Three moving average model.

Delving into Moving Average Convergence and Divergence

When the price crosses over a moving average, or one moving average crosses over another, you have a chart event with an embedded trading decision. But the crossover is a blunt instrument. You can often see a crossover coming, but if you're following rule-based discipline, you're twiddling your thumbs waiting for the actual crossover.

If you look at any two moving average crossovers, you see that at a turning point, the short moving average converges to the price and the long-term moving average converges, a bit later, to the short-term one. By the time the crossover actually occurs, the price peak (or trough) has already passed.

Similarly, after a crossover, the two moving averages diverge from one another. Wouldn't it be nice to quantify the convergence and divergence? Then you'd have a measure of market sentiment. You could say that sentiment is turning against the current trend when the moving averages are converging and market sentiment is confirming the current trend as the moving averages diverge.

Here are the convergence and divergence basics you need to know:

- **Convergence:** When two moving averages converge, the trend may be coming to an end. Convergence is therefore an early warning. Because moving averages are always lagging indicators, measuring convergence is a way of anticipating a crossover.

  At a peak, one way to look at the convergence is to say that short-term demand is faltering — traders are failing to produce new higher closes. The trend is still in place, as shown by the long-term moving average. At a price bottom, you can interpret the short-term moving average falling at a lesser pace as selling interest (supply) falters.

- **Divergence:** Conversely, when you can see a lot of daylight between two moving averages, they're diverging, and that means the trend is safe from a crossover, at least for another few periods. In practice, abnormally wide divergence tends not to be sustainable and can be a warning of prices having reached an extreme ahead of reversing.

To get the ins and outs on how to calculate and use convergence and divergence to maximize your trading, check out the following sections.

Calculating convergence and divergence

To calculate convergence and divergence, you simply subtract the long-term moving average from the short-term one. That sounds backwards, but stop and think about it for a minute. If the price and moving averages are rising, the long-term moving average is a smaller number, say $10, than the shorter-term moving average, say $15. The short average minus the long average equals $5. Now the price passes its peak and falls. The short-term moving average loses steam and the next day it is $13, while the long-term moving average is still climbing. Today's price drop is a drop in its bucket. The long-term numerical value is $12. Now the difference is only $1. From $5 to $1 is convergence.

The inventor of the moving average convergence-divergence indicator (MACD), Gerald Appel, designed it to use exponential moving averages of 26 and 12 days, although the MACD is a model into which you can insert any moving average that suits your fancy and backtests well on your security. (I discuss backtesting in Chapter 4.)

The chart in Figure 12-6 shows a 12-day and 26-day moving average in the top window. In the bottom window is the result of subtracting the 26-day moving average from the 12-day moving average, which is the convergence-divergence indicator. When the indicator line is rising, the two averages are diverging. When the line is falling, the averages are converging. At zero difference between the two averages, you have the crossover. You can verify this crossover by checking the actual moving averages on the price chart.

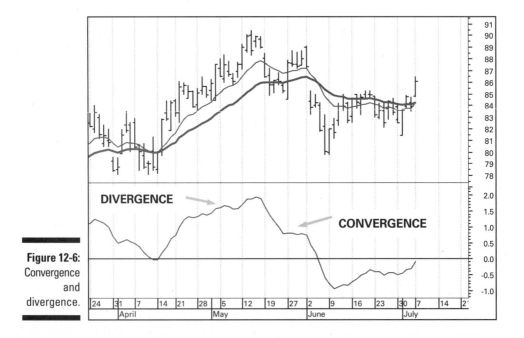

Figure 12-6: Convergence and divergence.

Creating a decision tool

So far all you have is an indicator line. To transform it into a trading tool, you need to give it a trigger. Appel (who I introduce in the preceding section) designed the trigger to be a moving average of the indicator, superimposed on top of the indicator. Normally, it is a 9-day exponential moving average. The full MACD indicator is shown on the next chart, Figure 12-7.

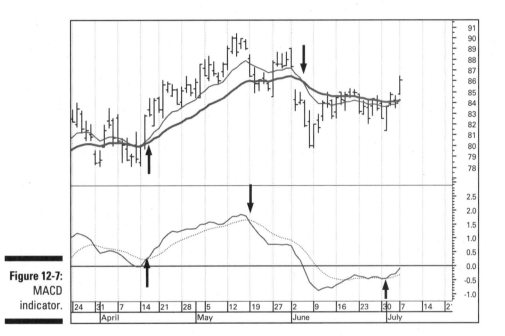

Figure 12-7:
MACD
indicator.

The arrows again show where you would buy and sell. In the MACD indicator window, notice that the crossover of the trigger and the MACD indicator occurs earlier than the crossover of the two moving averages in the top window. Looking from the left, the MACD tells you to buy two days earlier than the moving average crossover. The real benefit comes at the next signal — the exit. Here the MACD tells you to sell over two weeks ahead of the moving average crossover, saving you $4.68, or almost 5 percent. Finally, at the right-hand side of the chart, the MACD tells you to reenter, while the moving averages are still lollygagging along and haven't yet crossed. Actually, you get a crossover of the indicator line about two weeks earlier, but here I waited until there was some daylight between the two lines.

A refinement in applying the MACD is to note that last upside crossover, but to wait until both the indicator and trigger lines are actually above zero to make the buy trade.

The MACD seems to have predictive power, because it gets you out of the trade ahead of the big breakdown, more than two weeks before the shorter moving average crosses the longer moving average to the downside. The plain moving averages don't save you from the gap, either (for more on gaps, see Chapter 7). The MACD's forecasting ability makes it one of the most popular indicators. But watch out for attributing too much to it. A shock can come along and cause the price to vary wildly from the trend, whereupon the tendency to converge or diverge becomes irrelevant. A new price configuration develops, and because the MACD is comprised of moving averages, the indicator still lags the price event like any other moving average.

Interpreting the MACD

You may find it hard to "read" the MACD indicator, except when the trigger is actually crossing the indicator line. You're not alone. Another way of displaying the MACD, in histogram format, is much easier on the eye. See Figure 12-8.

In Figure 12-8, each bar in the histogram represents the difference between the two moving averages on that date. You don't use the trigger line in the histogram, because you can choose by eye how fast the histogram bars are closing in on the zero line, or diverging from it. At zero, the two moving averages have the same numerical value — they have zero difference between them. As the bars grow taller, the difference between the two averages is increasing (divergence), and this movement favors the trend continuing. When the bars stop growing and start to shrink, the two moving averages are converging — watch out for a signal change.

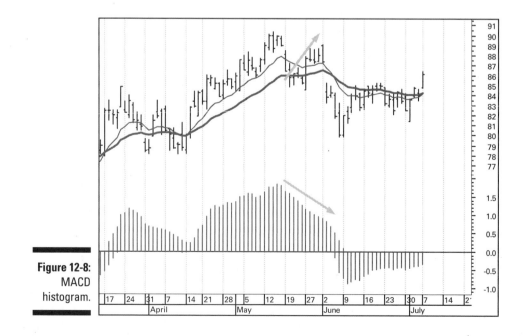

Figure 12-8:
MACD
histogram.

The histogram format gives you more flexibility in interpretation, but in the process, takes away a guide — the trigger. You want to use your eye rather than a number.

When the bars are upside down (below zero), the signal is to sell. What do you do when the bars become less negative? This indicator means selling pressure (supply) is running out of steam. Technically, you don't get a buy signal until the bars are actually over the zero line, but it's up to you whether to act in anticipation that it will cross the line. Notice that in Figure 12-7, the trigger line does signal a buy on the last day, while on the histogram format in Figure 12-8, the bar isn't quite up to the zero crossover level. This minor discrepancy is inherent in the calculation method of the software used to make this chart.

Chapter 13

Measuring Momentum

In This Chapter

▶ Figuring out what momentum means in trading

▶ Going over the math and using momentum

▶ Getting to know the relative strength index (RSI)

▶ Introducing the stochastic oscillator

*M*omentum is the strength of the speed of a moving object. In this case, the "object" is the price of a security. *Momentum* is also a generic term covering a number of technical indicators, although many momentum indicators don't use the word *momentum* in their names. In this chapter, I introduce you to some momentum indicators and give you tips on how to use them.

The terms *momentum* and *rate of change* are used interchangeably in technical analysis. The indicators look almost identical on a chart. Unless you plan to write formulas, the tiny differences don't affect your analysis. I use the general term *momentum* throughout this chapter because it's easier.

In general, you can use momentum indicators to generate buy/sell signals or to evaluate buy/sell signals generated by other indicators. Momentum is a leading indicator and can be used to offset the lag inherent in trend-following indicators like moving averages. Momentum indicators excel at spotting an impending move when the market is moving sideways, and certain momentum measures are central to recognizing when a security is overbought or oversold. (See Chapter 2 for a discussion of overbought and oversold.)

Doing the Math: Calculating Momentum

Everything you really need to know about momentum is that it compares the price today with the price *x* periods ago. A higher number means a faster speed — and momentum is all about speed. But how do you reach that calculation? In the following sections, I outline the basics of calculating momentum and show you how to further apply and refine the data so it can be useful as you trade.

Remember that you can choose any lookback period when calculating momentum indicators. In this section, I use 5 days, but you usually see 12 or 14 days — the standard parameter used in most software. Why 12 or 14 and not 10 or 15 (two or three trading-day weeks)? Because the inventors of these indicators found 12 or 14 to be the most efficient lookback period.

Using the subtraction method

The core concept of momentum is to measure the rate of change of a price over a specific period, such as one week. The formula is therefore as follows:

Momentum = Price Today – Price Five Days Ago

Momentum = $15 – $10 = $5

The number 5 means that the price has risen by $5. As a single number, this momentum reading isn't useful, but put it together with the momentum output from every day, and now you have a working indicator. In Figure 13-1, the momentum indicator crosses into negative territory (meaning that the latest price is lower than the price five days before) *one day before* the price opens gap down (see Chapter 7 on gaps). A little later the momentum indicator reaches the positive-negative line but fails to hold it for longer than a day. Finally, momentum crosses above the line while the price is still falling. But sure enough, momentum accurately forecasted a price rise. Three days later, the price matches a previous high and breaks out to the upside.

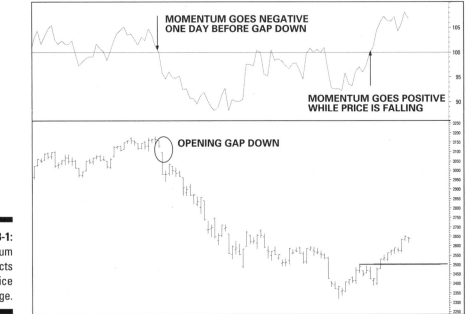

Figure 13-1:
Momentum
predicts
price
change.

Note that on Day 6, assuming the same $1 rise, the following calculation is true:

Momentum = $16 – $11 = $5

On Day 6, the momentum indicator starts going sideways. The price still rose $1 on Day 6, but momentum didn't change. The price is still rising, but the momentum value didn't change.

Utilizing the rate-of-change method

In practice, what I present as momentum is really what math nit-pickers call *rate of change*. The actual momentum indicator most technical traders use and software packages offer is calculated differently from the subtraction method outlined in the earlier section, "Using the subtraction method."

Here's how you calculate the rate of change:

1. **Divide today's close by the close five days ago.**
2. **Multiply that number by 100.**

   M = (Price Today/Price Five Days Ago) x100

   M = (15/10) x 100 = 150

The result is information presented as a ratio (times 100) rather than the simple difference between the two prices. If today's price is equal to the price five days ago, the centerline now reads 100, meaning that the new price is equal to 100 percent of the price five days ago, which is the same as saying that there is zero change between the two prices.

Stop and think about the arithmetic for minute. Imagine that a price is rising at the same pace every day, say $1, and you're using a five-day indicator. On Day 6, if you use the rate-of-change division method, the price today is $16 and the price five days ago was $11, so your calculation would look like:

M = (16/11) x 100 = 145.45

It now appears that momentum is moving down. In the subtraction method of calculating momentum section example, you see a flat line at the zero level. In the rate-of-change method, you get a *drop* from 150 to 145, showing that even though momentum is changing at a constant rate ($1 per day), it isn't accelerating.

The difference between momentum and momentum investing

Momentum is an arithmetic calculation technical traders use to identify the speed of a trend. Momentum investing, on the other hand, entails buying a security just because it is going up without actually measuring the rate of change or considering any other factors. The idea behind momentum investing is that a security that's already rising will continue to rise at least a little longer. This idea sounds like Dow Theory — prices move in trends — but it is incomplete and gives people the wrong idea about the meaning of the word *momentum* to real technical traders.

In the late 1990s, momentum stocks included Internet, telecom, and high-tech stocks that rose on the exuberance of the crowd to valuations many times any reasonable estimate of value. A momentum strategy came to be summed up in the phrase: "If it's rising, buy it."

However, to buy a security just because it's rising is not momentum-based technical analysis because the momentum trader has no systematic entry and exit criteria. To hijack a hot-button word like *momentum* is a silly effort to dress up an undisciplined approach to trading, and obscures a really important use of momentum, using the relative momentum of two or more securities (named *comparative relative strength*) to pick the one that has the best chance to deliver a gain. To chose a security from the universe of securities on the basis of comparative relative strength is a legitimate methodology and one of seven core concepts in William O'Neill's "CANSLIM" approach to stock-picking, beyond the scope of this chapter.

The momentum indicator can move up or down only if the price is accelerating or decelerating. The momentum indicator can flat line while the price is still moving if the relative pace of change is the same.

Adding context: Percentage rate of change

Now that you have your calculations (see preceding sections), you want to refine the arithmetic to make it more useful. One problem with the momentum indicator is that you miss a frame of reference — you don't know whether the move is a huge change over a short period or a minor event hardly worth considering. To add context, you put the rate of change into percentage terms that everyone can understand.

To calculate percent rate of change, you

1. **Take today's close minus the close from ten days ago.**

   This calculation provides you with basic rate of change. You can use the close from any day in the past, but I chose ten for this example.

2. **Divide the difference from Step 1 by the close from ten days ago.**

3. **Multiply the answer in Step 2 by 100.**

   The resulting indicator looks virtually identical to the rate of change calculation using subtraction alone, but the arithmetic process converts it to a percentage basis. If you use charting software, it puts numbers on the vertical axis of the chart denoting that a move is (say) 15 percent from ten days ago, or 30 percent from ten days ago.

If the price is higher today than ten days before, the indicator delivers a positive number. If the price is lower today than ten days before, it will be a negative number — but now you know by what amount in percentage terms.

For example, say your security typically doesn't reach a speed of more than 30 percent in any ten-day period before pausing or retracing. You can use this useful ingredient to predict a new move, using momentum as a leading indicator. When you see the indicator reach the 30 percent mark, you expect traders to do what they usually do: Cause a price pullback by taking profit. You can anticipate them and exit early, join them at the same time, or wait it out, depending on the other conditions on the chart and your trading plan.

By observing momentum over time, you can discover the maximum speed that your security is likely to reach in a specific period of time, like ten days. You may, of course, choose three days, or five days, or any other number of days. Most charting software allows you to backtest historical data to find the optimum number of days that would have generated the most profit when using rate of change as a buy/sell indicator.

Pondering the Trickier Aspects of Momentum

When you see a momentum indicator on a chart, your eye automatically tries to line it up with the price move. Usually the most noticeable thing about a price series is its direction, so you may think you see a correlation between the indicator and the price. Often this observation is true and useful, but sometimes it's an illusion and may lead you astray. To help you avoid mistakes, I describe some of the trickier aspects of momentum in this section.

The momentum calculation displays speed. When your momentum indicator line is horizontal, you may think that momentum has stopped. This isn't so. *Acceleration* has stopped.

Smoothing price changes

When you look at Figure 13-1 earlier in this chapter, you probably notice that the momentum indicator looks a lot like the price series, only smoother, and with the indicator's highest highs and lowest lows a day or two off the price's highest highs and highest lows.

Momentum sometimes mirrors the price move. This reflection is because, like a moving average (see Chapter 12), the momentum indicator is tracking the close relative to the close a certain number of days back. The more days you put in your lookback period, the smoother the momentum line. Unlike the moving average, momentum doesn't include all the days' closes in between, and by omitting that extraneous information, you get a smoother line.

However, if you have a one-day price spike, you may see a jump in momentum, but ten days later you're going to see a sudden drop in the momentum indicator, too, as that spike (see Chapter 7) leaves the data series. This type of situation is when it pays to look at the price bars and not just the indicator. If the spike was a one-day anomaly, the information you think you're getting from momentum can be misleading.

Momentum isn't a trend indicator like a moving average, and yet it seems to track the trend. How can this be? The answer lies in the nature of price moves, which are caused by human beings and all their emotions (see Chapter 2). When a price starts to rise, traders jump on the bandwagon and cause the price to move to higher prices at a faster pace. So it's not surprising that the slope of the price move often steepens at the same time as the slope of the momentum indicator. When traders stop adding to positions, closes may still be higher, but by less than they were at the beginning of the move. The trend remains in place and is still delivering profits to you, but at a slower pace.

Filtering momentum

A smooth line is visually more helpful, but you may want momentum to be more responsive to price changes. Therefore, you could shorten the number of days in the comparison from ten to (say) three. A three-day momentum indicator is more sensitive, but it also crosses the zero/100 line repeatedly when the price isn't trending, or is trending only slightly, generating small losses called whipsaws. (See Chapter 12 for more on whipsaws.)

The standard solution to whipsaws is to filter the signal. Instead of making the zero/100 line the buy/sell rule, you can dictate that the indicator has to rise (say) 2 percent over the zero/100 line for a buy and fall 2 percent under it for a sell. You can also delay accepting the buy/sell signal for one or more days. You can backtest both kinds of filters by using historical data.

Depending on the security, up moves and down moves aren't ordinarily symmetrical in size, duration, or speed. Sometimes your security has up moves that accelerate strongly but decelerate in a sloppy, slow manner. Remember, every security has it owns habits.

For instance, if a security usually delivers a momentum reading of plus 130 to minus 130, this reading means that the price tends to speed up or slow down by not more than 30 percent over the course of any ten-day period. Some securities are like old Chevy pickups — their momentum lumbers from plus 120 to minus 120 over many months, while other securities are sprightly Aston Martins that zip between plus 150 and minus 150 in a few weeks.

Many commentators speak of a *momentum cycle* as though it were a scientific fact of life. It's not, but you must make up your own mind on whether price cycles are real, and if they *are* real, whether they're useful to your trading. Sometimes you can see an eerie regularity in the momentum indicator, especially in longer time frames (like weekly and monthly data).

Applying Momentum

The momentum trading rule is simple: Buy when the indicator crosses above the zero line and sell when it crosses below the zero line. The *zero line* is the level at which the current price is equal to the price x number of days ago. When the momentum indicator crosses above zero, the price trend is upward, and the indicator is signaling you to buy. When it crosses below zero, the trend is downward, and the indicator is signaling you to sell.

However, because momentum measures the rate of change and not the price itself, it has some peculiar properties, which I discuss in detail in the following sections.

Discovering divergence

Momentum can be a confusing indicator, because your eye is accustomed to interpreting a line that is pointing upward as having to do with the dollar value. But in this case, this upward line refers only to the speed of the price change. The distinction is driven home when you have a price that is rising while momentum is falling.

Divergence refers to momentum that moves in the direction opposite to the direction of the price trend. Divergence also refers to momentum higher or lower, but less high or low than a previous peak or trough, while the price trend is making a new higher high or lower low. Technically, they're both going in the same direction, so it's a misnomer to call it a divergence, but when momentum falls proportionately short of the price move, you can think of it as a failure to confirm. See Figure 13-2 for a visual of the divergence concept.

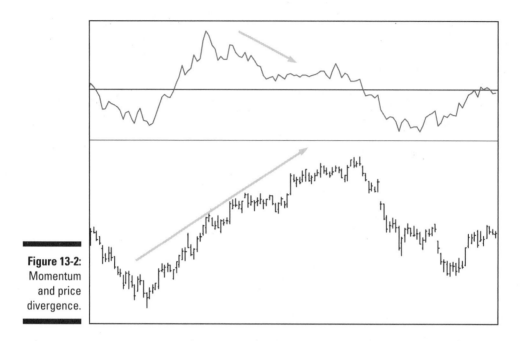

Figure 13-2:
Momentum
and price
divergence.

In Figure 13-2, the price is making a series of new highs, but about midway through the rise, momentum stops making new highs and starts going in the other direction. Then it flattens, meaning that the new price gains aren't as robust as the older price gains. Notice that momentum crosses the buy/sell midline on the very next day after the highest price high. This instance is an ideal example of using momentum as a buy/sell indicator in its own right. If you sell when the momentum indicator crosses the buy/sell line, you exit near the peak.

Volume can be a useful adjunct to momentum-price divergence. As I note in Chapter 11 regarding breakouts, as a price trend is peaking, you usually see an abnormal rise in volume. A volume spike often foreshadows the end of a strong trend. If you have both spiking volume and momentum-price divergence, get ready to bail out — the end of the move is nigh.

Confirming trend indicators

A change in momentum is a reliable guide to a change in price trend. A new uptrend is almost always preceded by rising momentum. Most of the time, momentum peaks ahead of the price peak, generating divergence in the direction of momentum and price — a valuable warning that the trader should be getting ready to exit.

You can use momentum indicators alone to generate buy/sell signals, but momentum indicators are excellent confirming indicators, too. A confirmation rule requires that both indicators agree before you make a trade. Using momentum to confirm another indicator

- Raises the probability of a trade being profitable
- Reduces the total number of trades
- Reduces the proportion of whipsaw trades

Determining the Relative Strength Index (RSI)

You may wonder why you have to wait for the momentum indicator line to cross the zero line. Why not make the buy/sell decision when the momentum indicator changes direction — just after an indicator top or a bottom? After all, you expect a move to keep going in the same direction after it starts.

A technical trader named J. Welles Wilder, Jr. answered the question. He pointed out that you want to make the trading decision at the change of direction only by ensuring that the *average* up move is greater than the *average* down move over a certain number of days (or the other way around for a sell signal). In other words, the average momentum is relatively higher (or lower), hence the name relative strength. Be sure to differentiate between the *comparative* relative strength between two securities and the *internal* relative strength I discuss here.

The RSI is much faster than momentum in signaling an impending price change, making RSI a good tool for timing profit-taking, especially if you are using a shorter-term version (say 5 days rather than the standard 14 days). However, the RSI falls short in the reliability department when it comes to buy/sell signals. For that reason, traders use RSI more often as a confirming indicator, while they use other indicators to obtain the buy/sell signal.

In the following sections, I outline how you can do the relative strength index (RSI) math and visualize it on a chart. Plus, you can also discover some of the nuances of using the RSI.

Calculating the RSI

The RSI measures the relative speed of price changes. The relative strength index uses averages over several days rather than single price points. However, it uses the ratio method, like momentum. To figure the RSI, you first calculate relative strength (RS) over a specific number of days. The calculation looks like this:

RS = Average of Close – Previous Close on Up Days/Average of Previous Close minus Current Close on Down Days

RSI = 100 – (100/(1+ RS)

Reversing the order of Close/Previous Close on Down Days eliminates negative numbers and delivers absolute values. This arithmetic process creates an oscillator that is limited to a range of zero to 100. When the indicator is at or near zero, it means that the security is fully oversold. When it is at 100, the security is overbought.

The relative strength index and indeed most oscillators rarely go all the way to zero or 100 percent, but rather vary between the 30 and 70 percent mark of the entire range. In some instances, you may find that the 20 to 80 percent mark is better, or even 10 to 90 percent.

The RSI, like most oscillators, is limited by one of its arithmetic components, the high-low range over x periods. You may have a 75-day uptrend, for example, that has five or six sell signals generated by an RSI that is using 14 days as the base range. They're false signals if you're a long-term trend-follower, but splendid opportunities to goose return if you're a swing trader. As I explain in Chapter 4, the trend-follower has one set of buy/sell signals, while the swing trader has multiple entries and exits. The RSI is a top swing trader tool.

Picturing RSI

In Figure 13-3, the RSI is shown in the top window, with two momentum indicators in the second window (a raw momentum indicator and a smoothed one containing more days), and the price chart itself in the main window. The gray trendlines are hand drawn, just for orientation.

On the left of the chart, as the price is rising, the RSI and momentum rise, too. RSI, however, hits and surpasses the 70 percent limit and starts turning down the very next day after the highest close. Momentum also turns down, but doesn't cross the center sell line for another two weeks. The RSI then falls to the bottom of its range at an index reading of 30 percent.

Because you're using averages, the indicator has a normal range of between 30 and 70 percent of the maximum range, although touches of the maximum extremes do occur as follows:

✔ **Overbought:** When the RSI is at or over the 70 percent level, the security is considered overbought (which I describe in Chapter 2). An overbought condition is when the security has moved so far and so fast that traders want to take profit. You can automatically sell when the security becomes overbought (when it crosses the 70 percent line), or you can use the line as a confirming indicator with other indicators.

In Figure 13-3, using the crossover of the 70 percent line as a sell signal in its own right is the correct trading action.

✔ **Oversold:** When RSI hits the 30 percent level, the security is considered oversold. A security is oversold when everyone who was going to sell has already sold, and the security is now relatively cheap (inviting buyers back in).

But notice that the RSI in Figure 13-3 first hits the oversold level about two and half weeks before the price itself actually makes its lowest low. That's because the price was making new lows, but the 14-day *average* down move was getting smaller each day — the down move was decelerating. In *this* instance, the RSI was giving a premature signal and it would've been better to consider crossing the oversold line as a warning rather than a sell signal.

When trends are strong, securities can remain overbought or oversold for long periods. However, a divergence between the price and the indicator is a warning sign that the price move may be coming to an end. In Figure 13-3, for example, the RSI serves as a sell signal at the overbought level, but doesn't provide an equally clear buy signal when it first meets the oversold level. Instead of reversing smartly, the RSI indicator meanders down around the oversold line for several weeks. So, on one occasion it's a buy/sell signal, and on the next occasion, it's a warning.

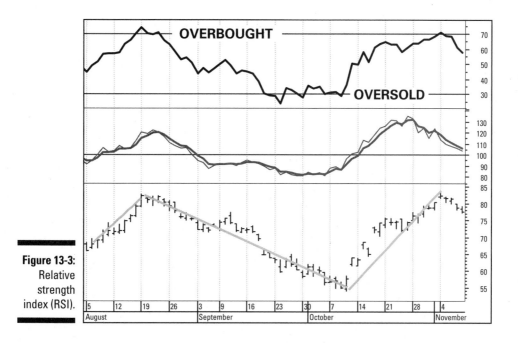

Figure 13-3:
Relative
strength
index (RSI).

In the place on the chart in Figure 13-3 between the overbought and oversold areas, the indicator is going sideways near the 30 percent line and the price is still falling. By analyzing the *internal dynamics of the price* (the ratio of average up days to average down days), the RSI indicator tells you not to sell the security short at this point, even though the price is still falling, because it is about to reverse to an up move. (Remember, to *sell short* is to sell the security first and buy it back later at a cheaper price.)

If you're a buy-only trader, hang on. Your chance is coming. Finally, you can see that an up move starts again and hits the overbought level on the right-hand side of the chart in Figure 13-3. Again, the RSI peaks on the same day as the price high. Notice that momentum peaks a week earlier, but has not crossed the buy/sell centerline before the chart ends.

Using the Rest of the Price Bar: The Stochastic Oscillator

So far, the momentum indicators all use the closing price. But a lot can be going on in other parts of the price bar, such as closes near the high versus closes near the low. When the close is near the high and each high is higher than the day before, you not only have an uptrend, but an uptrend that is accelerating. In a rally, you expect prices to close near the high of the daily high-low range. In a sell-off, you expect the price to close near the low of the daily high-low range.

Two relationships are particularly important: The high-low range over x number of days, and the relationship of the close to the high or the low over the same x number of days. (If you use the low, the resulting indicator is named the *stochastic oscillator,* and if you use the high, the indicator is named the *Williams %R,* after its inventor, Larry Williams.) In the following sections, I outline how to use the stochastic oscillator as an indicator.

No indicator name is worse than this one. The word *stochastic* refers to randomness, which of course is the exact opposite of what you're trying to achieve in applying technical concepts — finding order. It gets worse — the first component of the indicator is named the *%K,* because that was the letter of the alphabet assigned to the list of experimental formulas by its inventor, George Lane. The second component of the indicator is called *%D,* for the same reason. %K is called the "fast" stochastic and %D is called the "slow" stochastic, as you can discover in the next section. The good news: %K and %D appear only in the stochastic oscillator and aren't used anywhere else in technical analysis.

Step 1: Putting a number to the fast stochastic %K

The %K indicator takes the difference between today's close and the lowest low of the past five days and divides that by the widest high-low range of the past five days. The ratio is then multiplied by 100 to make it an oscillator that ranges between 0 and 100, again with a normal spread between 30 and 70 percent or from 20 to 80 percent. Five days is the standard parameter used for the indicator, although you can use software to find a number of days that better fits your particular security.

The %K indicator shows you how much energy the price move has relative to the range. If today the closing price is higher than it was yesterday, it is farther away from the lowest low than it was yesterday, too. If neither day put in a new high or low, the high-low range usually remains the same. Arithmetically, therefore, today's %K is a higher number than yesterday's, and the line on the chart has to rise, as follows:

%K = (Current Close – Lowest Low)/(Highest High – Lowest Low) x 100

But here's a brainteaser: What about the case in which the high-low range over the past five days is $5 to $12 and today's price is $12? If today's close is $12, the highest high, the top part (numerator) of the ratio is today's close ($12) minus the lowest low, $5, or $7, exactly the same as the five-day range, or the bottom part of the ratio (denominator). As you discovered in grade school doing fractions, $7 divided by $7 is 1, and if you multiply it by 100, your oscillator reading is 100. The indicator is telling you that the price is as high as it gets relative to the range.

And a lot of good that does you! You already know that the price made a new closing high today. When that happens, the %K gives a reading of 100 percent, which by definition is an *overbought condition* — even if the price is still trending upward! This is exactly what happens in the section of the chart in Figure 13-4 marked by an ellipse. You see that the price has moved smartly up, with several gaps to boot (see Chapter 7 for a discussion of gaps). When the %K indicator (the thin line) reaches 100 percent, it's telling you that the security is overbought. If you used the %K line alone as a buy/sell indicator, you might sell at this point — and miss out on another $10 rise in the security.

The stochastic oscillator gives a false overbought or oversold reading at a new highest high or lowest low, because the highest high or lowest low is then used in both the numerator and denominator of the ratio. Therefore, the stochastic oscillator works best in a sideways price movement. This is also true of the Williams %R, which is essentially the same indicator, only upside down.

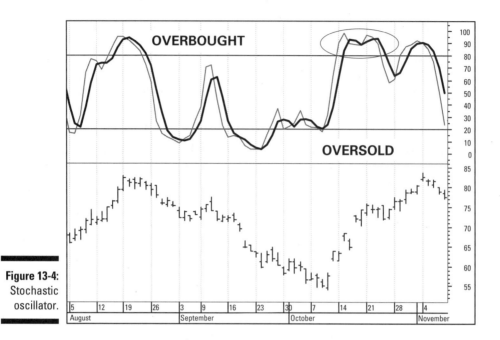

Figure 13-4:
Stochastic
oscillator.

Step 2: Refining %K with %D

So far you just have one line in the indicator. What you really want is the equivalent of the zero/100 line in momentum — some kind of crossover guideline to tell you whether to buy or sell, so you don't have to guess by eye. In the stochastic oscillator, the crossover line is named *%D* and is formed by a short-term simple moving average of %K (the higher line in Figure 13-4). A moving average always smoothes and slows down the price series so %D is sometimes called the *smoothed indicator* as well as the "slow" indicator. When you put the two indicator lines together, you get crossovers of the first indicator line by the smoothed shorter-term indicator line that give you exact buy/sell signals.

You can calculate %D with the following formula:

%D = Three-Day Simple Moving Average of %K

When %K crosses above %D, it's a buy signal, and the other way around for a sell signal. It's convenient when crossovers occur promptly at overbought or oversold levels but you will see plenty of crossovers that occur when the security is not overbought or oversold. Note that you can add numerous fancy modifications to the stochastic oscillator, including a "slowing" factor in %K. And as with any indicator, you can change the number of days in the lookback period.

Fiddling with the stochastic oscillator on the chart

You can sometimes see patterns on a chart of the stochastic oscillator that are meaningful. For example, see Figure 13-5 that shows some of the nuances of the stochastic oscillator. Here the stochastic oscillator shows a series of three higher highs in the indicator that have %D rising over %K in "right" crossovers (to the right-hand side of the peak), implying hidden power is in the up move on the left-hand side of the chart that cannot be discerned from just looking at the prices themselves.

But look again. Under the first bump up in the stochastic, only two days have lower closes (and one duplicate close). You could also draw a support line under the lower closes or series of "knees," as Lane called them. As it happens, this time the final downside crossover beats the break of the support line by five days, but that is not always the case.

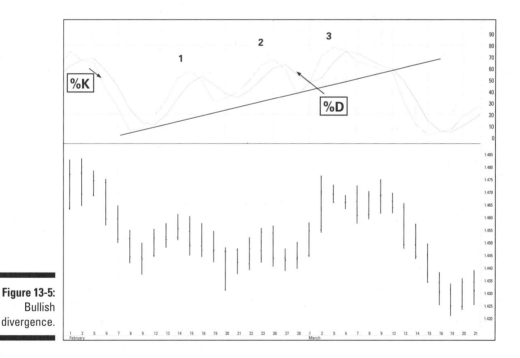

Figure 13-5:
Bullish
divergence.

You can become obsessed with the stochastic oscillator. Aficionados study charts for divergences, like when the price hits a new low but the stochastic oscillator fails to confirm and in fact shows a higher low. This type of situation is what you can see in Figure 13-5 and is named a *bullish divergence.* Similarly, a *bearish divergence* is when the price is making a higher high but the stochastic forms a lower high. The point is that momentum isn't confirming the price action.

After looking for divergences, traders then move on to pinpointing the number associated with the divergence. Is it above or below the midpoint at 50 percent? A bullish divergence over the 50 percent line is favorable. In a very real sense, the stochastic oscillator is bar reading on steroids.

The stochastic oscillator became fabulously popular in the 1990s as technology permitted the spread of swing trading to the general public. "Trade like the professionals!" was the sales pitch, and an accurate one, too, in the sense that professionals are heartless about not holding a security that isn't performing. The fad for this indicator, however, resulted in some technical writers making exaggerated claims for it. The stochastic oscillator has some serious drawbacks, such as having almost no trend identification capability and often signaling a premature exit.

Do not use the stochastic oscillator in a strongly trending market. When your security exhibits an abnormally long period of trendedness, you can get jumpy wondering how long it will last. However, this type of situation is when the stochastic oscillator isn't useful and can be downright dangerous. See Figure 13-6. The stochastic oscillator rises up from the oversold level in the oval and a little later the price rises over the hand-drawn resistance line. Surely this is a buy signal! But the price turns around after only a few days and puts in a lower low. If you're a very short-term trader, you may have been able to eke out a small gain from the buy signal, but not from this instance of the stochastic oscillator alone.

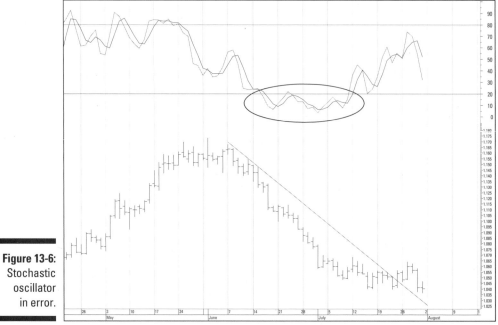

Figure 13-6:
Stochastic oscillator in error.

Chapter 14

Estimating Volatility

● ●

In This Chapter

▶ Introducing volatility

▶ Doing some volatility calculations

▶ Getting the hang of Bollinger bands

▶ Focusing on volatility breakout as a trading tool

● ●

*V*olatility is a measure of price variation, either the total movement between low and high over some fixed period of time or a variation away from a central measure, like an average. Both concepts of volatility are valid and useful. The higher the volatility, the higher the risk.

A change in volatility implies a change in the expected price range to come. A volatile security offers a wide range of possible outcomes. A nonvolatile security delivers a narrower and thus more predictable range of outcomes. The main reason to keep an eye on volatility is to adjust your profit targets and your stop-loss to reflect the changing probability of gain or loss.

In this chapter, I describe three ways you can measure volatility, and discuss their virtues and drawbacks. Then I describe the most popular way traders incorporate consideration of volatility into their trading plans — the Bollinger band. I also introduce another kind of band — the average true range band.

Catching a Slippery Concept

Volatility is a concept that can easily slip through your fingers if you aren't careful. Just about everybody uses the word *volatility* incorrectly from a statistician's viewpoint — and even statisticians squabble over definitions. To the mathematically inclined trader, volatility usually refers to the standard deviation of price changes (see the "Considering the standard deviation" section). Standard deviation is not the only measure of volatility, but it suffices for most technical analysis purposes. In general usage, volatility means variance, and that's how I use it in this chapter.

Variance is a statistical concept that measures the distance on each bar between the high and low from the mean (such as a moving average). You calculate variance by taking the difference between the high or low from the average, squaring each result (eliminating the minus signs), adding them up, and dividing by the number of data points. Squaring magnifies wildly aberrant prices, so the bigger the variation from the average and the more instances of such big variations in any one series, the higher the volatility.

Traders do not use variance as a stand-alone measure or indicator, and it's not offered in software charting packages. Why? Because variance isn't directly useful as a separate measure from the standard deviation, which is essentially the square root of variance.

Time frame is everything. How you perceive volatility depends entirely on the time frame you're looking at. Failure to specify a specific time frame is why you see so many conflicting generalizations about volatility. The period over which you measure volatility has a direct effect on how you think about volatility and, therefore, what kind of a trader you are. Your trading style isn't only a function of what indicators you like, but also of how you perceive risk. Two traders can use the same indicators but get different results because they manage the trade differently by looking at volatility differently (scaling in and out, choosing a stop-loss level, and so on).

In Figure 14-1, your eye tells you that the low-variance prices on the left-hand side of the chart are less volatile and therefore less risky to trade than the high-variance prices on the right-hand side of the chart, even when the high-variance prices are in a trending mode. And that's the point about volatility — it describes the level of risk. In the following sections, I go into more detail about the nature of volatility, including both high and low levels.

How volatility arises

Think of volatility in terms of crowd sentiment. Volatility rises when traders get excited about a new move. They anticipate taking the price to new highs or lows, which arouses greed in bulls putting on new positions and fear in bears, who scramble to get out of the way in a cascade of stop losses. The start of a new move is when you get higher highs and lower lows. Volatility tends to be abnormally low just before a turning point and abnormally high just as the price is taking off in the first big thrust of a new trend. It is also, however, a sad fact of trading life that sometimes volatility is high or low for no price-related reason you can find.

High volatility means trading is riskier but has more profit potential, while low volatility means less immediate risk.

Volatility isn't inherently good or bad. Stability of volatility is a good thing because it allows you to estimate maximum potential gains and losses with greater accuracy. Every security has its own volatility norm that changes over time as the fundamentals and trader population changes. Sometimes you can impute a "personality" to a security that is really a reflection of the collective risk appetite of its traders.

Low volatility with trending

Go to Figure 14-1. As the price series begins, you instantly see that it's trending upward. Your ability to see the trend is due in part to the orderliness of the move. You see the trend, not variations away from it.

A trending security that has low volatility offers the best trade, because it has a high probability of giving you a profit and low probability of delivering a loss. It is also easier on the nerves. Here's why low volatility means the best trade:

✔ You can project the price range of a low-volatility trending security into the future with more confidence than a high-volatility security.

✔ You generally hold a low-volatility trending security for a longer period of time, reducing trading costs such as brokerage commissions.

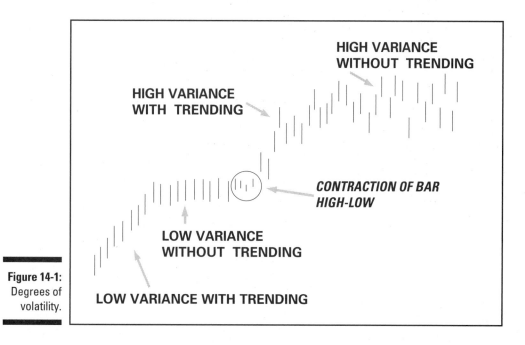

Figure 14-1:
Degrees of
volatility.

Low volatility without trending

A security that's range-trading sideways with little variation from one day to the next is simply untradeable in that time frame. You have no basis on which to form an expectation of a gain, and without an expectation of gain, don't trade it. You can reduce the time frame (from one day to one hour, for example) to make visible and tradeable the minor peaks and troughs. Note that options traders don't care about trendedness and see trading opportunities in both extra-low and extra-high volatility environments.

If a price is trading sideways without directional bias but the high-low range of the bars contracts or widens, now you're cooking with gas. Range contraction and expansion are powerful forecasting tools of an upcoming breakout. You can start planning the trade. In Figure 14-1, every bar is the same height except the ones in the circle, which are narrowing. The drop in high-low range and therefore in volatility often precedes a breakout, although you don't know in advance in which direction unless you also have a reliable pattern (Chapter 9), including candlesticks (see Chapter 8).

High volatility with trending

You may think that the degree of volatility doesn't matter when your security is trending, but an increase in volatility automatically increases the risk of loss. You may start fiddling with your indicators to adapt them to current conditions. Tinkering with the parameters of indicators when you have a live trade in progress is almost always a mistake. A better response to rising volatility is to recalculate potential gain against potential loss (Chapter 5).

High volatility without trending

When a security isn't trending but has high volatility in a wide range, it's called "trader's nightmare." This is the right-hand section of the price series in Figure 14-1. In this situation, the range is so wide you can't identify a breakout; you see spiky one- and two-day reversals as bulls and bears slug it out, making it hard to find entries or to set systematic stops.

The solution to high volatility in a nontrending case is to stop trading the security, or to narrow the time frame down to an intraday time frame. Often you can find tradeable swings within 15-minute or 60-minute bars that don't exist on the daily chart. (Another choice is spread trading in options.)

Measuring Volatility

Volatility is the degree of variation of a price series over time. You can measure volatility in plain or fancy ways. In financial analysis, volatility usually means one thing — the standard deviation, which I discuss in the "Considering the standard deviation" section later in the chapter. Before tackling that, look at other useful measures of volatility.

Tracking the maximum move

One way to measure volatility is to capture the *largest* price change over *x* number of days — the *maximum move,* also called *gross move.* You subtract the lowest low from the highest high over 10 days or 100 days or some other number of days. You use the resulting maximum move to set a profit target (*maximum favorable excursion*) or worst-case stop loss (*maximum adverse excursion*). See Chapter 5 for information on setting stops.

In Figure 14-2, the top window shows the highest high in a rolling 30-day period minus the lowest low in the same 30-day period — the maximum move. Notice that at the beginning and middle of the chart, you could make as much as $30 in a 30-day period in this security, but then the volatility of the price change tapers off to under $10 by the end of the chart. At that point, you're taking less risk of a catastrophic drop in the price over any 30-day period, but your profit potential has just been cut to one-third of its previous glory, too — the usual trade-off between risk and reward. Keep reading for more on the maximum and minimum moves in the following sections.

Volatility changes. Projecting the volatility of the last 30 days to the next 30 days is to assume conditions will not change — but conditions always change.

Maximum move and trend

In Figure 14-2, seeing the connection between the 30-day maximum move in the top window and the prices in the bottom window is hard. The straight line starting at the middle of the bottom window is the linear regression (see Chapter 10). The line slopes upward, meaning that the price is in a slight uptrend — but at the same time, volatility is on a downtrend. This is a good combination for you — trendedness is delivering new profits at an ever-lower risk of a big one-period loss. But remember, low volatility precedes a break-out, so it may not be a good deal for long.

The *price* trend can differ in size and slope from the *volatility* trend. Sometimes they're in sync, rising or falling together, or they can move in opposite directions. Knowing something about the trend in the maximum move doesn't necessarily tell you anything about the trend in prices, and vice versa. In other words, volatility is often independent of price trendedness.

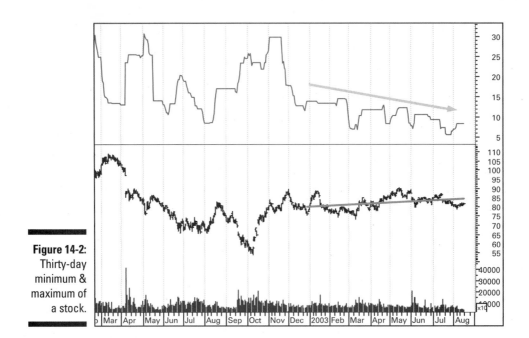

Figure 14-2:
Thirty-day
minimum &
maximum of
a stock.

Maximum move and holding period

In Figure 14-3, the orderly price series has a net change from the lowest low
to the highest high (A to B) of exactly the same amount as the disorderly
price series below it. But obviously the disorderly series implies a greater
risk of loss *if you have to exit before the period ends.* The trendedness of each
security is the same, as shown by the identical linear regression slopes.

Figure 14-3 illustrates that measuring the maximum high-low range over a
fixed period of time fails to capture the risk of holding a position *during* the
period, so don't write your expected holding period in stone.

Considering the standard deviation

Maximum move (see preceding section) measures the gross low-to-high
move over a period, but the bottom chart in Figure 14-3 exhibits a different
kind of volatility that isn't captured by the maximum move. The disorderly
price series has the same degree of trendedness and the same low-to-high
outcome over the period, but it's obviously a riskier trend. What is the right
way to express that riskiness?

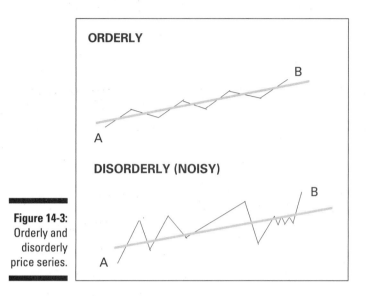

The answer is the standard deviation. The *standard deviation* is a measure of the dispersion of prices away from the average. The wider the spread, the higher the standard deviation. The concept is in the same statistical family as standard error, which I introduce in Chapter 11. The standard deviation is measured from a moving average and measures the actual variance of each price away from the centerline.

I bet you were expecting a chart showing standard deviation right about here. Well, charting software does offer it but it's not very useful as a stand-alone measure. Hardly anyone actually looks at the raw standard deviation on a chart, because we have better applications for it. See the section "Applying Volatility Measures: Bollinger Bands" later in the chapter.

Using the average true range indicator

Another way to view volatility is to look at the average high-low range over *x* number of days. The best version of the high-low range is the *average true range (ATR)*, which incorporates gaps by substituting the close for the gapped high or low. See Chapter 7 for the calculation method and for illustrations of expanding and contracting ranges. To summarize here:

- ✔ **Range expansion:** The highs and lows are getting farther apart; volatility is rising. Range expansion provides a bigger profit opportunity and an equivalent increase in risk of gain or loss.

- ✔ **Range contraction:** The highs and lows are moving closer together, and you may think that risk is lower, too. But this is true only up to a point — the point of a breakout.

In Figure 14-4, the ATR indicator in the top window starts falling after the one-day big-bar rise that marks the beginning of the support line. You don't know whether you can draw the support line until afterwards, but you can see the ATR indicator failing to match that spiky high and continue to fall. The price is rising, but the indicator is falling. And as usual, a divergence between indicator and price is a warning sign. Sure enough, right after the highest high, you get a series of lower highs and can draw a resistance line (see Chapter 10). Pretty soon the price breaks under support.

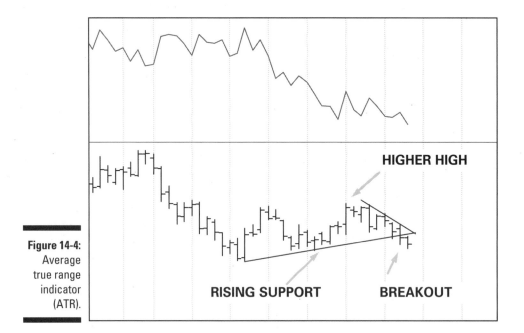

Figure 14-4:
Average
true range
indicator
(ATR).

HIGHER HIGH

RISING SUPPORT

BREAKOUT

Applying Volatility Measures: Bollinger Bands

The most popular volatility measure is the Bollinger band, invented by John Bollinger. He charted a simple 20-day moving average of the closing price with a band on either side consisting of two standard deviations of the moving average, effectively capturing about 95 percent of the variation away from the average. See Figure 14-5.

You use Bollinger bands to display the price in the context of a norm set at the 20-day moving average, which is the number of days that Bollinger's research showed is the most effective in detecting variance in U.S. equities. The bands display *relative* highs and *relative* lows in the context of the moving average — they're adaptive to the price by the amount of the standard deviation. The bands are, so to speak, moving standard deviations.

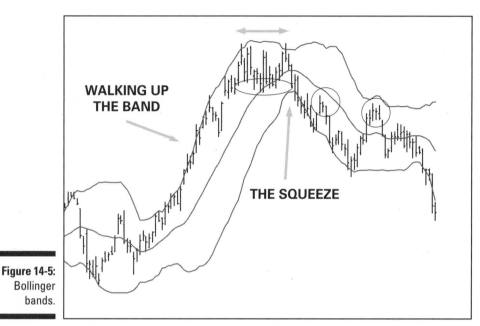

Figure 14-5:
Bollinger
bands.

The price touching or slightly breaking the top of the band is a continuation signal. Often the price continues to *walk up* or *walk down* the band, as shown in Figure 14-5. A Bollinger band breakout is just like any other breakout — you expect the price to continue moving in the same direction as the breakout.

At some point, every price thrust exhausts itself. Bollinger bands display the end of the up move in two ways:

- ✔ **The price bar stops hugging the top band in an up move, and slides down to the center moving average (or farther).** In Figure 14-5, the retreat to the moving average occurs at the ellipse. As a general rule, the failure to make a relative new high signals the end of the move, although this time, the bulls made a second effort to keep the rally going. In this case, the price was forming a double top (see Chapter 9).

- ✔ **The bands contract.** When the bands contract, the range is narrowing. Traders are having second thoughts. They aren't willing to test a new high, but they aren't willing to go short and generate new lows, either.

The narrowing of the trading range is named the *squeeze* and implies an impending breakout. Figure 14-5 displays a reversal, but a reversal isn't the inevitable outcome. Breakouts can occur in the same direction as the original move, too. In this case, the downside breakout of the bottom of the band occurred unusually quickly after an upside breakout of the top band.

A rapid break of the opposite band is sometimes a *head fake.* In the case of a downside move like the one in Figure 14-5, traders could have been overly exuberant in taking profits after such a big run up to the high. See the upward pullback from the down move in the two circles. Sometimes pullbacks keep going, and the price resumes the uptrend — although hardly ever after breaking the bottom band like this one. To detect head fakes, use Bollinger bands with other confirming indicators, especially momentum indicators like the relative strength index and MACD (Chapter 12).

Applying Stops with Average True Range Bands

Bollinger bands are not generally used to set stops. The bands are equidistant from the moving average, so an upside breakout has the same statistical strength as a downside breakout. When you have a strongly trending security, you can't make a reversal move face a tougher breakout test — but logically, you should. I call it a "prove it" test. Given that false breakouts are so common, this reason makes it necessary and sufficient for you to consider another type of band, as observed by system designer Steve Notis.

To use a band for a stop, you want the band to be asymmetrical, so that in an uptrend, a down move has to be more severe than recent up moves to trigger your stop. But you can't filter Bollinger bands. Instead of using the standard deviation to form the upper and lower bands, you can use a version of the average true range (ATR). You can adjust the ATR as follows so that a breakout "proves" that it is statistically significant:

- **Uptrend:** Widen the distance of the lower band from the average.
- **Downtrend:** Widen the distance of the upper band from the average.

The greater width of one of the bands from the center moving average separates corrective moves from real reversals. This move can become labor intensive, not least because before you can widen either band, you must be sure of the trend direction.

In Figure 14-6, the price makes a bottom on the left-hand side and starts an up move. The centerline is a moving average of the *median price,* or the average of the high, low, and close. The bands are formed by taking a moving average of the ATR and adding and subtracting it from the moving average.

This process creates an ATR test that a breakout has to pass to qualify as a true breakout. When the price starts a new uptrend, the price breaking the upper band confirms that you have identified the trend correctly.

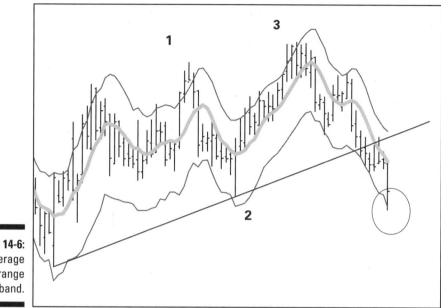

Figure 14-6:
Average
true range
band.

A downside breakout has to pass a bigger test in an uptrend. Accordingly, you widen the lower band by adding a percentage of the ATR to it. On the chart in Figure 14-6, the lower band is 50 percent wider than the upper band (it is 150 percent of the ATR). The last bar on the chart breaks the band, just after the support line is broken. This is no mere retracement! You have a double breakout of the trend (support) plus a volatility breakout (ATR band).

As with Bollinger bands, a breakout above the upper band signals continuation, but because breakouts are a sign of abnormally high volatility, you can usually count on a pullback to the median. A longer-term position trader would buy at the left-hand low and hold the break of the support line. A swing trader, on the other hand, would sell at breakout "1" and go short the security to the touch of the support line at point "2." Now he becomes a buyer again to point "3," where high volatility again triggers a short position that he holds to the break of the support line or final ATR band breakout.

Few traders would use the ATR breakout alone as the sole deciding factor. On Figure 14-6, I put only a support line, but in practice, you would be looking at other indicators. I didn't do the profit-and-loss arithmetic in this case, but it's pretty clear that swing trader using volatility would have made a series of gains that collectively added up to a higher profit than the trend-following buy-and-hold trader.

Chapter 15

Ignoring Time: Point-and-Figure Charting

· ·

In This Chapter

▶ Figuring out point-and-figure charting

▶ Looking at patterns

▶ Taking a look at breakouts

▶ Using point-and-figure with other indicators

· ·

*P*oint-and-figure ("P&F") charting strips away time and displays only significant prices on the chart. *Significant* prices are those that exceed the high or low of a recent trading range by a specified amount. You ignore minor moves — literally. You don't even record them on your chart. The result is filtered price action. You don't see a price move in the opposite direction of the current trend until it's meaningful, according to a rule you set yourself, so that you can have confidence when a reversal signal is accurate.

You can also easily identify patterns on point-and-figure charts, especially support and resistance, and therefore, breakouts of support and resistance. Point-and-figure charts look very different from standard bar charts, but after you get used to them, you may find their directness and simplicity addictive.

P&F charting emphasizes a shift in the price *range* as the basis of trading decisions, which is in keeping with the idea of measuring crowd behavior (see Chapter 3). The purpose of the display method is to filter out irrelevant prices to isolate the trends.

P&F analysis is suitable for trading that has a medium- to long-term holding period — weeks and months. The only way to know whether point-and-figure charting is for you is to try it out on your chosen securities and see what gains you would've made, how many trades it requires of you, and so on. In general, point-and-figure charting on a daily basis is the easiest technique of all and the best way for a beginner to start getting a feel for making rule-based trading decisions. So what are you waiting for? This chapter is ready to guide you through what you need to know about point-and-figure charting.

Creating a Point-and-Figure Chart to Visualize What's Important

Technical indicators aim to identify trend tuning points and, if a trend exists, how strong it is. But all charts contain a lot of data that isn't meaningful — it's filler or noise. For example, a standard bar chart (see Chapter 6) has an entry every day, even when nothing interesting happened. What if you could isolate just the juicy nuggets of price information and forgo the noise?

Displaying the price only when it makes a significant move is the essence of point-and-figure charting. If nothing noteworthy happened on a particular day, you put nothing on the chart. Because chart events like a breakout or reversal often follow real-world events (breaking news, for example), you can consider the point-and-figure chart to be event driven.

The point-and-figure method of displaying data takes time to get used to. Some people think that it looks weird, while others take to it like a duck to water. Stick with me through this section, and by the end, you'll have the hang of it.

Putting each move into a column

In point-and-figure charting, you put a price entry on the chart only if the price is higher than the previous high by a certain amount or lower than the previous low by a certain amount.

When a price is going sideways — not making a new high or low — nothing is happening in the security, and you have nothing worth entering on the chart.

For a new high that is higher than the previous high, you enter a dot or an X. For a new low that is lower than the previous low, you enter a dot or an O. You place the Xs and Os in a column that represents a continuous move, either up or down. The point-and-figure chart contains alternating columns of Xs and Os, where each column is a move. A column of Xs is an up move and a column of Os is a down move. Each X column is reserved for rising prices and each O column is reserved for falling prices. You can't put an X into an O column or an O into an X column.

Say you're considering a security whose price has been rising. The high today is $9. You start a new chart and enter an X next to the $9 label on the vertical axis, as I've done in Figure 15-1. The next day, the price high is $10, so you enter an X *in the same column* at the $10 level. When the high reaches $12 the next day, you add two Xs to denote the move from yesterday's $10 to today's $12. You keep adding Xs in the same column until the price climb ends. In the example in Figure 15-1, the price stops climbing at $13. You see a column of Xs that represents the price rise from $9 to $13 in a single move.

**PRICE RISES
FROM $9 TO $13**

**NEW LOW $3 BELOW
PREVIOUS HIGH**

When the up move is over and the price makes a new low below yesterday's low by a specific amount, you *must* start a new column, using an O and placing it at the dollar level of the new low. (I tell you more about this topic in a minute in the "Defining box size" section; for now, consider that the new low suffices to consider that the up move is over.) Figure 15-1 tells you that the new low came at $10. You now expect the next entry to be another O where the question mark is placed on the chart. Whatever happens next, the formation of a new column alerts you to a change in the price dynamics.

Each column on the chart represents an up move or a down move, regardless of time. On a daily chart, a column can represent 2 days, 10 days, 100 days, or any other number of days. You start a new column only when the last directional move is over. On the chart in Figure 15-1, you have an up move from $9 to $13 and thus five Xs, but that doesn't mean it took five days. It may have taken 30 days, because on days showing no new high, you skipped over that price data and did not make a chart entry.

Most P&F software exhibits dates at the bottom of the chart along the horizontal axis. These dates aren't spaced evenly at regular intervals because they are in the usual chart format. In fact, the dates are there only for convenience — they don't actually measure time because in point-and-figure charting, the date is irrelevant and only price action matters.

Dealing with box size

The *box size* is the minimum amount that the security needs to move above the recent highest high (marked by the last X) or below the lowest low (marked by the last O) before another entry is made on the chart. The following sections discuss how to get the box size right in P&F charting.

Defining box size

The horizontal axis suppresses dates and compresses time, but the vertical axis is spaced in the conventional way. In the days when traders used actual graph paper, they filled in the little boxes of the grid with the Os and Xs set at some appropriate dollar amount, such as $.50 or $1. In futures markets, traders use the number of points corresponding to dollar amounts. The choice of spacing on the vertical axis is still called the *box size,* even if you're using a computer program and not actual graph paper.

When your security has a highest high of $10, for example, and it regularly varies by $.50 per day, you might set your box size at $1. If today's new high is $12, you acknowledge that this is a price extreme — four times the usual daily trading range — and deserves a new X in the X column. In fact, in this case, the new high is a full $2 over the last high, so you fill in two $1 boxes with the X notation. What happens if the price changes by $.98? Nothing. The new price is close to the box size of $1, but close doesn't count.

Choosing a box size

When you select a small box size, you're asking to see a lot of detail, including small retracements. By increasing the box size, you're filtering out filler data, just like when you make a rule that requires a price to cross a moving average by *x* percent (see Chapter 12 for a discussion of filtering).

The smaller the box, the more sensitive the chart is to price changes. The bigger the box, the less sensitive the chart is. If you're risk averse, you may prefer a small box size. If you want to see the big picture, you prefer a bigger box. Table 15-1 contains the standard box-size guidelines.

Table 15-1	Approximate Guidelines for Box Size
Security Price	*Box Size*
$5–20	$.50
$20–100	$1
$100–200	$2
$200–300	$4
$300–400	$6

Computer charting programs adjust the box size to fit the screen if you leave the program in default mode. You may wind up with a box size of $.67 or some other arbitrary number. Box size is too important to leave to a program, because many other traders use a standard round-number box, like $.50 or $1. Besides, software adjusts box size to accommodate the amount of data you select, so you get different point-and-figure charts (and hypothetical trading decisions), depending on how much data you display. The software uses the box size that fits the highest range in the data series in order to get everything on one chart. But the trading range of any single security changes over time, and you want to take note of that rather than let software obscure the changing range. If you use P&F charting software, fix the box size so you know whether the range is expanding — the columns of Xs and Os get taller — or contracting — or whether the columns get shorter and there are more of them.

Adding the reversal amount to the picture

The purpose of the box size (see earlier section on this topic) is to note a significant change in price. But how do you know how far a price has to move below the X (upward) column to warrant starting an O (downward) column? For that, you establish a second criterion, the *reversal amount*. The traditional reversal amount is three boxes. If your box is $1 and you're now in a rising X column, you have to get a new low that is $3 lower than the low today to start a new O (downward) column.

You can backtest a variety of box sizes and reversal amounts to arrive at the best numbers to use for any particular security. As a general rule, though, point-and-figure chartists recommend sticking to the three-box rule for reversals and adopting different box sizes for chart entries, depending on the absolute level of the prices.

A box size of $4, the appropriate box for a security selling over $200, with a three-box reversal, works out to $12. If you have 100 shares, you would exit on a reversal of at least $1,200, which is a fairly hefty sum of money. If you use the three-box reversal as a stop level (see Chapter 5 for stops), you have to accept that big of a loss when the price goes against you. If you judge that $1,200 is too big a loss to take on a single position, you can trade a smaller number of shares (an odd-lot) or trade a cheaper security.

Drawing the daily chart

To draw the chart, every day you check the highest high and lowest low of the day. Is the price higher than the previous high by $1? If so, enter another X above the last X in the column. Is the low lower than today's low by $1? Enter nothing. By $2? Again, enter nothing. By $3? Aha! That's three boxes worth, the reversal amount, and you start a new column, entering the O at a level $3 below the last X. Because it's a reversal, now you expect the next entry to be one box lower. The next day, is the low price lower than yesterday by $1? If so, enter another O. If it's higher, it has to be higher than today's high by $3 to abandon the falling-price O column.

If you see a lot of reversal columns that contain only one entry, chances are your box size is too small — or your reversal amount is wrong.

What if you get a new high by one box and on the same day, also get a new low by the reversal amount — three boxes? This is an *outside* day (see Chapter 6). The new low trumps the new high, and you should start a new column of Os. After all, you're looking for a threat to the trend (and your pocketbook). A new low by the reversal amount constitutes a serious threat.

Applying Patterns

Patterns pop out on point-and-figure charts. Some of the most common patterns include support and resistance, but also simple patterns like double and triple tops and bottoms appear. This section outlines how you can use these common point-and-figure chart patterns.

Support and resistance

Point-and-figure charting offers two versions of support and resistance: The horizontal historic-level version I describe in Chapter 5 and the conventional version that slopes along a series of highs or low, which you can discover in Chapter 10. I show you how to approach both types when using point-and-figure charting in the following sections.

Horizontal support and resistance

In Chapter 5, I talk about the historic high or low. Traders remember the highest high ever or the lowest low in three months as benchmarks when the price approaches the same level. In point-and-figure charting, the horizontal line that you draw to mark the top or bottom of columns becomes a kind of recent-history support or resistance. Therefore, you often get a series of columns that all end at a floor or a ceiling, regardless of whether they're Xs or Os. Floors and ceilings are very handy both for spotting a breakout and setting a stop (see Chapter 5 for a discussion of stops).

In Figure 15-2, the top-left chart shows a breakout X above the resistance line. Using conventional charting, you wouldn't have known that line was there unless you were on the lookout for historic highs and lows. But point-and-figure chartists draw them all the time to denote where supply becomes abundant or demand falls short, halting a price rise.

Conventional support and resistance

On a standard bar chart (see Chapter 6), you draw a support line along a series of lows or a resistance line along a series of highs. These lines almost always have a slope that describes the trend and are hardly ever horizontal except in a consolidation. You can draw sloping support and resistance lines on point-and-figure charts, too.

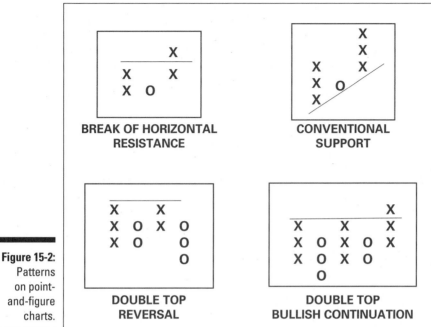

You trade point-and-figure support and resistance the same as you do when using conventional support and resistance — a breakout to the upside triggers a purchase and a breakout to the downside triggers a sale. As with conventional support and resistance lines, don't erase a support line after it's broken — it has a good chance of becoming the new resistance line. An old resistance line may become the new support line, too.

Because a point-and-figure chart filters out noisy prices and compresses time, your chart often displays authentic long-term support or resistance that you'd miss on a regular daily bar chart. You may also see *triangles,* which are support and resistance lines that converge. Chapter 9 covers triangles.

The top-right chart in Figure 15-2 shows a conventional support line. You could have a conventional (sloping) resistance line, too. Notice that if your boxes are perfectly square, you can draw a 45-degree line and extend it out into the future by starting with just two columns when one of the columns is one box higher or lower than the other. The 45-degree technique allows you to start a support or resistance line more simply and sometimes earlier than in conventional bar charting. The upward-sloping 45-degree line is named a *bullish support line,* and a downward-sloping 45-degree line is a *bearish resistance line.*

Double and triple tops and bottoms

Double and triple tops are formed when demand falls off as the price nears a previous high. When bulls fail to get a breakout above the established high, it's a pretty good sign that sellers are happy to unload the security at that price. When you get more than one low at about the same level, it's a double or triple bottom, where buyers think it's a bargain, and the price is likely to rise. See Chapter 9 for a discussion of double and triple tops and bottoms.

A double or triple top or bottom can be either a reversal pattern or a continuation pattern in point-and-figure charting, depending on the behavior of the opposite-direction columns. In conventional time-based bar charting, you have to wait for confirmation of these patterns — chewing up time. Point-and-figure, therefore, can speed up the process of helping you decide whether you're getting a reversal or a continuation.

In regular bar charting, a confirmed double top has a high probability of resulting in a price drop. A qualified double bottom leads to a price rise. They're reversal patterns, which you can see in chart form in Figure 15-2. In point-and-figure, however, chartists find that in an uptrend of Xs, if the intervening Os are on a rising line (the lowest low in the last O column isn't as low as the lowest low in the previous O column), a double top may turn into a triple top and then an *upside breakout* — in other words, a continuation pattern. This configuration is shown in the fourth pattern in Figure 15-2. If the opposite-direction columns are horizontal, though, the traditional reversal interpretation is probably correct.

Projecting Prices after a Breakout

Point-and-figure chartists forecast prices after a breakout by using the box count, either vertically or horizontally. However, vertical projections work more often than horizontal projections. The following sections discuss how to make your own forecasts based on point-and-figure chart breakouts.

In point-and-figure charting, you buy when the new price surpasses the highest X in the previous X column, and you sell when the new price surpasses the lowest low O in the previous O column. When the price surpasses a previous high or low, you have a breakout. (See Chapter 10 for a full discussion of breakouts.)

Using vertical price projection

Say that your security has just made a double or triple top breakout like the one shown in Figure 15-2. You want to know how high the price will go. Or your security has fallen to a new low but is now rising up off it. You want to know the potential gain if the bottom is really in and the up move continues. You know that the price will retrace to the downside over the course of the move, and you don't want to mistake a retracement for the end of the trend. If you have faith in the forecast, you decide to ride out the retracement.

Point-and-figure chartists create forecasts in each case with an ingenious version of momentum. Here's how you can do it:

1. **Find the bottom of the last X (upward) column if you have an upside breakout (or the bottom of the lowest X column if you suspect a reversal to the upside).**

2. **Count the number of boxes in the column (say four boxes).**

3. **Multiply the number of boxes by your reversal amount (see the reversal amount section earlier in the chapter), say the standard three.**

   4 x 3 = 12

4. **Multiply that product by the box size, say the standard $1.**

   12 x $1 = $12

5. **Add the product to the lowest low in the starting column to get your new price target.**

   If the lowest low was $10, you add $12, and your price target is now $22.

Figure 15-3 shows a sample vertical point-and-figure projection.

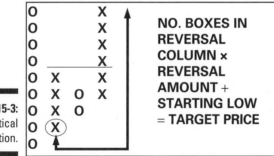

Figure 15-3: Vertical projection.

The price objective is only a guide. The actual new high may fall short of $22, or it may be a great deal more than $22. You don't automatically sell at $22 if the price is still making new highs. But you may want to evaluate the risk-reward ratio in terms of the price projection (the reward) and the lowest low in the starting column (where you may place your initial stop). As I discuss in Chapter 5, you always want to manage the trade so that the expected gain from a trade is higher than the worst-case loss you allow.

To estimate how far a down move may go, reverse the process. You start from the highest-high box before the down move column begins, count the boxes, multiply by three, multiply again by the box size, and voilà! You have an estimate of where the drop may stop.

Applying horizontal projection

You use a horizontal count to project the ending price of a breakout after a period of consolidation. Say the price has been going mostly sideways for some period of time. Yes, it has alternating X and O columns, but your eye can detect a base, or bottom formation. (For a downside breakout, you need to see a top formation.)

Figure 15-4 shows a base forming after a five-column downtrend ahead of an upside breakout. To calculate the projected price, follow these steps:

1. **Identify the number of columns in the base, which is the sideways period before the breakout. Exclude the breakout column.**

   In this example, say you identify five columns.

2. **Multiply by the number of columns in the base by the reversal amount you choose — say the standard three-box reversal.**

   5 x 3 = 15

3. **Add the product to the lowest low in the base to get a price target.**

   Say the lowest low is $10.

   Now you have a price target of $10 + $15 = $25.

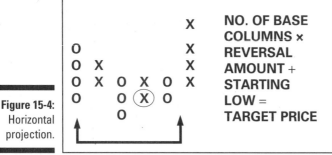

Figure 15-4:
Horizontal
projection.

Combining Point-and-Figure Techniques with Other Indicators

The innate simplicity of point-and-figure charting is appealing, but you can add value to decision making by speeding up the buy/sell signal or seeking confirmation or lack of confirmation from other indicators. Because other indicators are time based, how can this merger be done?

Here's how you can use point-and-figure charting along with other indicators I mention in this book:

- **Moving averages:** You use the price at the center of each column in calculating a moving average in P&F charts, instead of the usual method of averaging prices over a fixed number of periods. Thus you are using the average price per reversal. If the moving average shows that you had a downtrend and now you get a new column of Xs that rises over the moving average, you have more confidence that the Xs really do imply a rising trend and thus a safer buy signal.

- **Parabolic stop-and-reverse indicator:** The parabolic stop-and-reverse (SAR) indicator delivers a speedier reversal than waiting for a new column of Xs or Os. (See Chapter 5.) The parabolic SAR has the advantage of tightening your stop as the momentum of a price move decelerates.

- **Bollinger bands:** Data displayed in the P&F format can't display momentum and thus overbought or oversold, a shortcoming that can be partly addressed by applying Bollinger bands (see Chapter 14). If your columns of Xs persist in pressing against the top of the band and sometimes breaking it, you have confirmation of the uptrend. When the next column of Os crosses the centerline (a simple moving average) to the downside, you expect a swing all the way to the bottom band.

  Finally, Bollinger bands are wide apart when volatility is high, and they "squeeze" narrower as volatility dissipates and prices become congested. In a congestion, P&F prices are in a series of short columns that you can't trust to deliver a reliable buy-or-sell signal. When you see the short columns together with the narrow Bollinger band, you can guess that the market is fickle — it's not trending, and you should go find something else to trade.

Chapter 16

Combining Techniques

· ·

In This Chapter

▶ Finding out just how straightforward trading can be

▶ Looking at complexity

▶ Figuring out positive expectancy

▶ Discovering setup trading

· ·

*I*ndicators are roughly grouped into three types — trend, momentum, and sentiment. Technical heads argue over which category to file any particular indicator. Relative strength, for example, is a momentum concept that is used to measure market sentiment (overbought or oversold).

The key point is that using one indicator increases profits and lowers losses. Combining two indicators works even better. You can add as many indicators and trading rules to your charts as you can hold in your head or program into your computer.

This chapter surveys some combinations of techniques and offers guidance on the process of putting techniques together to forge a systematic approach to trading. Before you get to full-scale trading systems (see Chapter 17), though, you need to examine the compatibility of indicators. You also need to know that adding indicators multiplies the difficulty of the trading decision. That's where this chapter comes in handy.

Standing the Test of Time: Simple Ideas

Many professional traders make a living by applying the same simple indicators and the same simple rules, over and over again, on the same small set of securities. "It can't be that easy!" you think. But it is. Professionals have a superhuman ability to focus on a single narrow set of circumstances. They know from experience that the indicator and rule produce a profit most of the time. If it fails to produce a profit this time, too bad. They put it behind them and move on to the next trade.

One of the oldest trading concepts is also one of the simplest — Richard Donchian's 5/20 system, which uses a trend-following principle. You buy when the 5-day moving average crosses above the 20-day moving average and sell when the closing price crosses below the 5-day moving average. Both the buy-and-sell crossover signals are qualified according to additional filtering criteria, specifically that a crossover has to exceed the extent of the previous crossover in the same direction, proving its street credentials, so to speak. (See Chapter 12 for information on moving averages and filtering.)

Another simple but effective one-rule concept is to buy when the price moves above the range established in the first *x* number of minutes of trading. Its inventor, Toby Crabel, calls this strategy the opening range breakout. The *opening range breakout* is a volatility breakout setup (see the section on "Evaluating Efficient Entries and Ruthless Exits: Setups" later in the chapter). With the opening range breakout, you can improve the odds of getting a successful trade by adding one or more confirmation qualifiers, such as:

- ✔ The preceding bar was an inside day or doji (see Chapter 8).

- ✔ The x-minute opening range over the past three to ten days was narrowing (see Chapter 14).

- ✔ The opening is a gap from the day before (see Chapter 7).

As the two classic cases illustrate, even the simplest trading rule based on a single indicator uses confirming filters, patterns, or another indicator.

But which two indicators should you choose? Or should you choose three, or four, or more? Because technical analysis has produced thousands of stand-alone indicators and patterns, the number of possible combinations and permutations is humungous. By the time you add time constraints, such as "Buy 30 minutes after the open (or high or low or close) if *x, y,* and *z* occur," the number of potential trading regimes is in the millions.

The key reason for adding confirming indicators is to overcome the inconvenient little fact that every indicator fails some of the time. By requiring a second indicator that gives the same buy or sell signal, you increase the probability that your trades are profitable.

As I say in Chapter 5, you must take five steps in planning and managing the trade. At each step you have to decide which indicators to follow, but you don't have to use the same indicators for each step. Your entry rule can be based on one set of indicators that is different from the set of indicators you use to exit. You can change your indicator set at any time if your eye spots something on the chart that normally you wouldn't use but is too big and obvious to neglect. You can even change your stop-loss rules, either the initial stop when the trade is young or the trailing stop as the trade progresses — as long as you have an indicator-based reason and you still have a stop at all times.

Adding a New Indicator: Introducing Complexity

An indicator used to establish a new position usually has an inherent implied exit rule, as in the case of the Donchian 5/20 moving average from the earlier section, "Standing the Test of Time: Simple Ideas." You enter on the up-cross and exit on the down-cross. But what if the down-cross doesn't occur until after you have started taking losses?

Another big issue arises after you have been stopped out or taken the preset profit. How do you know whether to reenter? Do you use the same or different rules to reenter in the same-direction trade? I have asked this question of about 30 high-level system designers and traders. About half say that the indicators and rules for reentry are the same as for the entry and about half say that you should have a different set of indicators and rules for reentry.

Adding a new indicator piles on complexity and can get tricky. When you combine indicators, sometimes they contradict one another. One indicator says buy, while a different indicator says sell. This conflict is very common.

The price of your security, for example, crossed above its moving average and you bought it. The trend has been in place for a while. Now a momentum indicator like RSI or MACD is signaling that the security is overbought and will retrace. You don't know if the retracement will be minor or become a full-blown reversal. You know that the moving average lags the price action — no help there. Do you accept the sell signal from the swing indicator?

No single correct answer exists. Sometimes momentum indicators are wrong, and the retracement doesn't occur at all, leaving you with the problem of where to reenter your trend, which is running away without you. But even after the most exhaustive backtesting and observation, you still are wrong some of the time no matter which decision you make. The purpose of combining indicators is to improve the odds of being right about the next price move, but you will never be right 100 percent of the time.

The only way to know whether two or more indicators work well together is to backtest them together, with the trading rules meticulously stipulated. Testing a single indicator is easy. Testing multiple indicators and rules for various contingencies is hard work and often raises more questions than it answers. And many people don't have the time or aptitude for backtesting. In that case, at the least take the time to observe the indicators on the chart and estimate how well they work together. After reading the following section and some practice, you should be able to see matching signals, divergences, support and resistance, and patterns. Expert traders say, "Trade what you see on the chart," and it's good advice.

Choosing a ruling concept

Here's the bottom line: You have to choose a ruling concept. Making that choice establishes whether you are a trend-follower or a swing trader, or if you are a swing trader through and through, how fast and how frequently you want to trade.

Switching indicators, even in mid-trade, is okay if you see something compelling on the chart — as long as you appreciate that you're changing your trading plan. To override your ruling concept is like abandoning your date at the prom when you spot a prettier girl. You can't evaluate an indicator properly if you don't apply it consistently, and you can't evaluate your skills as a trader if you switch focus. But at the same time, your ultimate purpose in trading is to make money, not to prove that your indicators are valid. Just be aware that you may be taking more risk when you adopt a new technique that you have not used before or backtested. If set properly, your stop can save you if your embrace of a new indicator goes south.

For example, your security may be on a rising trend when suddenly you notice a candlestick, like a hanging man (see Chapter 8), that is a big warning and decide to exit early even though your indicators are not signaling a sell and your stop is still far away.

Figure 16-1 shows another example. In this case, say you decide to use the Donchian 5/20-day moving average crossover. You get a sell signal. A little later, the price bounces and you get a buy signal followed in a few weeks by another sell signal — a whipsaw. But before then, you can't avoid noticing the double top, even though pattern recognition is not one of the indicators in your toolkit. But it's the gorilla in the room on this chart, so you run right out and research it. The rule in double-top analysis is that after the confirmation point is reached, the price often pulls back above it before resuming the downtrend, giving you a better opportunity to go short. This time you follow the double-top rule and avoid the moving average-generated whipsaw. Pattern recognition served you well.

A wide knowledge of indicators can help make your trading more adaptive and flexible. But it's human nature that when you have a hammer, everything looks like a nail. Beware of imagining double tops on every chart after the successful trade exemplified in Figure 16-1 and beware of believing that every double top delivers this outcome. A series of successful trades on a single indicator doesn't make it a magic indicator that always works. I can't say it often enough — no indicator works all the time.

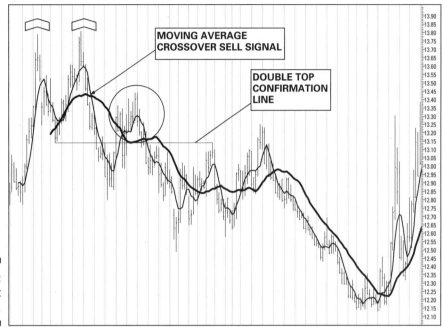

Figure 16-1:
Trade what
you see.

Studying a case in complexity

Combining indicators can be messy and complex. By studying the case I present here, you can see just how complicated one security trade can be and how choosing your indicators can make all the difference.

A trend-following concept like the moving average crossover accepts late entries and lower profits, because moving averages always lag the price action. Say you decide that you want to improve the moving average system, so you add two additional indicators:

- ✔ You want to enter earlier, so you add a momentum indicator.
- ✔ You want to exit closer to the high, so you also add an overbought indicator (a sentiment indicator).

In Figure 16-2, the main window shows the primary trading concept, a version of the moving average crossover. You buy when the 5-day moving average closes above the 20-day moving average (the thicker line) and sell when the price closes below the thinner 5-day moving average. Say you want to identify the entry sooner. You jazz it up by adding a momentum indicator at the bottom of the chart that tells you when momentum is on the rise, giving you an earlier entry than the moving average by three days. At the top is a different momentum indicator (relative strength) telling you when the price is coming down off an overbought level. This gives you an exit one day earlier.

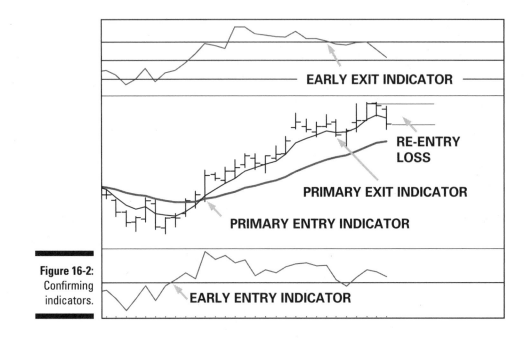

Figure 16-2:
Confirming
indicators.

Using the moving average alone makes you a profit of $2.51 in three weeks, but when you accelerate the entry and exit by using the additional indicators, you boost profitability by over 50 percent, as shown in Table 16-1.

Table 16-1	Indicator Trading Results		
Indicator Trading Rule(s)	*Buy*	*Sell*	*Profit*
Moving Average Concept	$64.35	$66.86	$2.51
With Momentum and Relative Strength	$63.38	$67.32	$3.94

At a glance, the case in Figure 16-2 seems to be a successful integration of three indicators that accelerates entry and exit and makes you more money. But in reality, you may have opened a can of worms. The following are some examples of problems that can arise when you combine indicators.

Trading decisions multiply exponentially

Indicators add up arithmetically, but trading decision complexity multiplies exponentially. For example, what if the momentum indicator gives you a false reading? As I mention in Chapter 4, indicators are wrong a lot. In the example in Figure 16-2, the early entry worked, but plenty of times it doesn't. You need an exit strategy — a stand-alone, stop-loss rule — for that early entry when it's incorrect. The best rule for this type of situation may be to exit when you lose a simple percentage of capital at stake.

Concepts can mirror each other

The purpose of using multiple indicators is to get confirmation that a signal is likely to be correct. Obviously, if you're using a momentum indicator, you don't get independent confirmation from another momentum indicator, because they're both using the same conceptual principle.

In the case of Figure 16-2, the confirming indicators are a near match for one another. The relative strength indicator in the top window looks suspiciously like the momentum indicator in the bottom window. And it is! A technical trader named Tushar Chande studied the correlation among various momentum concepts. He found that momentum and the relative strength indicator shown on this chart (Mr. Chande's own version) are over 90 percent correlated. (See Chapter 13 for a discussion of all the guises momentum can assume.) When two things are highly correlated, it means that they move more or less in lockstep.

Concepts sometimes clash

Two or more concepts don't always play well together. For example, see Figure 16-3. The stochastic oscillator, momentum, and MACD are all used to improve the timing of entries and exits. On this chart, you have a sell signal from the moving average crossover. You use a trailing stop-loss based on the average true range (see Chapter 5). It gets hit. Should you exit? Dumb question! Of course you should exit. You should always follow your stops.

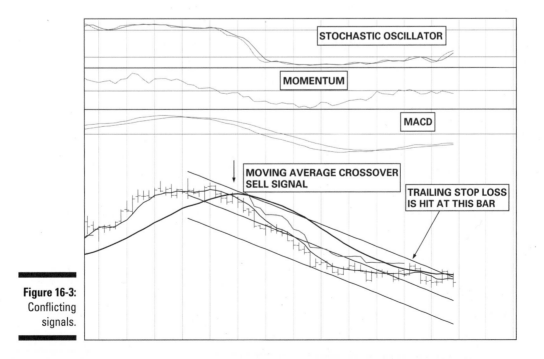

Figure 16-3:
Conflicting
signals.

But after the exit, now what? Look at the stochastic oscillator. It says not only should you exit the short position, but you should buy. The two moving average crossover indicators do not confirm, and momentum in the next window is wavering around the center buy/sell line and doesn't confirm that you should exit the short position, let alone create a new long position. MACD in the next window has a crossover to the upside but the entire indicator remains under the bull/bear line. This situation suggests a trend change might be coming (or might not).

Here's how to reconcile these clashing indicators:

1. **Backtest or observe on the chart which of the momentum indicators is right a greater percentage of the time and use only that one.** In particular, decide whether a crossover in the MACD suffices or you need the buy signal to be over the center buy/sell line, too.

2. **Obey the stop and wait for a clearer picture of where this price move is going.** In other words, this chart isn't suited for stop-and-reverse trading.

3. **Consult the big-picture linear regression-based channel trendlines (see Chapter 10).** The basic assumption is that a trend once in place tends to remain in place until something comes along to break it. In Figure 16-3, you have three highs over the channel top but *no closes* over the channel top. You, therefore, suspect that the trend might be changing (from the stochastic oscillator and MACD) but you do not have a preponderance of evidence.

When looking at multiple indicators, add up the ones that say buy, the ones that say sell, and the ones that say "stay out" or are hard to read, and go with the course of action that has the preponderance of evidence on its side. You seldom have a trading decision that is proven beyond a reasonable doubt, and so preponderance of evidence is the reasonable course.

Additional entry and exit issues may arise

You don't know what to do next. You have obeyed your stop-loss and exited the trade, but you are chomping at the bit to get back in this security.

Don't get back into a security until you get a confirmed buy signal from two or more indicators, and they don't have to be the original indicators you used on the last trade as long as they are indicators that you understand and trust. You're not taking any risk when you have no position. See Figure 16-4 that shows what happens next after the Figure 16-3 chart.

You have a buy signal from the stochastic oscillator. But you don't get confirmation from the channel breakout for a whole month. Three days after that, you get the moving average crossover. Now you're back to Step 1 of the trade plan outline, determining the basic direction of the price.

Oddball combinations are not that odd

In practice, no combination is oddball. Any combination that works on *your* securities in *your* time frame is perfectly acceptable. I know one trader whose setup consists of the divergence of support and on-balance volume in a very short time frame (minutes, in fact). He finds it over 90 percent reliable — and that's awfully good.

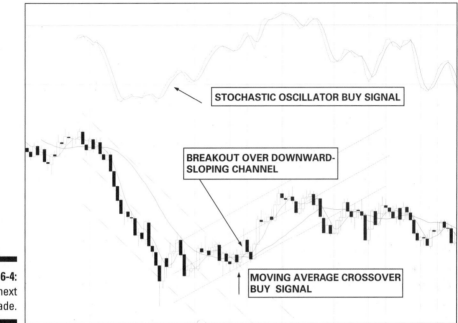

Figure 16-4:
The next trade.

STOCHASTIC OSCILLATOR BUY SIGNAL

BREAKOUT OVER DOWNWARD-SLOPING CHANNEL

MOVING AVERAGE CROSSOVER BUY SIGNAL

You don't need to use moving averages and momentum as essential ingredients in your indicator combinations. They are basic indicators that many traders use, and not "beginner's indicators" at all. But some traders find confirmation from others indicators altogether, such as combining pivot point lines with candlestick interpretation to get viable trades, complete with stops. Other traders use Fibonacci counts to figure out where the price lies in the wave continuum. Even traders who observe Fibonacci counts are unproven may use Fibonacci or Gann retracement levels to guess where to place a stop, which is less costly than using maximum adverse excursion (although usually more costly than a trailing stop).

Use the KISS approach — keep it simple, stupid. Especially if you are a novice at technical analysis, don't add too many conditions and try to account for every contingency.

Expecting a Positive Result

The main reason to add bothersome complexity is to improve gains or reduce losses, or both. But you need to have some idea that the overall conditions are right to make any trade in the first place. This section can help you do just that.

Calculating positive expectancy technically

The first question to ask yourself is whether the security in front of you right now offers an opportunity to make a profit. As statisticians say, you want to have a positive expectancy that a gain is possible. Not every security offers a profit potential. If it is range-trading sideways with low volatility (see Chapter 14), profit potential is low unless you know how to trade options.

In general terms, a positive-expectancy trade is one that

✔ Displays a bar configuration or pattern that generates profits a high percentage of the time

✔ Has multiple confirming indicators, as discussed in the "Adding a New Indicator: Introducing Complexity" section earlier in the chapter

✔ Offers an obvious exit, like a spike high or the downside break of a support line that occurs before your stop-loss kicks in

Think of the trade as a *process* in which the evidence mounts that the indicators are correct. Don't neglect the configuration of the price bars themselves and obvious patterns. See Figure 16-5 and take a look at the following numbered list that corresponds to the numbers on the chart:

1. The price puts in three days of higher highs and higher lows, and then rises above a resistance line (see Chapter 10).

2. The price gaps to the upside (see Chapter 7).

3. At the same time, the price crosses above the 20-day simple moving average inside the Bollinger band (Chapter 14).

4. A few days later, the relative strength indicator in the top window crosses the buy/sell line to the upside.

5. A few days later, the MACD in the bottom window crosses its buy/sell line to the upside, confirming RSI.

6. Finally, the price breaks out above the Bollinger band top, a continuation signal that suggests the trend will keep going up.

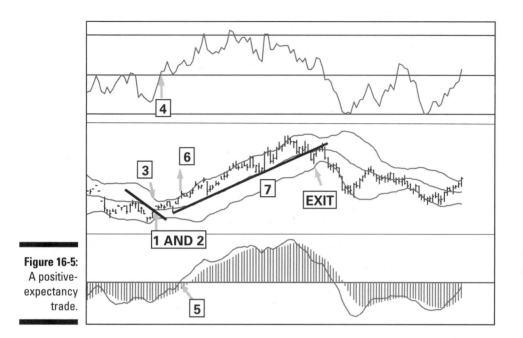

Figure 16-5:
A positive-
expectancy
trade.

You can trade this chart any number of equally valid ways, depending on your appetite for risk. You can say to yourself, for example, that the first indicator (three higher highs with three higher lows plus break of resistance) gives you a 25 percent expectancy that the price is going to rise farther. The gap gives you another 25 percent. The cross of the 20-day moving averages gives you a further 25 percent. You now assign a 75 percent probability of a further price rise — in fact, a full-blown trend. By the time you get to the fourth confirming indicator, you're 100 percent convinced.

Where does the 25 percent come from? *You* determine it — from experience, from backtesting, and from reading other traders' work. Go back and look at the history of gaps in this security. If you're trading a security that has gaps only once a year or so and every time the move continued in the same direction, you're safe in giving it a pro-entry value. On the other hand, you may be looking at a security that gaps a lot without delivering the expected move in the direction of the gap. In that case, be sensible — don't assign the gap any weight toward the trade.

You may not like the number 25 percent. Okay, pick a different number. Just be careful not to pick such low numbers that you postpone entry until the move is practically over. Each individual views risk differently. Some traders enter on the three higher highs (with higher lows), and get in before the break of the resistance line and the gap, for example, improving their gain from this trade over the trader who waits for confirmation from the gap.

The probability of a trade generating a profit isn't an objective number that you can determine scientifically at the start of a trade. You can *estimate* the chance of any particular trade being successful by subtracting the margin of error from the historical success rate from your backtests, assuming that you did a very large backtest. (See Chapter 4 for a discussion of backtests.) The *margin of error* is a statistical concept that programmers are just starting to include in technical analysis software. Say that a particular set of indicator-based rules delivered 80 percent profitable trades over a large number of hypothetical trades on historical data. Your margin of error is 20 percent, meaning that the rule-based trade delivers a loss 20 percent of the time.

Math whizzes say that if a technique works 80 percent of the time on, say, Blue Widget over a gazillion trials, it should work the same (or nearly the same) on Pink Widget. In other words, the probability of the outcome is a function of the statistics — and independent of the quality or character of the security. Non-mathematicians have a hard time swallowing this one. You can show identical backtest results for Blue Widget and Pink Widget, but feel in your bones that you should increase the margin of error judgmentally when trading Pink Widget. Don't dismiss instincts like this one. Maybe Pink Widget has lower liquidity or some other characteristic that didn't throw up a hairball in the backtest but is still vulnerable to doing it someday.

Developing a positive expectancy of gain by having your indicators pass successive tests is not the same thing as having found a "high probability trade." There is no such thing as a high-probability trade. Trades can go wrong because of events that you cannot foresee or control. To speak of high-probability trades is to buy into the huckster and con man mindset. The only time to use the high-probability label is when you fix the stop and target at trade entry. The high probability applies to the stop as well as the target.

Enhancing positive expectancy by entering gradually and exiting at once

Figure 16-5 discusses the trade in terms of a single purchase and sale. In practice, you can enhance profitability by scaling into the trade (Step 3 of the trading plan outline). To *scale into the trade* means to add to the position as each confirmation appears. Say you have $5,000 to place on this security. You start by placing a portion of that capital ($1,000) when the first or second indicator signals buy. Then you place additional lots of $1,000 as each benchmark is reached, until you have 100 percent of the capital allocated to the trade. One clear place to add more to the trade is at Point 7, where the price tests support and bounces off it to the upside.

In Figure 16-5, the price breaks below the support line and also crosses below the 20-day moving average, and the two indicators in the top and bottom windows turn downward. Chances are this up move is over. You exit as shown.

Notice that you scaled into the trade but exited all at once. This chart doesn't show a trailing stop-loss line, but in practice, this trend was fairly long lasting, and a trailing stop, if hit, would still have resulted in a nice gain.

Evaluating Efficient Entries and Ruthless Exits: Setups

Setup trading is a form of swing trading that's very popular today. A *setup* is a particular configuration of bars, usually with one or two other confirming conditions like a pattern or an indicator, that delivers an expected outcome in a high proportion of trades. The opening range breakout I describe in the "Standing the Test of Time: Simple Ideas" section earlier in the chapter is an excellent example of a setup. Candlestick trading can be considered setup trading, too (see Chapter 8).

Setups usually have catchy names (like *pinball* and *coiled spring*). Do these setups work? If you identify the setup correctly, yes, the price does often behave in the predicted manner. Unfortunately, statistics on exactly what percentage of the time they do work don't exist, but experienced setup traders say that setups work often enough that early entry gives you an edge.

Each setup identifies a specific market condition that can be explained in terms of market psychology. Setup analysis is promiscuous, borrowing from bar reading, pattern identification, and indicators. Setups are effective tools when you can read the supply and demand dynamics on the chart — you can imagine what traders must be thinking, such as the predictable burst of buying after a test of support. In general, you're counting on the normal swing of Newtonian action-reaction and the principles of support and resistance.

One benefit of setup trading is that you can be out of the market until you spot a setup situation. You take no risk when you're out of the market. Some setup trades are intraday, where you enter and exit the trade on the same day. Other setup trades are more long lasting because they lead to authentic trends that you stick to until your exit rules or stop is hit. In the next section, I describe some aspects of trading setups.

Starting off early

A setup identifies the conditions that precede and accompany a price move, giving you a head start in entering a trade. When you correctly identify the setup, the price goes in your direction immediately. And when a strong move begins, the first few days can account for 25 percent or more of the total move. That's the thrust or impulse aspect of new moves.

The key to setup trading is early identification of a trading opportunity and early entry into the trade. As a general rule, your goal as a setup trader is to take a profit bite out of a move without necessarily having a position over the entire move.

Entering early in setup trading is in stark contrast to trend-following, where you wait until the move has proved itself according to some definition of trend-edness before you take a position. In setup trading, you enter a position on the same day or the next day as the chart event, whereas in trend-following, you may not enter until several periods (usually days) later.

Efficient entries are the hallmark of setup swing trading, but being quick on the trigger doesn't imply that the trader is a wild-eyed risk taker. Quite the opposite. Risk management is the key feature of setup swing trading and thus appropriate for beginners. You must

✔ *Never* give up profits by sitting out a retracement (as you often do when trend-following).

✔ Absolutely, positively use stops and keep them updated.

Exiting the setup game

For the most part, you do not scale into and out of setup trades. You determine the amount to trade only once. The next part of the trade — the exit — borrows a page from the professional playbook: Ruthless stops. The playbook offers the following tips:

✔ **If the setup is a dud — it fails or you have not identified it right — you need a stop at a level of loss that you can tolerate.** (See Chapter 5 on stops.) All good traders use stops but if you have a problem obeying your stops, setup trading might be for you. You go broke fast without stops, and recognizing that, force yourself to use them.

✔ **If the setup succeeds, you keep moving your stop upward to secure each new level of gain as it occurs.** Generally you hold until the price moves against you by some specified amount. Sometimes setups are so short lived that an initial stop is all you need and you are not in the trade long enough to use a trailing stop. Setup trading can be hit and run.

Working hard while trading like a pro

Here's the catch: Not every setup works every time, and you have to adopt the professional's attitude to a losing trade — get out of the trade and move on to the next one. Amateurs sometimes feel an emotional attachment to their securities — pros don't.

In the pros' world, the only thing that counts is making money. If a security doesn't offer a good setup today, they abandon it for a new one without a backward look. If your job required you to make a specific sum of money trading *every day,* you'd feel hard hearted toward securities that fail to offer setups, too.

Other drawbacks to using setups include

- ✔ A setup that you like may not appear every day or even every month. With a small universe of securities, you'd have to memorize a dozen setups if you want to be in the market most or all of the time. If you like only one or two setups, you have to monitor a large universe of securities.

- ✔ If you focus on setups to the exclusion of all the other concepts in technical analysis, you're at a loss for what to do when setups don't appear.

- ✔ To find your favorite setups, you have to scan a list of securities, and the best setups may appear in securities that you wouldn't touch with a bargepole on a fundamental or value basis.

- ✔ Setups require intense concentration and often the ability to trade actively during market hours. If you have a day job, this task can be impossible to do. And remember, active stop management is critical to success, meaning that you really should be out of the market altogether when you go on a vacation or business trip. War stories about hair-raising losses usually involve not having placed a stop and learning about some market-moving event only after arriving in an exotic location.

Reading promotions carefully

Because many professionals use setups to make trading decisions, some trading system vendors play off this nugget of information to claim that they have a "magic secret" that'll get you trading like a pro. The secret identifies "high-probability trades," and sometimes the vendor promises that "You can't lose!" Sometimes setups are called power strategies, which is more promotional than anything else.

Be wary of such promotions. For one thing, vendors who use exaggerated claims aren't showing respect for your brainpower or common sense. Razzle-dazzle ads may intend to deceive and bamboozle rather than to share wisdom. Keep in mind that

- ✔ Pros don't have any secret indicators or techniques. *All* the trading techniques and tricks, including setups, are available to you in books, magazines, newspapers, Web sites, and seminars.

- ✔ As for claims that you can't lose — don't be silly. Of course you can lose. In fact, you will lose. The point is to lose little and gain big. You don't need to spend thousands of dollars on a program or seminar to grasp the principle of the five-step trading plan.

✔ If trading discipline is a problem for you, trading psychologists and coaches can help — but discipline is a set of personal habits that you can't acquire from anyone else — you can only build it internally. The heart of "trading like a pro" is the trading discipline, not the indicator.

Some reputable technical traders offer follow-along setup trading in seminars or online, for a fee, in which you can see the price action on the chart and hear the trader's commentary every few minutes. What you find out from participating in such a training course has less to do with identifying the setup and more to do with sharing the pro's attitude toward exploiting a promising situation, but knowing how to retreat from a loser — without regret.

Chapter 17

Considering a Trading System

*T*he technical-based trader uses indicators and trading rules to plan as many decisions as are possible. To remove human judgment entirely, some technical traders go whole-hog and design trading systems. A strict, fully mechanical trading system automates the trading process by making *every* decision a rule-based decision. You have no discretion over any aspect of any trade.

By the time you enable your computer to execute the trades as well as determine them, you have built a *robot*. Robo-trading or algorithmic trading is all the rage now that computing power has grown so enormous. Even a modest robot can have 5,000 (or 50,000) lines of code for just the indicators, and that's before applying trading rules to generate the buy/sell signals.

But should you build a trading system? The straightforward answer is "no." For nearly everyone, building (or buying) a trading system is a bad idea. To build one, you must have advanced mathematical and computational skills. Plus, you need literally thousands of hours to devote to it. A complete trading system can take years of full-time work to develop (or hundreds of thousands of dollars to have custom built). Third, after you get started, it's hard to stop. You can always find one more contingency you want to cover or one more technique to try out. And even if you have the scientific mind-set to do this complex work, you may not have the right mentality to place the trades in real time. The technical landscape is littered with engineers turned system designers who can't trade their way out of a paper bag.

Next, consider that *you* change. Your risk appetite changes. Your patience in dealing with complexity may go down (or up). Finally, the market changes. By this I mean that until traders can make indicators instantly adaptive to changing volatility, the human mind is still a faster and more accurate computer than a computer. Where robots do excel is in speed of execution, which can be critical in trading on news releases and in arbitrage models.

Having just poured cold water on the idea of building a system, why include this chapter at all? Two reasons. First, building a system forces you to examine indicator effectiveness and reliability in a strict and fact-based way. It also opens the door to refining your money-management rules, which often yields as much or more profit than replacing indicators or adjusting indicator parameters. Second, the process is a scientific one. You create a hypothesis, you test it, and you get results that can be evaluated to refine the hypothesis for another round of tests. The scientific process is disciplined. If you aren't scientifically trained or oriented, having a system is invaluable to help you discard sloppy thinking, unwarranted assumptions, and general bias.

Defining a Trading System

The term *trading system* has different meanings to different people. *Systematic trading* can be as simple as a single indicator and a stop-loss rule (for more on these topics see Chapters 4 and 16). In fact, most folks in the technical analysis field now refer to any trading regime as a *system,* even when it doesn't meet the strict requirement of full automation. In this chapter, I speak of a *trading system* in the strictest sense — every decision is dictated in advance by the indicators and trading rules that you set down.

A trading system is built, block by block, by accumulating trading rules to convert indicators or other data inputs into buy/sell signals. A trading system becomes a robot when it executes the trades as well as determines them. These decisions include position size and other aspects of the trading plan. Instead of laboriously figuring out how many shares of Blue Widget to buy or sell depending on your changing risk preference and market volatility (see Chapter 16), the machine does it for you. Instead of selecting from among a menu of indicators and trading rules to reenter after a stop or target is hit, the machine does it for you.

Super systems

Algorithmic trading is the fusion of technical analysis with efficient order entry, and banks and fund managers initially used this method to get an advantage in execution speed. One subset consists of "high-frequency" traders whose machines can place trades at literally the speed of light (or just under it), whereas the human trader may take as long as five or ten seconds to make a trading decision after the release of news or the appearance of a trading opportunity.

Information input needs to be as fast as output (the trade orders). Data and news vendors, for a special price, make information available to big institutions fractionally faster than to the general public, too. The innate fairness of this fact is under question today. Algo trading may account for as much as 75 percent of all securities trading in the U.S. Does this mean the trading game is rigged against the little guy? If you want to do lightning-fast arbitrage, yes. If you are trend-following, maybe not. You can find any number of equally valid ways to trade the same security.

The same problems arise in algo trading as in any system. Computer programming is deeply specific. If the program fails to include every contingency, it doesn't have a brain that automatically falls back to some kind of default mode. Data errors caused a "flash crash" in May 2010, when the Dow fell 998 in under an hour and some $40 stocks were priced at $1. Experts doubt that this type of occurrence due to data error is the last.

When a trade goes bad in some unprecedented way, humans have a fallback — they exit. But computers don't watch TV or read newspapers, so if the trade goes bad, it may have no programmed instructions on what to do until after the event starts being reflected in prices. Markets are notoriously slow to respond to event shocks. This is one time the human is faster.

The idea of automating trading is not innately wrong. After all, the equivalent of robots can fly an airplane and even land it. But the mechanical and electronic contingency planning underlying avionics is vast and has taken decades, and superlative as it is, would still not be able to land a very large plane on the Hudson River after a bird strike. At a guess, engineers are working on it.

Algo trading is newer and presumably less far advanced than avionics, although the big institutions aren't disclosing information on their top-secret systems. We can draw inferences, though. First, big institutions have made big investments in algo trading that are delivering a big payoff. In theory, you could duplicate the effort in every way except high-frequency trading (unless you're willing also to pay for advance information) and market making — offering a two-way price to any comer for any size trade.

The second deduction is that vendors of automated systems or robots have almost certainly not put hundreds of million of dollars into the design. If they had, they wouldn't be promoting it to you for $500 or $5,000. It would literally be worth more than that. If the system were a fabulous design, they would sell it to a big institution for millions. A third flaw in retail-level systems and robots is that the designer has embedded into it his own trading philosophy, by which I mean choice of indicators and risk appetite. Risk appetite is deeply personal, as I discuss in Chapter 16. The robot designer may be willing to lose, say, $3 in an $8 initial buy whereas your stop would be half that, or $1.50. Buying somebody else's system is always going to disappoint.

Meeting the designers

Books, articles, and Web sites abound on the topic of technical trading systems, but who are these gurus and system designers behind it all? Usually they're self-trained "experts" (and a surprising number are drop-outs). They have mastered one or more of the software packages designed solely for technical analysis. Sometimes they program their own software. System designers are college math professors, engineers, medical doctors, economists, historians, musicians, and practitioners of dozens of other lines of work. They run the gamut from brilliant, insightful, and inspiring to self-important, argumentative, and petty (just like any other field).

System designers are usually adept at math and computer programming, although often they're not very good traders, as they themselves may admit. This reality isn't really surprising because math and computer programming are complex and intricate, while trading can be mind-bogglingly simple. Some designers start with programming and apply it to markets. Some start with markets and use programming as a tool. It's amusing and intriguing that many technical traders barely passed high school algebra but take home high six-figure profits, while many know-it-all system designers barely scrape by.

Why pay attention to system designers if they're not successful traders? Because you never know when you'll get a "Eureka!" moment and discover one indicator or one rule that makes all the difference to your own trading performance.

Meeting the strict requirements

A trading system is a *mechanical trading system* when it dictates every single decision, leaving no latitude for the operator to inject a subjective decision. Definitions for a mechanical trading system vary, but most systems designers would agree on the bare minimum:

- ✔ You backtested every indicator and combination of indicators over a large set of historical data and have determined that the indicator set generates a favorable gain-loss ratio.

- ✔ The system contains enough trading rules so that whatever the contingency, you never need to make a judgment call. You have already provided directions ahead of time. As noted in a previous section, this really cannot be done in full. Why? Because of what Nassim Nicholas Taleb named black swans — highly improbable events. Do traders ever get a *new* black swan? In other words, an event shock of a type never seen before? Maybe not. Human history is a long affair and perhaps nothing is ever really new. But programming every contingency into trading rules is a vast and probably impossible task.

- ✔ You follow the system without fail and without overriding the signals by using judgment. You take every trade that the system gives you, if only because you never know which signal is the one that'll generate the juicy profit. And in most systems, the successful backtest track record depends on those big profits to offset many small losses.

Building a mechanical trading system is a major undertaking that requires knowledge of statistics, computing, and risk management as well as technical trading methods. You could spend years developing a comprehensive mechanical trading system, and many people do.

Finding your place on the spectrum

You don't have to embrace a fully mechanized computer program-based system to be a technical trader. But when you take losses, you start imagining that some indicator, rule, or risk-management concept might have saved you from the loss, so you think you should trade more systematically. Yearning for more systematic trading is especially heartbreaking if you have a spectacular winning year and then a losing one, and honestly can't remember how you did it in the winning year.

You can start small. The first step is to review various indicators and their associated trading rules. You can develop a buy/sell system fairly easily, choosing indicators that seem logical and workable to you, and then adjust the trading rules until you get a satisfactory hypothetical gain-and-loss profile. *Hypothetical* is the right word because the chief reason to combine techniques in a trading system is to backtest indicators and trading rules to see how they would have worked in the past. I discuss backtesting in Chapter 4. For all its faults, backtesting is the only way to know whether an indicator works on your security. After you find good indicators and rules, you can take them out for a trial run in real time.

Discovering Why Mechanical Systems Fail

Training yourself to be a fully systematic trader is hard. The virtue of a well-designed trading system is that real-time results come in as the backtest leads you to expect. The challenge of a mechanical trading system is . . . you.

You have to trade *exactly* as the system dictates in order to duplicate test results. For some, following every single system dictate is impossible. More than one advanced system designer has had to give day-to-day control of trading his system to another party, because he can't help second-guessing it. Here are some ideas to help you sidestep some of the common pitfalls of mechanical trading systems.

Fooling around with new ideas

Mechanical trading systems often fail because the trader can't resist fiddling with system components — either indicators or rules. Most traders' systems are never really finished. They evolve as the trader experiments with new ideas. The problem with new techniques is that people are impatient and try to fit the new idea into an existing system without fully backtesting it — or sometimes without backtesting it at all. Even experienced technical traders (late at night, after a few martinis) confess to reading about a new idea or hearing about it at a conference, and running right back home to trade it — using actual money. Needless to say, this decision usually ends in tears.

Backtesting until you're blue in the face

To find the "perfect" parameter for your indicator on your securities, you can spend countless hours backtesting. No sooner do you discover the ideal parameters than market volatility shifts, and the parameter is no longer optimum.

A lot of indicator testing is just spinning your wheels. Indicator signal accuracy isn't 100 percent reliable to begin with, and fiddling with indicators never cures the accuracy problem. To add more indicators to "fix" the shortcomings of an existing indicator can result in excessive complexity without a commensurate improvement in accuracy. The one exception is if you're able to make your indicators more *adaptive* to market conditions, either arithmetically or with filters or additional indicators.

Performing backtesting research while working toward a fully automated trading system has two virtues. You not only find out about indicator effectiveness and reliability, but you also get the opportunity to refine your money-management rules.

Before you spend a zillion hours adding or perfecting indicators, remember that your goal isn't to have the perfect indicator; your goal is to make money. You spend time more wisely by perfecting your money-management rules than by backtesting indicators until 2 a.m. Maybe nothing is wrong with your indicators — it may be your risk management that needs work. See Chapter 5 for a discussion of managing the trade.

Not knowing your time frame

No rule is always right. Technical analysis contains rules that are valid in the context of their own time frame but work a whole lot less well in a different time frame. Candlesticks (see Chapter 8), for example, tend to be most effective in a short time frame (intraday or three to five days). If your preference is for trades lasting many months, you need indicators and risk-management rules that match up to that time frame.

Practicing self sabotage

The success of technical trading systems is due to one characteristic — they keep you in winning trades for a relatively long time while getting you out of losing trades relatively quickly. Therefore, over a large number of trades, your profit exceeds your losses. In this sense, fully systematic technical trading is a numbers game.

While a mechanical system imparts confidence in the eventual profit-and-loss profile over some period of time, it has the drawback of occasionally being wrong on any single trade. Sometimes you can see the wrong trade coming, which makes you want to override the signal. To override technical signals is called *discretion*. Discretion is an innocent-sounding word, but in fact, it's dynamite. To exercise discretion means to abandon your hard-earned, high-probability systematic trading signals in favor of personal judgment.

Just about every technical trader allows himself the luxury of discretion to some extent. Professionals tend to exercise discretion a lot more than non-professionals. System purists point out that to override signals is to defeat the purpose of having a system, while experienced traders say they have a "gut feel" about when a signal is bad.

Overriding system signals is the main way that traders sabotage themselves. Sabotage can take the form of overtrading (trading too often) or being unable to pull the trigger (indecisiveness), despite clear directions from your own system on what to do.

One of the chief reasons to use technical analysis and a systematic approach to trading is to give yourself a break from emotion. You may get away with a little overriding once in a while if you have good instincts, but if you do it on more than a few rare occasions (in other words, more than a quarter of your trades), you're still a technical trader but no longer a system trader.

Because you can't backtest judgment, the only way to evaluate discretionary overrides is to keep a diary and write down every override you want to do. Every so often, go back and do an honest accounting of your judgment. A trading diary is a prose rendering of what you're seeing on the chart. Print out the chart and write your override idea on it. Then a few periods later, print out the chart showing what happened.

A trading diary has many benefits:

- ✔ You get ideas about additions to your system to overcome a shortcoming. The diary becomes a wish list. Then while perusing the technical literature, you can *see* a gem when you come across it — it's the solution to an issue on your wish list.

- ✔ You may discover that your eye was detecting patterns that math-based indicators don't catch. If you had a feeling that you should stop out a position but your indicators didn't agree, and in retrospect you can see a pattern that was correct, you may have a hidden talent for patterns. See Chapters 7 and 9 for more about patterns.

✔ You discover personal characteristics you didn't know about yourself (and may or may not like). A common finding is that you saw a continuing trend because you wanted to see it and willfully ignored reversal warnings from other indicators that were present on the chart.

Following Big-Picture Rules

Having a positive expectancy of a gain is the key element of taking a trade (for more on this topic, see Chapter 16). Whether you're aiming for a full trading system or working more informally toward a more systematic approach, this section gives you a short list of other considerations that have a big impact on overall long-term profitability.

Stopping out versus the stop-and-reverse

Stopping out is a function of having met the maximum loss you're willing to take. When the stop is hit, you have to decide whether to go short. Hitting a stop doesn't necessarily mean you want to reverse direction. Maybe you prefer to be out of the market altogether. As a practical matter, most individual traders are buy only and never go short.

Some professionals are required by the rules of their firms to be in the market nearly all the time. They're not "working" if they're not trading. Individuals don't bear this burden. The flip side is that when you're out of the market, you're potentially missing an opportunity.

Trading more than one security

You may have a valid and systematic way to trade a single security, but you still face a high risk of loss due to a one-time catastrophe. The obvious solution is to apply your systematic trading regime to a broader array of securities. Diversification reduces risk. When one security is falling in price, some other security is rising. A solid track record may require offsetting some losses with gains in an inversely correlated or noncorrelated security.

A good portfolio is diversified, and so are good trading systems. Using spreadsheet software, you can easily discover whether any two securities are correlated. Or you can plot both securities on the same chart and eyeball whether they move in tandem. If they do, you may not have to dump one if you can find something else that is inversely correlated. The process of diversification is named *portfolio optimization.* Portfolio optimization isn't, strictly speaking, a technical analysis idea, but it's a natural extension of the systematic approach to trading.

Optimization may make for some strange bedfellows. Don't reject a noncorrelated security on fundamental grounds and pass up the opportunity to smooth your earnings path. You don't have to *like* the security to trade it successfully. If you're building an equity system and find that adding soybean futures would reduce total system risk by half, then resign yourself to finding out how to trade soybean futures.

The same thing is true when you buy a system that requires you to trade each security of a basket of securities. If you cherry-pick the securities, you're violating a core principle of the trading strategy — its diversification. Diversification may be its best feature on which results depend. See the section "Buying a Trading System" later in this chapter.

Don't forget that correlation or the absence of correlation is not written in stone. Two securities that are uncorrelated today may become highly correlated at some point in the future. Keep your correlation data updated.

Don't trade on too little capital

A good system designer acknowledges that every system takes losses, and the trader must have enough capital to remain standing afterward. If the system is capable of generating a $3,000 loss, the minimum capital required to trade the system is obviously higher than $3,000. You must know in advance the amount of money you could lose on any single trade, named a *drawdown.* Whether you're building your own system or buying one, you should know the expected *average* drawdown and the expected *maximum* drawdown.

A standard rule is the Turtle rule — never risk more than 2 percent of total capital on any single trade. In practice, the maximum drawdown many traders accept is 20 to 30 percent of capital, or ten times the conservative amount. You can take only three or four worst-case losses in a row before you're out of business. Alas, this happens all too often because many brokers encourage newcomers to trade with a small capital stake and high leverage.

This situation is particularly prevalent in foreign exchange trading, where you can open an account with $1,000 and control (say) $20,000 in face value of contracts. If you applied the 2 percent rule using your true capital, your stop loss would have to be $20, which is two points in a currency futures contract like the Canadian dollar. The Canadian dollar has an average daily range of about 80 points, so you can forget about using the average true range (see Chapter 5) as a guide or indicator. The stop is obviously unrealistically tight — you will get stopped on the first random move. Instead of accepting that $1,000 is too little capital to trade, beginners widen their stops. But widening the stop is a mistake when it's done for this reason. One thousand dollars is simply too small an amount.

Buying a Trading System

You may see ads for trading systems that promise huge returns, practically no risk, and 80 percent accuracy on trade recommendations. Never forget that if it sounds too good to be true, it's not true. These trading systems are usually *black boxes,* which are systems that claim to select high-probability trades but don't reveal the trading rules and indicators that the system uses. The promotional material may say that the inner workings of the system are self-adaptive (it's a "neural network" that "learns" from its own mistakes) and is simply too complex to display.

Even in the case of a self-adapting system, chances are that the system worked well on certain securities in a certain time frame in the past. But that's no guarantee that it is working today, will work in the future, will work on the securities you like, or will work for you. You have to ask yourself why anyone would sell such a gold mine to you (at any price) instead of keeping it to himself. This section can help you avoid these too-good-to-be-true trading systems and find one that can work for you.

Overcoming phony track records

If you choose to buy a trading system, be aware that crooks and charlatans are found in the technical analysis business just as they are in any other business. You see fraudulent track records, track records that mysteriously include only certain periods, and other chicanery. One trick is to adjust the track record by excluding the performance of securities in a portfolio when they produce losses in the period, but to add them back when they produce gains. You can see through this financial foolishness by doing the following:

- ✔ **Get disclosure of all the indicators and rules and verify results yourself by testing the system on the same historical data as the vendor's track record.** Make sure that you get data covering several years, and verify that the prices shown on the vendor's track record actually existed on each trade date.

- ✔ **Examine the vendor's actual brokerage statements, if possible.** If the vendor doesn't trade his own system and disclose real-life results, why not? To be fair, some system designers may have some good reasons why he doesn't trade his own system, including a fondness for systems and deep dislike of the trading process. Forget testimonials. Everyone has a Cousin Fred who will say the system is fabulous for the price of a pizza.

Evaluate carefully what it means if performance results are "hypothetical." Regulatory agencies require the hypothetical label if the vendor doesn't have brokerage statements. But this requirement applies equally to systems published in real time for same- or next-day day execution and systems that are only curve-fitted to the past. Any 12-year-old can "fit" trading indicators to historical data to produce 100 percent plus gains. A system that gives you trading signals, with stops and targets, for tomorrow's market and then calculates a track record on this outcome is a better bet.

Looking under the hood

Only a few system vendors are crooks. Most are perfectly legit. Still, you want to get good value for money spent. You want

- ✔ **Original ideas that are fully disclosed:** In some cases, you could pay $250 to $5,000, only to get nothing more than a formula or two that you could have acquired free from a book or the Internet. Often the vendor has a near-religious attachment to some theory of price movements that is unproven or unprovable. You're welcome to share beliefs, but remember that technical analysis is an empirical exercise. If a belief doesn't translate into profitable trading outcomes, why pay for it?

- ✔ *Scalability,* **which means that you can trade the system with a variable amount of money, including small amounts:** Some trading systems require $50,000 or $100,000 in risk capital, amounts that are unrealistically high for a newcomer. Usually the vendor has a good reason for requiring so much capital — the system depends on diversification among many securities to get the published track record, for example, or the system tends to generate big drawdowns. If you buy a high-capital requirement system but then allocate too little money to it, you must cherry-pick the trades, defeating the core concept.

- ✔ **Fully defined money-management rules:** Most trading systems don't contain money-management rules and leave so much decision making up to the user that duplicating the advertised track record is virtually impossible. At the very least, a trading system should tell you the recommended entry and exit (stop and target). An estimate of riskiness and advice on adding and subtracting from positions would be nice, too.

Picking the Tool, Not the Security

Say that you just arrived from another planet, and you have no attachment to the concept of blue chip stocks and no difficulty seeing soybean futures in the same light as IBM or the Swiss franc. To you, a security is a security, and you care nothing about its underlying value or fundamental characteristics.

Welcome to the realm of professional traders, chartists, and system designers. They all have a peculiar and wonderful ability to see a price as just a price. Using this mind-set, you're free to pick indicators and securities without regard for fuddy-duddy ideas of what is "proper." Who knows? Maybe your talent is for applying candlesticks to silver futures when you thought you wanted to trade equities.

An accomplished technical trader can sit in front of a live price screen and before an hour is out, spot a method to trade the security. Even if he's an equities trader and you're showing him the Japanese yen, he can "read" the price action. You can do this, too, if you focus on the tools and not on the security.

Rather than seeking the best indicators to trade your favorite securities, consider finding good indicators and matching the securities to them. If your only goal is to make money by using technical indicators, why not reverse the usual order? The process goes by several different names, the most generic of which is *scanning*. You scan a universe of securities to find the ones that fit the criteria you specify. Each technical analysis software package has its own name and method of scanning. Say you like the breakout concept. You can tell the software to search or explore for every security in your database that has just risen above its 20-day moving average. Now you have a candidate list of securities to check out for other technical criteria.

That list will be too large, of course, so next you seek out the securities that have other characteristics that suit your indicators and risk preference, such as a volatility filter. Note that some software vendors have scanning capability for fundamental characteristics, too.

Part VI

The Part of Tens

The 5th Wave   By Rich Tennant

"I was so into my charts that one day she came in and told me she was running away with the pool boy. Now there's a trend I didn't see coming."

In this part . . .

Every trade has two parts — the security and its technical characteristics, and you. After you master a few key concepts, exactly how you apply technical methods is a matter of personal preference. No one technical method is "right" — the right method is the one that consistently makes you more money than you lose. To do that, your chosen method must match up with your risk profile and be practical — you have to be able to execute it.

This part — the legendary Part of Tens — gives you easily digestible tips and tricks to do just that. I cover some of the tricks of the trade many top-performing traders use on a daily basis, as well as some basic rules for "playing well" with indicators. Finally, I wrap up this part with ten ways that the market has changed and what that means for technical analysis and you.

Chapter 18

Ten Secrets of the Top Technical Traders

In This Chapter

▶ Putting your faith in the chart rather than the "experts"

▶ Getting to know the virtues and drawbacks of technical indicators

An old saying has it that "money is how we keep score," but trading is about more than making money. We trade for many other reasons — to keep busy or to get the adrenaline rush of trading. If you trade for a living, keeping your sanity isn't a bad goal, either. In this chapter, I point out ten issues that you must confront to succeed in technical trading.

You can trade technically in any number of equally valid ways. In fact, technical traders come in all stripes (and some are plaid). At any technical analysis conference or online chat room, you meet people ranging from the geeky math whiz to the benchmark-oriented fund manager to the retired schoolteacher. You can't tell from appearance or vocation what technical methods they use. Some are quick-trade artists who make rapid-fire trades lasting less than an hour every day. Other technical traders immerse themselves in charts for hours every day but hardly ever make a trade. Another kind of technical trader is always in the market, long and short, and willing to take big losses for the chance to make spectacular gains. They're all genuine technical traders.

Whatever their styles, successful technical traders all have one thing in common — they've each built a trading plan that uses the technical tools that suit their personality and appetite for risk, and they follow it.

Trust the Chart

The essence of technical analysis is to analyze the price action on a chart to arrive at buy/sell decisions. You determine whether the security offers a positive expectancy of making a profit by looking at indicators on the chart, not on the fundamental characteristics of the security itself. This approach does *not* mean selecting securities without judgment. With thousands of securities to choose from, you are free to pick the ones you deem to be fundamentally sound, and time your trades from there.

After you select your personal universe of securities, nearly every decision to initiate a trade is based on chart events and not on news developments, fundamental factors, or what some "expert" says. The chart contains all the information you need to make trading decisions. If information is truly important, the chart reflects it. Don't forget to look at charts of the same security in different time frames. The best of all possible worlds is when the price is moving in the same direction in multiple time frames.

I say *nearly* every decision because some wildly exceptional news shocks take time to be reflected on the chart, like September 11, 2001 (after which the U.S. stock market closed for several days). Giant rare or unprecedented events like this one will always trump the chart in the first few days or weeks. The best way to handle monumental historic events like these is to exit and wait.

Befriend the Trend

The single-best way to know what's happening and likely to happen to your security's price is to follow its trends. If you buy when an uptrend is forming and sell when the uptrend peaks, you make money over the long run. Remember, your job is to define *trend* for yourself. A trend can be as small as six bars on a ten-minute chart or hundreds of bars on a weekly chart.

Sometimes you can't see a trend in the security you have selected. Patience is a virtue. If the security is usually trended, sit back and wait for the trend to appear. Staying out of the market when the security is not trending is okay — as is getting out of the trade temporarily when a pullback occurs. A security purchase isn't a life-long commitment. You're not being disloyal to your security if you sell it during a pullback.

Understand That You Make Real Cash Money Only When You Sell

On many occasions, securities rise and fall according to overall market sentiment and through no credit or fault of their own. Selling a falling security to lock in a profit or to stop a loss is common sense, even if you intend to buy the very same security again when it starts moving up.

A policy of buy and hold is hardly ever the optimum long-term strategy. Many people rode the bull market in the 1990s to great fortunes — on paper. Then when the crash came, they saw their net worth go down the drain. They were afraid to sell because they were holding onto the idea that to buy and hold is the best rule, always and under every circumstance. Obviously, it's not.

Take Responsibility

You should have a reason for making every trade — the expectation of a positive gain at a level of risk you can live with. If your broker, trust fund manager, or Uncle Fred proposes that you sink some money into a security but the chart shows that the price is on a downward trajectory, just say no. You may be astonished at how many otherwise intelligent and sensible people yield to the supposed superior expertise of their money managers when even a 12-year-old kid can see that the security is tanking. "It'll come back," they say. The only sane reply is, "Okay, let's wait for it to prove it's coming back."

Never take a tip without first consulting the chart. No excuses! You can get free charts at a dozen Web sites. You don't need to become a full-fledged market technician to observe whether a price is rising or falling. And you should never buy into a falling price. What if your broker or Uncle Fred was right, and the falling price abruptly turns up? Well, too bad. You have an opportunity loss. Missing a trade is okay. You had a good reason to miss the trade — it didn't qualify under your trading plan.

If you do succumb to the broker or Uncle Fred, acknowledge that taking the trade is gambling and doesn't belong in the same mental box as trades made under your carefully thought-out risk-reward trading plan. Good trading is not gambling. In good trading, you don't have unknown outcomes and therefore you have no such thing as "luck."

Avoid Euphoria and Despair

You should make the trading decision on the empirical evidence on the chart and not on some emotional impulse. It's human nature to bet a larger sum of money when you've just had a win, perhaps on less evidence than you normally require to take a trade in the first place. Likewise, you may become timid after taking a loss and pass on trades that offer a fabulous profit opportunity by your own technical standards.

A good technical trader follows his trading plan and disregards the emotions created by the last trade. This basic rule is why technical traders use indicators as systematically as possible, even the ones who modestly shy away from claiming to have a "trading system." A good trading regime employs trading rules that impart discipline to every trading decision in a conscious effort to overcome the emotions that accompany trading. Trading is a business, and business should be conducted in a nonemotional manner.

Focus on Making Money, Not Being Right

When you ask brokers and advisors for the single biggest character flaw of their customers, they all say the same thing, "The customer would rather be right than make money." One case stands out: Refusing to take a loss. Either the trader didn't have a stop-loss rule in the first place (a situation you can avoid by checking out Chapter 5), or he refused to obey it. To take a loss says to him that he's wrong about the direction of the security, and he takes it as a personal affront.

Some people have an unusually hard time facing losses, and because they can't take a small loss, they end up taking big ones, which only reinforces the fear and loathing of loss. Soon you're not trading systematically, but on emotion — and worse, the single emotion of fearing losses. If you start falling into this morass, stop trading. Develop a different trading plan that is designed to takes fewer losses.

Don't Let a Winning Trade Turn into a Losing Trade

You can have a fine trading system with excellent indicators properly backtested for the securities you're trading but still be a lousy trader if you don't have sensible trading rules. A good trader differentiates between indicators (which only indicate; see Chapter 4) and trading and money-management rules (which manage the risk; see Chapter 5).

How can a winning trade turn into a losing trade? Many ways, including

- **Failure to use a stop-loss.**
- **Adjusting perception of risk while the trade is in progress by looking at a new indicator that's not backtested and not part of the trading plan.** It's okay to use a new indicator in mid-trade if you're sure of what the new indicator really means, but not if it's only a wild guess, or worse, the advice of some guru.

> ✔ **Tricking yourself into thinking that the market "owes" you the highest price it already attained.** Your indicators tell you that the price is not likely to go back to the old high but that's the amount of money you want to make. You're trying to tell the market what to do, which never works. This is how you start to see what you want to see on the chart rather than what's there — in other words, wishful thinking.

Following your trading plan takes guts. Quantify the amount of loss before placing the trade and accept the losses that do occur (and they will!). Eat your spinach — take the darn loss and move on. This principle is trader discipline, and if you don't have it, you will not be a successful trader.

Sidestep the Temptation to Curve Fit

Just because an indicator "fits" your chart of historical data doesn't make it a workable indicator for the future. *Curve-fitting* refers to backtesting your indicators on historical data to see which parameters would have worked the best (see Chapter 4). A good technical trader doesn't curve fit but rather backtests indicators by using realistic assumptions. If you overanalyze indicators so that they're a perfect fit for the past, they almost certainly fail to work in the future.

Acknowledge that it's okay to have numerically more losing trades than winning trades as long as the gain-loss ratio is more than 1:1. In the same vein, if you're buying someone else's trading system, be sure that it's not just some bright idea that would've worked in the past but is so complex and detailed that it won't work on a broader range of conditions.

Know When to Hold 'Em and When to Fold 'Em

Position sizing is a thorny subject on which statistics experts disagree. Is there a single best portion of your capital stake to bet on any one round of trading? Yes, depending on which theory you accept. You may not want to get into the theoretical discussion of position sizing, but even so, you know that in poker, if you have four aces, you bet more than if you have a pair of sevens.

Likewise, in securities trading, you need to rely on your indicators to tell you whether you have a good hand and can scale up the amount at risk, or have a dud and may need to tighten stops or even fold. The more confirmation of a buy/sell signal you can get, the safer it is to place the trade. For example, if you have only one indication that the trend is turning your way, you can bet small, and add to the trade as confirmation comes in from other indicators. Or you can just wait for all the confirmations. Either method is "right," but only one method is right for *you* and your risk appetite.

Diversify

Diversification reduces risk. The proof of the concept in financial math won its proponents the Nobel prize, but the old adage has been around for centuries: "Don't put all your eggs in one basket." In technical trading, diversification applies in two places:

- **Your choice of indicators:** You improve the probability of a buy/sell signal being correct when you use a second, noncorrelated indicator to confirm it. You don't get confirmation of a buy/sell signal when you consult a second indicator that works on the same principle as the first indicator. Momentum (see Chapter 13) doesn't confirm relative strength because it adds no new information. Widen your horizon beyond a few indicators, and seek different concept indicators instead of torturing old indicators to come up with better parameters.

- **Your choice of securities:** You reduce risk when you trade two securities whose prices move independently from one another. If you trade a technology stock, you achieve no diversification at all by adding another technology stock. Instead, you may get a better balance of risk by adding a stock from a different sector. If you trade metals futures, add something from agriculture or finance to get diversification. You can estimate degree of correlation scientifically with a spreadsheet or informally by eye (charting both securities in the same space).

Chapter 19

Ten Rules for Working with Indicators

*I*ndicators measure changes in market sentiment — bullish, bearish, and blah. Indicators are only patterns on a chart or arithmetic calculations whose value depends entirely on how *you* use them. You use indicators for many trading-related decisions, including identifying a trend, knowing when to stay out of a security that isn't trending, and knowing where to place a stop-loss, to name just a few. This chapter is all about a few tips and tools you need to know to maximize your use of technical analysis indicators.

Listen to the Price Bars

Price bars contain a ton of useful information, but bar-reading takes patience. Indicators take less time, but indicators are only the result of manipulating the price bar data into a different format. Think of the bar as a miniature indicator. For example, when you have a series of higher highs and suddenly the next bar closes far down and at the low of the day, the crowd is sending you a message with a foghorn — this move is over.

Every bar tells a story about crowd behavior. Exceptional bars tell you more than ordinary bars, but try to listen to all bars. Floor traders complain that electronic trading lacks something valuable that being on the exchange floor offers — the noise of the crowd. As an individual trader, you can't hear the crowd, either, so you have to rely on your imagination. (See Chapter 6 for more on bar basics.)

Understand Your Indicator

Use indicators that make sense to *you* in terms of crowd behavior. You need to use an indicator that you trust, and you can't trust an indicator if you don't understand how it reflects crowd behavior. Don't use an indicator mechanically because some self-styled expert says that it has magical properties. The world is full of great indicators. Get your own.

If math isn't your strong suit, don't let it hold you back from using math-based indicators. You don't need to know the math behind an indicator if you understand how it works. Think of technical analysis as a giant department store full of indicators. One department or another has an indicator that can work for you. If you can't find it, keep looking.

Trade What You See

Patterns are indicators, too. Prices never move in a straight line, at least not for long, and patterns can help you identify the next price move. When you see a double bottom, you can feel confident that the right trade is to buy — and this principle is true well over half the time and normally returns a gain of 40 percent. Some patterns are easy to identify and exploit, while others may elude you. If you can't see it, don't trade it. Patterns also aid you in seeing a big picture when you change your chart's time frame (from daily to weekly, for example). Finally, you don't have to believe in elaborate theories about cycles or Fibonacci numbers to use a Fibonacci retracement pattern. Many experienced traders eschew math-based indicators and use only patterns, and for this reason alone, it pays to find out how to see patterns.

Use Support and Resistance

Support and resistance (see Chapter 10) are valid concepts that all technical traders respect. You can pinpoint support and resistance by using any number of techniques, including hand-drawn straight lines or bands and channels created out of statistical measures. Momentum and relative strength indicators can help estimate support and resistance, too. To preserve capital, always know the support level of your security and get out of Dodge when it's broken.

Follow the Breakout Principle

The breakout concept (which I cover in Chapters 10 through 12) is universally recognized and respected. A *breakout* tells you that the crowd is feeling a burst of energy. Whether you're entering a new trade or exiting an existing one, trading in the direction of the breakout usually pays. Studying the conditions under which real breakouts occur is also beneficial so that you don't get zapped by false breakouts.

Watch for Convergence and Divergence

When your indicator diverges from the price, look out. Something's happening. You may or may not be able to find out why, but divergence often spells trouble. Convergence is usually, but not always, comforting. (This rule refers to convergence and divergence of indicators versus price, not the internal dynamics of indicators like the MACD.) For more on convergence and divergence, check out Chapter 4 and 12.

If your security is trending upward and the momentum indicator is pointing downward, you have a discrepancy. The uptrend is at risk of pausing, retracing, or even reversing. If you're risk averse, exit. Look for divergence between price and volume, too. Logically, a rising price needs rising volume to be sustained. The most useful divergence is a paradoxical one, where the price is falling but by less than abnormally high volume would suggest. This divergence may mark the end of a major downtrend and is more reliable than the percentage retracement or round numbers touted by market "experts."

Backtest Your Indicators Properly

You're free to use the standard indicator parameters in software packages and on Web sites. Experience shows that the standard parameters are useful over large amounts of data and large numbers of securities — that's why their inventors chose them. For this reason, some traders never feel the need to perform their own backtests. They accept the standard parameters and put their effort into something else, like bar or pattern reading.

But if you *are* going to backtest indicators to refine the parameters, do it right. Use a large amount of price history when testing an indicator — and don't make the indicator fit history so perfectly that the minute you add fresh data, the indicator becomes worthless (a waste of time called *curve-fitting*). Observing price behavior and estimating the range of sensible and reasonable parameters is better than finding the perfect number. The perfect number for the future doesn't exist.

Acknowledge That Your Indicator Will Fail

Indicators are often wrong. Support lines break for only a day or two instead of signaling a new trend as a breakout is supposed to. Textbook-perfect confirmed double bottoms fail the very next day instead of delivering that delicious 40 percent profit. And moving averages generate whipsaw losses even after you've added every clever and refined filter known to man.

It's a fact of life — your indicator will fail and you will take losses in technical trading. Don't take it personally. Indicators are only arithmetic, not magic. You will take losses in winging-it trading, too. Console yourself with knowing that using indicators reduces losses over winging it, but indicators never eliminate all losses.

Accept That No Secret Indicators Exist

Technical traders have devised thousands of patterns and math-based indicators. They can be combined in an infinite variety of ways over an infinite number of time frames with an infinite number of qualifying conditions. So the idea that somebody has discovered a superior combination of indicators is possible. But none of the indicators is a secret, and no indicator combo is going to be right all the time.

The secret of successful trading doesn't lie in indicators. Shut your ears to the guy trying to sell you an indicator that "never fails!" Of course it fails. If it never fails, why would he sell it to you? And why should you have to pay for an indicator in the first place? You don't. Every indicator ever invented is easily available in books, magazines, and on the Internet.

Play Favorites

Indicators are addictive. You read about a new indicator that seems so logical and appropriate that it becomes your new darling. Suddenly you can apply it everywhere. It's good to be adaptive and flexible, but remember that the purpose of using indicators is to make money trading, not to get a new vision of how the world works. Always check that your new indicator plays well with your old indicators. You picked your favorite indicators for a good reason — they help you make good (profitable) trading decisions. Keep discovering new indicators, but don't fall in love unless the new indicator meshes well with the old ones.

Chapter 20

Ten Ways the Market Has Changed

....

In This Chapter

▶ Realizing that human nature doesn't change — but markets do

▶ Overcoming fear of the math monsters

....

*N*early all the basic observations about technical analysis in this book could as easily have been made a hundred years ago as today, except for references to personal computers and software. Pioneers such as W. D. Gann, Richard Wyckoff, Richard Schabacker, and Charles Dow, all from the early 1900s, would have recognized just about everything I mention here.

And yet . . . the markets have changed in the last five to ten years. They changed in ways that traders could pretty much foresee, but still struggle to understand and adapt to them. Much of the change arises from technological advances and from the new prominence of math whizzes who are able to harness technology in ways mere mortals like myself can barely grasp. But fear not — these changes do not wipe out the opportunity for regular folks who are not math whizzes to trade profitably by using technical analysis. In this chapter, I not only point out what changes are occurring, but also give some advice for navigating these advances in the market.

Technical Analysis Is Universally Accepted

In 1980, traders viewed technical analysis largely as an oddball or even crackpot backwater of investment theory. The explosion of interest in technical analysis since then can be attributed to numerous forces, including

✔ The failure of fundamental-based advisors and managers to deliver consistent and high returns

✔ The spread of personal computers to almost every home

✔ The Internet

So pervasive has technical analysis become that today you can find it in social networks like YouTube and Twitter. Someone who mentioned MACD in 1980 may have been considered a nut job; today if you don't know the term, you're hopelessly outdated. Note that change in the investor and trader mind-sets are arising from the retail masses and the software geeks and brokers who serve them, rather than from the academics or the conventional investment management firms. Technical analysis is the tool of a democratic revolution against security market elites. Now the crackpots are the ones denying the usefulness of technical analysis.

Algorithmic Trading Is on the Rise

The rise of algorithmic trading is the logical extension of the acceptance of technical analysis. *Algorithmic trading* is automated order-entry designed in advance by traders employing computer programming but executed entirely by computers. Algo trading is also named *robot trading* (and the program is named a robot). Algo trading identifies high-probability trades by using indicator analysis, arbitrage opportunities, intermarket analysis, or some other aspect of price behavior. Traders widely use algorithmic trading in equity and commodity markets, including foreign exchange, and it accounts for a high and rising percentage of total volume.

A special variety of algo trading is high-frequency trading that seeks to exploit tiny and momentary price gaps identified directly from electronic information, usually price information but also volume and other inputs. Because computer data processing is far faster than human brain data processing, trades can be executed in rapid-fire manner, with hundreds of trades executed in a minute or two.

Foreign Exchange Is More Prevalent

Those individuals discouraged by the difficulty of beating the market or even just keeping even in equities are often seduced by the idea that trading foreign exchange (or FX) is somehow easier and, because of the use of leverage, more profitable. Client standards are low because the broker has the right to close any trade the instant it falls to breakeven, thereby preventing a loss the customer may not be able to cover. A trader is allowed to open an account with a small charge (as small as $500) on a credit card and begin trading the same day.

A new breed of spot FX retail brokers promote the idea that FX trading is an easy way to get rich quick, even though it should be obvious that in all trading, the little guy is *always* up against big institutions with deeper pockets. Having said that, the FX market is the biggest in the world at about $4 trillion per day and operates virtually 24 hours per day, reducing liquidity risk and the ability of any single player to move the market. The FX market is also fairly immune from insider information, and best of all, it is highly trended and thus suitable for technical analysis.

Hard Assets Have Revived Interest

Technical analysis can be applied to any security, even when you know absolutely nothing about the fundamentals. Technical skills encourage traders to feel qualified to foray into hard assets as well as equities.

Hard assets include precious metals such as gold and industrial metals such as nickel and copper, as well as oil and more perishable commodities like grains, cocoa, and sugar. Interest in hard assets as an investment class waxes and wanes throughout history, but until recently, trading them was too expensive for the average trader to attempt. Now brokers offer mini-contracts, exchange-traded funds, and complex structured deals that allow anyone to participate in the hard-asset markets.

In addition, during the early 2000s, U.S. commodities exchanges modernized the reporting of volume from next day to same day. Commodity traders still don't get live real-time volume, as on the equity exchanges, but at least they get it before the sun goes down. Volume can be a critical confirming or warning factor.

Intermarket Trading Is Blooming

Because you can apply technical analysis to any security, the resulting widespread embrace of trading multiple asset classes simultaneously has some odd side effects. Big price moves occur without any real connection to the fundamental supply-and-demand dynamics of one security and often without the technical indicators giving the customary signals (such as overbought or oversold) because of a change in either the fundamentals or technicals in another seemingly correlated security. Oil, for example, moves in an inverse correlation with the U.S. dollar, so you can't look at only your oil price chart — you also have to look at the chart of euro-U.S. dollar exchange rate. Sometimes gold is inversely correlated with the dollar and sometimes with the euro.

Intermarket trading capability has resulted in some bizarre and frightening outcomes, like the number of barrels of oil referred to in crude oil futures contracts exceeding the number of barrels of oil in existence during the late 2000s. The key concept behind intermarket integration is risk appetite and its mirror image, risk aversion. Traders become risk averse when indicators suggest a security is overbought, but now traders become risk averse when some other security's indicators suggest it is overbought. This factor adds another layer of needed work on top of the chart work you're doing on your security.

Leverage Is Dangerous

When your indicators fall in line one by one to increase your confidence in your trade, you may be tempted to increase your position by borrowing money to supplement your starting capital. *Leverage* is the use of debt issued by brokers to traders. In the U.S. equity markets, the most a trader can borrow from the broker is 50 percent of the face amount of the trade, with each broker applying its own standards so that the amount of leverage extended to the trader is often a great deal less. In commodity trading and in some foreign markets, the allowable leverage is a lot higher.

In foreign exchange, for example, leverage of 100 to 300 times used to be commonplace but was reduced in 2010 to 50 times. Even this reduction in leverage means that the trader with a capital stake deposited at the broker of $10,000 can trade contracts collectively worth $500,000. It should go without saying that trading with such high leverage is seldom a good idea, if only because you may be tempted to ditch your stops or otherwise engage in wishful thinking instead of heeding your trading rules. Technical analysis can't stand alone without trading rules.

Internationalization Is Becoming More Popular

Due to technology, foreign brokers are able to offer the same services as domestic brokers, often at vastly reduced costs, and escaping U.S. regulations. For example, in 2009, the National Futures Association instituted a new regulation disallowing a foreign exchange trader from creating a hedging position in the same account (in other words, the first position was long a currency and the new position is short to offset — or hedge — the first one). This regulation applies only to U.S. trading accounts and traders can circumvent it by having an account outside the United States.

Second, internationalization is seen in the form of domestic investors in a country (such as Japan) that is actively seeking higher returns in foreign markets and currencies, even when they're using domestic brokers who now offer special securities with embedded options like limited foreign exchange risk.

Last but not least, internationalization takes the form of corporations or sovereigns issuing securities, usually bonds or specialized forms of bonds, in foreign countries in its own currency or the foreign country's currency. Some of these securities are wildly complicated, such as a bond-like derivative contract that offers a fixed 8 percent return for five years on a foreign exchange contract of the Brazilian real-Euro cross rate with a 2 percent floor on foreign exchange losses. Eek!

Internationalization raises market participation and thus liquidity, but also introduces new uncertainties to your comfort level in your technical analysis. New regulations and the existence of these newfangled exotic contracts and blended securities make it very hard to backtest your indicators. Also, you may think that you know where support and resistance lie on your chart, but you will be wrong if some big institution has an options strike price under or over it. Plus, some event in a foreign country can move the price of your security in a new, never-seen-before way.

Hedge Funds and Sovereign Wealth Funds Are the New Big Dogs

Hedge funds were invented in the late 1940s and sovereign wealth funds in 1953 (Kuwait) but accelerated as a trend around 2000. Both types of funds embrace trading strategies that travel far beyond the buy-and-hold idea, including sophisticated technical analysis applications as well as the following:

- ✔ Taking short positions to benefit from down markets
- ✔ Diversifying holdings into asset classes previously dominated by a small group of specialists (such as oil, metals, and agricultural commodities)
- ✔ Getting into emerging markets

Hedge funds and sovereign wealth funds are run by well-educated, advanced-math managers who question conventional ways of thinking about markets, and in many cases engage in algorithmic trading, including high-frequency trading. They are the big new players or "agents" in many markets. As technical analysis-oriented players with deep pockets, they are market leaders and may promote more trendedness and higher volatility, which means that you need to stay on your toes and keep your indicators adaptive.

Platforms Are Emerging

A *platform* is a computer capability upon which software applications can be built. In trading applications, the platform provider offers two-way data transmission (prices and analysis to the user and trade orders from the user), usually with security, storage, and analytical options built in. Some platforms, such as Metatrader, allow open-source contributions from users that are then available to everyone.

Among the first major trading platforms was TradeStation, which started as a technical analysis software company and transformed itself into a broker that offers live, online technical analysis woven into the order-entry process. Interactive Data is another broker that joined with data and technical analysis vendor eSignal. Instead of doing your chart work on one PC and then switching to the broker's electronic order-entry Website, you perform all the functions in one space — and with the platform offering you ideas, analysis, and real-time alerts. Anyone can build an automated trading system using an advanced platform — this is, of course, both a curse and an opportunity.

Exchange-Traded Funds Have Made Their Mark

Exchange-traded funds (ETF) is a class of investment fund that bundles together related securities and trades like an individual stock on an exchange. An ETF consists of a basket of securities that trades in its own right as a proxy for the collection. For example, the SPDR ("Spider") exchange-traded fund serves as a proxy for the S&P 500 index.

From a single ETF in 1993, the range of ETFs expanded to nearly a thousand ETFs in the U.S. alone, with more being created by the month. Most ETFs replicate the performance of a stock, bond, or commodity market — or take a position that effectively shorts that market. ETFs are an alternative to mutual funds, which create a pool of generally unrelated securities and almost never outperform the market indices. ETFs, while designed to trade at about the same price as the net asset value of its components, are subject to supply and demand of their own, and prices can vary widely from the collective prices of the underlying securities. ETFs sometimes offer double or triple leverage and can trade erratically, which reduces confidence in your technical analysis.

Appendix

Additional Resources

· ·

Y ou may be overwhelmed the instant you start searching for material on technical analysis. A lot of the information you find is full of jargon and math, and some of it is downright crackpot (although you don't know that at first). Much of it is just intimidating.

Relax. You don't need *all* this stuff, just enough to get started. Of course, start with the main chapters of this book, which give you all the basics you need to know to launch your technical analysis career. However, if you want some additional reads, this Appendix lists some I find useful and complementary to *Technical Analysis For Dummies,* 2nd Edition.

Plenty of technical traders use a single, easy-to-master technique to achieve their financial goals. I know one trader who made his first million after reading one book (Edwards and Magee — see the "Additional Reading" section later in the chapter). Others try all the ideas and methods, and don't want to miss a trick.

Why spend time and money on research? Because you never know when you may come across an idea that strikes a resounding chord in you — the *Eureka!* moment, when you say to yourself: I can do this.

The Bare Minimum

You can use price quotes from the newspaper and graph paper, but realistically, you need charting software and an electronic data source, plus a few additional books as you discover what aspects of technical analysis and technical trading are most appealing and workable for you.

Online resources

Become familiar with charting conventions you can find on Web sites such as www.stockcharts.com, www.stockchartwizard.com, finance.yahoo.com, chartadvisor.com, and other free sites.

In no time at all you can find many excellent newsletters and blogs, too, but in the beginning, resist the temptation to start following them because you really should do some charting work yourself in order to be qualified to evaluate the newsletter or blogger.

Charting software

You want to survey what is out there for free because after you buy a charting package and invest the time and energy to master it, changing horses is hard. Many traders are satisfied with their broker's charting programs, which are becoming more advanced all the time. Using your broker's charting software saves time and reduces errors by combining analysis with order entry.

I have been using Metastock by Equis (www.equis.com) since the early 1980s and so to me it is the most user friendly. It comes with preset indicators, a user guide, and data to get you started.

Equally valuable is the TC2000 software from Worden (www.worden.com). The principle is to scan the equities universe on *fundamental* criteria, and then apply key indicators. Worden offers first-class free seminars, too.

Other charting software packages are

- eSignal (www.eSignal.com)
- EnsignSoftware (www.ensignsoftware.com)
- NeoTicker (tickquest-inc.software.informer.com)
- NinjaTrader (www.ninjatraderpro.com)
- TradeStation (www.tradestation.com)

What should you require of your software? At the least, your charting software should have an easy interface with your source of raw data. You should be able to switch time frames along a wide range (from three minutes to monthly). Your software should be able to show bars in regular OHLC format, candlestick format, and point-and-figure. It should allow you to draw an unlimited number of lines at any slope and contain at least ten standard parameter indicators, including moving averages, MACD, stochastic oscillator, Bollinger bands, and linear regression and linear regression channel. You also want it to be capable of writing your own formulas and modifying the ones included in the charting package.

Futures magazine (www.futuresmag.com) and *Technical Analysis of Stocks and Commodities* magazine (www.traders.com) both offer annual reviews of all the charting software, all the system vendors, all the brokers, and so on. *Active Trader* magazine (www.activetradermag.com) offers articles on trading system design.

Additional Reading

I like books. Books are the medium through which other traders deliver new ideas and offer guidance on avoiding mistakes. I begin this section with a list of my favorites. I recommend these resources because they are written by or about real traders who suffered through the process of figuring out how to trade profitably. Note that I organize each book section in the order of what I find most important and useful so you can know where to start reading.

My favorites

- *How I Made $2,000,000 in the Stock Market,* by Nicholas Darvas (Lyle Stuart)
- *How I Made $1,000,000 Trading Commodities Last Year,* by Larry Williams (Windsor Books)
- *Long-Term Secrets to Short-Term Trading,* by Larry Williams (Wiley)
- *Trader Vic — Methods of a Wall Street Master,* by Victor Sperandeo (Wiley)
- *Evidence-Based Technical Analysis,* by David Aronson (Wiley)
- *Candlestick and Pivot Point Trading Triggers,* by John Person (Wiley)
- *Profitable Candlestick Trading,* by Stephen Bigalow (Wiley)
- *Market Wizards: Interviews with Top Traders,* by Jack Schwager (HarperBusiness)

Encyclopedias

- *Trading Systems and Methods,* by Perry Kaufman (Wiley)
- *Encyclopedia of Chart Patterns,* by Thomas Bulkowski (Wiley)
- *Encyclopedia of Candlestick Charts,* by Thomas Bulkowski (Wiley)
- *Encyclopedia of Technical Market Indicators,* 2nd Edition, by Robert Colby (McGraw-Hill)
- *Technical Traders Guide to Computer Analysis of the Futures Market,* by Charles LeBeau and David Lucas (McGraw-Hill)

Classics

- *Technical Analysis of Stock Trends,* by Robert Edwards and John Magee (Saint Lucie Press)
- *Reminiscences of a Stock Operator,* by Edwin Lefevre (Wiley)
- *Extraordinary Popular Delusions and the Madness of Crowds,* by Charles Mackay (Harmony Books)

Special areas

- *The Definitive Guide to Point and Figure,* by Jeremy du Plessis (Harriman House)
- *New Thinking in Technical Analysis: Trading Models from the Masters* by Rick Bensignor (Bloomberg Press)
- *Bollinger on Bollinger Bands,* by John Bollinger (McGraw-Hill)
- *Beyond Technical Analysis,* by Tushar Chande (Wiley)
- *Street Smarts,* by Laurence A. Connors and Linda Bradford Raschke (M. Gordon Publishing Group)
- *PPS Trading Sytem,* by Curtis Arnold (Irwin)
- *Advanced Swing Trading,* by John Crane (Wiley)
- *The New Science of Technical Analysis,* by Thomas DeMark (Wiley)
- *The Master Swing Trader,* by Alan S. Farley (McGraw-Hill)
- *Price Pattern & Time: Using Gann Theory in Trading Systems,* James A. Hyerczyk (Wiley)
- *Channels & Cycles: A Tribute to J.M. Hurst,* by Brian Millard (Traders Press)
- *Elliott Wave Principle,* by Robert Prechter and Alfred Frost (New Classics Library)
- *Martin Pring on Market Momentum,* by Martin Pring (McGraw-Hill)
- *Steidlmayer on Markets,* by J. Peter Steidlmayer (Wiley)
- *Maximum Adverse Excursion,* by John Sweeney (Wiley)

Money management

- *When Supertraders Meet Kryptonite,* by Art Collins (Traders Press)
- *Trading for a Living,* by Alexander Elder (Wiley)
- *How To Take a Chance,* by Darrell Huff and Irving Geis (W. W. Norton & Company)
- *A Mathematician Plays the Stock Market,* by John Allen Paulos (Basic Books)
- *Van Tharp's Definitive Guide to Position Sizing,* by Van Tharp (International Institute of Trading Mastery)
- *The Mathematics of Money Management,* by Ralph Vince (Wiley)

Index

Notes

Notes

Notes

Notes

Notes

Apple & Macs

iPad For Dummies
978-0-470-58027-1

iPhone For Dummies,
4th Edition
978-0-470-87870-5

MacBook For Dummies, 3rd
Edition
978-0-470-76918-8

Mac OS X Snow Leopard For
Dummies
978-0-470-43543-4

Business

Bookkeeping For Dummies
978-0-7645-9848-7

Job Interviews
For Dummies,
3rd Edition
978-0-470-17748-8

Resumes For Dummies,
5th Edition
978-0-470-08037-5

Starting an
Online Business
For Dummies,
6th Edition
978-0-470-60210-2

Stock Investing
For Dummies,
3rd Edition
978-0-470-40114-9

Successful
Time Management
For Dummies
978-0-470-29034-7

Computer Hardware

BlackBerry
For Dummies,
4th Edition
978-0-470-60700-8

Computers For Seniors
For Dummies,
2nd Edition
978-0-470-53483-0

PCs For Dummies,
Windows
7 Edition
978-0-470-46542-4

Laptops For Dummies,
4th Edition
978-0-470-57829-2

Cooking & Entertaining

Cooking Basics
For Dummies,
3rd Edition
978-0-7645-7206-7

Wine For Dummies,
4th Edition
978-0-470-04579-4

Diet & Nutrition

Dieting For Dummies,
2nd Edition
978-0-7645-4149-0

Nutrition For Dummies,
4th Edition
978-0-471-79868-2

Weight Training
For Dummies,
3rd Edition
978-0-471-76845-6

Digital Photography

Digital SLR Cameras &
Photography For Dummies,
3rd Edition
978-0-470-46606-3

Photoshop Elements 8
For Dummies
978-0-470-52967-6

Gardening

Gardening Basics
For Dummies
978-0-470-03749-2

Organic Gardening
For Dummies,
2nd Edition
978-0-470-43067-5

Green/Sustainable

Raising Chickens
For Dummies
978-0-470-46544-8

Green Cleaning
For Dummies
978-0-470-39106-8

Health

Diabetes For Dummies,
3rd Edition
978-0-470-27086-8

Food Allergies
For Dummies
978-0-470-09584-3

Living Gluten-Free
For Dummies,
2nd Edition
978-0-470-58589-4

Hobbies/General

Chess For Dummies,
2nd Edition
978-0-7645-8404-6

Drawing
Cartoons & Comics
For Dummies
978-0-470-42683-8

Knitting For Dummies,
2nd Edition
978-0-470-28747-7

Organizing
For Dummies
978-0-7645-5300-4

Su Doku For Dummies
978-0-470-01892-7

Home Improvement

Home Maintenance
For Dummies,
2nd Edition
978-0-470-43063-7

Home Theater
For Dummies,
3rd Edition
978-0-470-41189-6

Living the
Country Lifestyle
All-in-One
For Dummies
978-0-470-43061-3

Solar Power Your Home
For Dummies,
2nd Edition
978-0-470-59678-4

Internet

Blogging For Dummies,
3rd Edition
978-0-470-61996-4

eBay For Dummies,
6th Edition
978-0-470-49741-8

Facebook For Dummies,
3rd Edition
978-0-470-87804-0

Web Marketing
For Dummies,
2nd Edition
978-0-470-37181-7

WordPress
For Dummies,
3rd Edition
978-0-470-59274-8

Language & Foreign Language

French For Dummies
978-0-7645-5193-2

Italian Phrases
For Dummies
978-0-7645-7203-6

Spanish For Dummies,
2nd Edition
978-0-470-87855-2

Spanish
For Dummies,
Audio Set
978-0-470-09585-0

Math & Science

Algebra I
For Dummies,
2nd Edition
978-0-470-55964-2

Biology For Dummies,
2nd Edition
978-0-470-59875-7

Calculus For Dummies
978-0-7645-2498-1

Chemistry For Dummies
978-0-7645-5430-8

Microsoft Office

Excel 2010 For Dummies
978-0-470-48953-6

Office 2010 All-in-One
For Dummies
978-0-470-49748-7

Office 2010 For Dummies,
Book + DVD Bundle
978-0-470-62698-6

Word 2010 For Dummies
978-0-470-48772-3

Music

Guitar For Dummies,
2nd Edition
978-0-7645-9904-0

iPod & iTunes For
Dummies, 8th Edition
978-0-470-87871-2

Piano Exercises
For Dummies
978-0-470-38765-8

Parenting & Education

Parenting For Dummies,
2nd Edition
978-0-7645-5418-6

Type 1 Diabetes
For Dummies
978-0-470-17811-9

Pets

Cats For Dummies,
2nd Edition
978-0-7645-5275-5

Dog Training For Dummies,
3rd Edition
978-0-470-60029-0

Puppies For Dummies,
2nd Edition
978-0-470-03717-1

Religion & Inspiration

The Bible For Dummies
978-0-7645-5296-0

Catholicism For Dummies
978-0-7645-5391-2

Women in the Bible
For Dummies
978-0-7645-8475-6

Self-Help & Relationship

Anger Management
For Dummies
978-0-470-03715-7

Overcoming Anxiety
For Dummies,
2nd Edition
978-0-470-57441-6

Sports

Baseball
For Dummies,
3rd Edition
978-0-7645-7537-2

Basketball
For Dummies,
2nd Edition
978-0-7645-5248-9

Golf For Dummies,
3rd Edition
978-0-471-76871-5

Web Development

Web Design
All-in-One
For Dummies
978-0-470-41796-6

Web Sites
Do-It-Yourself
For Dummies,
2nd Edition
978-0-470-56520-9

Windows 7

Windows 7
For Dummies
978-0-470-49743-2

Windows 7
For Dummies,
Book + DVD Bundle
978-0-470-52398-8

Windows 7 All-in-One
For Dummies
978-0-470-48763-1